THE GREATEST

BRIGADE

THE GREATEST BRIGADE

HOW THE IRISH BRIGADE CLEARED THE WAY TO VICTORY IN THE AMERICAN CIVIL WAR

* * * * THOMAS J. * * * *
CRAUGHWELL

This edition published in 2013 by
CRESTLINE
a division of BOOK SALES, INC.
276 Fifth Avenue Suite 206
New York, New York 10001
USA

This edition published by arrangement with Fair Winds Press.

Text © 2011 Thomas J. Craughwell

First published in the USA in 2011 by
Fair Winds Press, a member of
Quayside Publishing Group
100 Cummings Center
Suite 406-L
Beverly, MA 01915-6101
www.fairwindspress.com

10 9 8 7 6 5 4 3 2 1

ISBN: 978-0-7858-3055-9

Library of Congress Cataloging-in-Publication Data is available

Cover design by Peter Long
Book design by Sheila Hart Design, Inc.
Photo research by Anne Burns Images

Opposite page: A memorial, featuring an Irish wolfhound and cross, to the 63rd, 69th, and 88th New York regiments at Gettysburg. (National Park Service)

Printed and bound in China

CONTENTS

INTRODUCTION

In the midst of America's Civil War there was already a consensus in the army, the press, and the general public that the Irish Brigade was an especially impressive outfit. In the years after the war, historians, following the lead of the Civil War military historian William F. Fox, declared that the Irish Brigade was the greatest brigade in the Union army. Fox praised the Irish as "the best known of any brigade organization, it having made an unusual reputation for dash and gallantry. The remarkable precision of its evolutions under fire, its desperate attack on the impregnable wall at Marye's Heights, its never failing promptness on every field, and its long continuous service, made for it a name inseparable from the history of the war."

The service of the Irish Brigade is impressive: Beginning with the Battle of Bull Run in 1861 and concluding at Appomattox Court House in 1865, the Irish fought in every major battle of the war's eastern theater. The Irish Brigade played an essential role in the victory at Antietam, rescued artillery that was about to fall into enemy hands at Chancellorsville, and fought with reckless courage at Marye's Heights at Fredericksburg and the wheat field at Gettysburg. The Brigade suffered 4,000 casualties, arguably the highest of any brigade in the Civil War. Several times the Irish Brigade lost so many men as to be on the verge of extinction, yet fresh Irish recruits always stepped forward to replenish the Brigade's strength.

When the first shot was fired at Fort Sumter on April 12, 1861, it was far from certain that the Irish immigrants in the North would fight for the Union. For the most part, the United States had not been especially welcoming. Most of the population of America was Protestant, with a strong anti-Catholic streak and anti-Irish bias. In the 1840s and 1850s, about one million Irish flooded into the United States, most of them impoverished, uneducated refugees from the Potato Famine. Desperately poor, they crowded into squalid urban shantytowns. As former tenant farmers, they had few skills that were useful in the cities (where the overwhelming majority of the Irish settled), and so the men and boys took the dirtiest and most dangerous menial jobs, while the women and girls worked in the mills or hired themselves out as servants. Most Yankees of every class looked on the Irish with contempt.

Although many Irish immigrants found life in America difficult, they also recognized that there were opportunities in the United States that did not exist in Ireland. They could send their children to public or parochial schools. They could practice their Catholic faith freely. Once they became citizens, they could vote. Families who could set aside a little money could send their sons to a Catholic college such as Georgetown outside Washington, D.C., or Holy Cross in Worcester, Massachusetts, or a new school in South Bend, Indiana, called Notre Dame. That the son of a tenant farmer would acquire a college education and enter one of the professions such as medicine or law had been unimaginable in the Old Country.

The heart of the Irish Brigade was the 69th New York Infantry Regiment. In 1860, it was a regiment of the New York militia, composed mostly of Irish volunteers and commanded by Colonel Michael Corcoran, who was wanted by the police in Ireland for acts of vandalism and sabotage he had committed against landlords during the Famine. In 1860, Corcoran won the hearts of all Irish when he flat out refused to lead the men of the 69th in a military parade honoring Edward, Prince of Wales. For this act of insubordination, Corcoran was arraigned before a court martial. His trial was proceeding when the war broke out. Because Corcoran called on Irishmen to fight in defense of the Union, the officers of the tribunal dismissed the charges against him and restored to him his command of the 69th.

By the end of the war the Irish Brigade was celebrated not just as a band of brothers, but as a band of heroes.

Inspired by Corcoran and the virtually all-Irish roster of the 69th, another, even more famous Irish immigrant in New York, Thomas Francis Meagher (pronounced "Mar"), conceived the idea of a much larger force, four or five times more numerous than Corcoran's regiment—an all-Irish brigade. Like Corcoran, Meagher was an Irish patriot, but unlike Corcoran, he had not managed to escape the law. Meagher was arrested for attempting to incite rebellion in Ireland and was sentenced to be hanged, drawn, and quartered; the sentence was commuted to banishment for life, and he was sent to Tasmania, known at the time as Van Dieman's Land. But Meagher escaped to America and settled in New York City.

ON JUNE 28, 1963, PRESIDENT JOHN F. KENNEDY ADDRESSED THE IRISH PARLIAMENT IN DUBLIN. AS THE PRESIDENT SPOKE,

A BANNER FROM THE IRISH BRIGADE WAS DISPLAYED BEHIND HIM.

THE JOHN F. KENNEDY PRESIDENTIAL LIBRARY AND MUSEUM

Shortly after the Battle of Bull Run, Meagher announced that he was forming an Irish Brigade, with the 69th Regiment as its keystone. Overnight, thousands of Irishmen turned out to enlist, all of them eager to fight with fellow Irishmen under the command of Irish officers. The war offered adventure, a chance to prove their courage, and an opportunity to prove that the Irish were as good as the Yankees. And they did. By the end of the war the Irish Brigade was celebrated not just as a band of brothers, but as a band of heroes.

The memory of the Irish Brigade has not merely survived; it has been celebrated for 150 years. Perhaps the most moving tribute ever offered to the Irish Brigade occurred on June 28, 1963, when President John F. Kennedy addressed the Irish Parliament in Dublin. He brought with him the Brigade's green regimental banner, which was displayed in the chamber as the president spoke of the Battle of Fredericksburg in 1862. "One of the most brilliant stories of that day was written by a band of 1,200 men who went into battle wearing a green sprig in their hats," Kennedy said. "They bore a proud heritage and a special courage, given to those who had long fought for the cause of freedom. I am referring, of course, to the Irish Brigade."

What follows is the story of 7,000 gallant Irishmen who fought in America for something they had never known in Ireland—freedom.

REMEMBERING IRELAND AND FIGHTING FOR THE UNION:
The Origins of the Irish Brigade

It began with a fight over a book—specifically the Bible—and in particular, which version of the Bible children should use in Philadelphia's public schools. In 1844, the city's parochial schools could not accommodate all the Catholic children, most of them new immigrants from Ireland. Their parents' only alternative was to send their children to the local public schools, but this was not an entirely satisfactory solution. In the 1840s, studying the Bible and praying from the Bible were part of the daily routine of the Philadelphia public schools, and the Bible the schools used was the Protestant King James Version. Francis Patrick Kenrick, the Catholic bishop of Philadelphia, petitioned the city's board of education to permit Catholic children to use the Catholic edition of the Bible. The board granted the bishop's request.

The bishop and the board's timing could not have been worse. In recent years, thousands of Irish Catholics had poured into Philadelphia, many of them settling in the Kensington district, a heavily industrialized district where the Irish—men, women, and children—found jobs in textile mills and factories. Beginning in the 1820s, Philadelphia was being transformed from the neat, tidy, Quaker city of red brick houses into a major metropolis. The boom in manufacturing brought new wealth to the city, but also unprecedented squalor, as thousands of poor immigrants, most of them Irish, crowded into tenements near the new factories. The newcomers were altering Philadelphia in another way as well—the city that for generations had been dominated by Yankee Protestants was experiencing its first large influx of Catholic immigrants who would eventually compete with native-born Americans for jobs and would very soon become involved in Philadelphia politics.

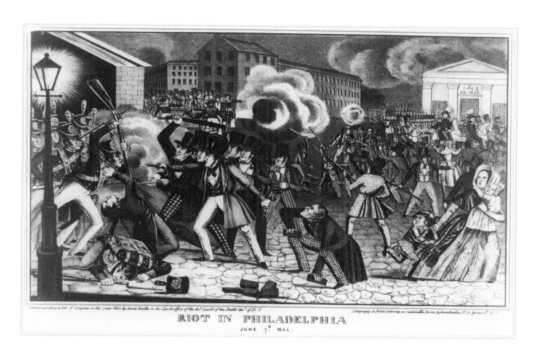

RIOT IN PHILADELPHIA
JUNE 7ᵗʰ 1844.

IN PHILADELPHIA, AFTER THE ANTI-CATHOLIC RIOTS OF MAY 1844 HAD DIED DOWN, A NEW SPATE OF RIOTS ERUPTED IN JUNE.

THIS TIME IT REQUIRED THE INTERVENTION OF THE PENNSYLVANIA STATE MILITIA TO CLEAR THE RIOTERS FROM THE STREET

Their arrival stirred up the resentment of the Native Americans, generally known as the Nativists, an informal political and social organization that was vehemently anti-immigrant and anti-Catholic. In the wake of the board of education's concession to Catholic students, Nativist demagogues claimed that the introduction of the Catholic Bible was the first step in driving the Protestant Bible out of the schools altogether. Irish Catholic priests and immigrants, they said, were the initial wave of the pope's shock troops, preparing the way for a full-scale invasion from Rome that would end with the overthrow of the U.S. government, the establishment of the Inquisition on American soil, and the open persecution of American Protestants.

On May 6, 1844, hundreds of Nativists began to march on the Catholic enclave at Kensington. They stopped at a covered outdoor marketplace called the Nanny Goat Market, where Lewis Levin, editor of a Nativist newspaper, began to fire up the mob with anti-Irish and anti-Catholic rhetoric.

Several Catholics who lived in the neighborhood came out of their houses to see what was going on. A Nativist broke away from the crowd, drew two pistols, and moved toward one of the Catholic bystanders. Several firefighters from the nearby Hibernia Hose Company saw the danger, grabbed fire axes, called for their friends, and ran out into the street. As Irish and Nativists brawled, someone's pistol went off, wounding Patrick Fisher, an Irishman, in the mouth.

More Catholics arrived at the scene, enough to temporarily drive back the Nativists. Then the Nativists made a counterattack, firing into the crowd, hurling clubs, bricks, and paving stones. The Irish scattered, and the Nativists pursued them. One young Nativist, George Shiffler, was chasing an Irishman when he was struck by a bullet and died. This first casualty enraged the Nativists. They stormed Catholic homes in the neighborhood, stealing what they wanted and destroying the rest.

At ten o'clock that night, a mob gathered outside the Convent of the Sacred Heart. One of the nuns, Sister Mary, thought a display of courage might shame the men into dispersing. She flung open the front door and stood silently before the mob. A moment later the mob rained a shower of rocks and paving stones at the nun; she fell to the floor unconscious. While two of the convent's pupils dragged her inside, then shut and locked the door, gunmen in the houses behind the mob opened fire. Two Nativists fell dead in the street, and the crowd ran for cover.

The next night, once again the Nativists gathered outside Kensington—this time someone had brought a large, battered American flag on which he had painted in large black letters, "This is the FLAG that was trampled UNDERFOOT by the IRISH PAPISTS." Behind this flag, thousands of armed Nativists marched on the Hibernian Hose Company.

IRISH CATHOLIC IMMIGRANTS WERE THE PRIMARY TARGETS OF THE NATIVIST POLITICAL PARTY
(ALSO KNOWN AS THE KNOW-NOTHINGS). A PHILADELPHIA PUBLISHING COMPANY ISSUED THIS MEMORIAL ENGRAVING
HONORING NATIVISTS WHO WERE KILLED OR WOUNDED DURING THE ANTI-CATHOLIC RIOTS OF MAY 1844.
THE PRINT IS ENTITLED, "COLUMBIA MOURNS HER CITIZENS SLAIN."

Word spread that the Nativists were on their way. The firefighters barricaded themselves inside their building; armed with muskets and pistols, they took up position in the windows. As the Nativists charged the firehouse, the defenders opened fire, killing one Nativist and wounding another. For an hour the gun battle raged until a Nativist set fire to the firehouse. The firefighters escaped out the rear windows, but the fire spread to the Nanny Goat Market, then to neighboring houses. By midnight the Hibernia Hose Company, the market, and thirty homes lay in ashes. Six Nativists were killed that night, and nine or ten Catholics; no one knows how many were wounded.

The next morning, Bishop Kenrick published a statement calling on the Catholics of Philadelphia "to avoid all occasion of excitement and to shun public places of assemblage, and to do nothing that can in any way exasperate."

The next morning, May 8, as many Catholic families in Kensington packed up and left the city, militia and fire companies entered the neighborhood to keep the peace and put out fires. By noon the Nativists were rampaging through Kensington once again, setting fire to houses as they made their way to St. Michael's Church. A detail of militiamen had been sent to protect St. Michael's, but they were vastly outnumbered by the mob. When three Nativists entered the church and set it ablaze, no militiaman tried to stop them. The militia did save the parish priest, Father John Loughran, escorting him in a cab through the mob to safety. As the cab dove off, the mob ransacked and burned the rectory, the school, and the convent of the Sisters of Charity. Then it headed for St. Augustine's Church. While a teenage boy started the fire inside the church, the mob trashed the residence of the Augustinian Fathers, carried the priests' library of 5,000 books into the street, and made a bonfire.

News of the riots spread across the country. In New York, newspapers blamed the Irish Catholics—if they had not insisted on their children reading the Catholic Bible in public schools, the editors claimed, there would have been no rioting, no killings, no acts of arson in Philadelphia. Other papers, such as the *Herald*, appeared intent on stirring up Nativist animosity in New York: Beneath St. Patrick's Cathedral, the paper reported, were dungeons where Protestant Americans would be imprisoned once the pope's armies had triumphed in the United States.

Nativists from Philadelphia planned to bring the so-called trampled flag to New York and display it at a huge rally outside City Hall. New York's Catholic bishop, John Hughes, expected that such a rally would lead to attacks on Catholics and Catholic churches. He placed armed Irishmen around each church and Catholic institution in New York City, then called on Mayor Robert Morris. "If a single Catholic church is burned in New York," Bishop Hughes warned, "the city will become a second Moscow."

The smug mayor asked, "Are you afraid, Bishop, that some of your churches will be burned?"

"No sir," Hughes replied. "But I am afraid that some of yours will be burned. We can protect our own. I come to warn you for your own good."

Bishop Hughes went back to his cathedral, the Nativists canceled the trampled flag rally, and there was no rioting or church burning in New York.

POPERY AND DESPOTISM

Almost all of the Irish who immigrated to the American colonies in the seventeenth century were Protestants. There were exceptions, of course. In 1643, when the Jesuit martyr Isaac Jogues had escaped from his Mohawk captors and was being sheltered by the Dutch in New Amsterdam (present-day New York City), an Irishman asked the priest to hear his confession. In Boston in 1688, Ann Glover, an Irish Catholic washerwoman in the house of John Goodwin, was accused of witchcraft by the Goodwin children. All the evidence suggests that Glover's real crime was her Catholicism. The notorious witch-hunter, Cotton Mather, denounced Glover at her trial as "a scandalous old Irishwoman . . . a Roman Catholic and obstinate in idolatry."

The Protestant immigrants from Ireland fell into one of two categories: Irish, who had renounced the Catholic faith, and the more common Scotch-Irish. They were Presbyterians from Scotland who had been encouraged by the English government to settle in Ulster, forming a population that was Protestant and loyal in a country that was overwhelmingly Catholic and resentful—if not outright rebellious—of English rule.

After the American Revolution and the ratification of the U.S. Constitution, a trickle of Irish Catholics emigrated to the New World, lured by economic opportunities as well America's promise of freedom of religion—something they did not enjoy in their homeland. In New York, there was a political dimension to who welcomed the newcomers. The Federalists, who were sympathetic to their old Mother Country, England, regarded all Irish Catholics as rebels and interlopers who, because they were willing to work cheaply, would steal jobs from honest, hardworking American Protestants. Members of Thomas Jefferson's party, the Democratic Republicans, were hostile to all monarchies and so they welcomed the Irish as political allies.

By the mid-1830s, there were so many Irish Catholics in New York as to provoke a serious backlash. Some Protestant New Yorkers of all classes were beginning to regard the Irish Catholics not merely as unwelcome, but as a threat. In 1835, they formed the Native American Democratic Association. Among the leaders of the Native Americans was Samuel F.B. Morse, inventor of the telegraph, and newspaper publisher James W. Webb, who called for limited immigration and warned his readers that "popery" was a form of despotism that presented a direct threat to the American way of life.

THE IRISH FAMINE

In the first half of the nineteenth century two-thirds of the population of Ireland worked as tenant farmers. They had small holdings, between 1 and 15 acres (0.004 to 0.06 square km). On such small farms, only the potato had the nutritional value and could be grown in sufficient quantity to feed a family. There had been widespread suffering in rural Ireland several times in the 1820s and 1830s when the potato crop failed in parts of the island. Then, about the year 1842, Ireland's potato crop became infected with *Phytophthora infestans*, a fungus, which reduced healthy potatoes to a soggy black mass. The resulting famine swept across Ireland, returning every year throughout the 1840s and into the 1850s. At least 1.5 million people died, and millions more emigrated to the United States, Canada, England, even far-off Australia and New Zealand.

The Irish were not only the largest immigrant group in the city, but they had also made New York City the largest Irish enclave in the United States.

Between 1847 and 1851, approximately 848,000 Irish arrived in New York City—163,000 of them in 1851 alone. Not all of them stayed; many moved on to Albany, or Buffalo, or went west to find work building railroads or digging canals. Nonetheless, a considerable number remained in New York. According to the U.S. census of 1850, 133,730 New Yorkers (26 percent of the city's population) had been born in Ireland. The New York State census of 1855 found 175,735 Irish-born residents in the city (27.9 percent of the population). In other words, the Irish were not only the largest immigrant group in the city, but they had also made New York City the largest Irish enclave in the United States.

AS MAYOR OF NEW YORK CITY, FERNANDO WOOD, SHOWN IN THIS IMAGE TAKEN BETWEEN 1855 AND 1865, DISTRIBUTED
PATRONAGE JOBS TO THE IRISH AND WAS OUTSPOKEN IN HIS SUPPORT OF IRELAND'S INDEPENDENCE FROM ENGLAND.
IN RETURN, MOST OF THE IRISH THREW THEIR POLITICAL SUPPORT BEHIND WOOD. IN THE 1858 MAYORAL RACE, THE DEAD RABBITS,
AN IRISH STREET GANG, PADDED THE VOTER LISTS WITH NAMES FROM THE CITY'S CEMETERIES.

Most of the newcomers had been tenant farmers in the Old Country, which meant they had no marketable skills in a city. Irish men took the heavy, dangerous jobs that required nothing more than muscle. Unmarried Irish women found work as domestic servants, typically in the homes of well-to-do Protestant families. Married Irish women sewed piecework at home so they could earn a little money and watch their children. Most of the immigrants were crammed into slums in the southern and eastern neighborhoods of Manhattan. The poorest lived in what is now Central Park, where they built shanties, raised pigs and goats, and scrambled for work as day laborers.

Education was the road out of poverty. There had been no schools for the rural poor in Ireland, but in New York, Bishop Hughes, himself an immigrant who had been a tenant farmer in Ireland, labored to establish Catholic schools in every parish.

While the immigrants dreamed of a better life for their children, most found themselves at the bottom of America's economic ladder—unskilled Irish laborers worked for the lowest wages in the city, and they were not happy about it. For a people accustomed to political insurgency, it was a small thing to make the transition to labor agitation. In 1846, 500 Irishmen who worked on the Atlantic Dock in Brooklyn went on strike: They demanded (unsuccessfully) a raise—87 cents per day—and a reduction of the working day to ten hours.

Nonetheless, for the Irish, life in America was not all grinding poverty, street battling against Nativists, and seeing their parish churches burn. By 1860, some of the immigrants had made progress. They opened saloons, opened little neighborhood grocery stores, or started small construction companies. They found jobs with the municipal police force or in the fire department. The Irish learned that joining the Democratic machine gave them access to good-paying government jobs, with a pension and connections to influential politicians. They were no longer tied to a few acres, their future limited to tenant farming; in America, there were job opportunities for the adults and schools for the children. Once they became American citizens, the Irish could vote and participate in government—something virtually unimaginable for peasants in the Old Country. Many, perhaps most, Americans were hostile to Catholicism, but freedom of religion was guaranteed in the U.S. Constitution, and under that freedom, the Catholic Church in America flourished. And here the Irish found another outlet for their ambitions: Across the country the overwhelming majority of cathedrals, chanceries, colleges, convents, and schools were administered by Irish bishops, priests, and nuns.

"THE BASE ALLOY OF HYPOCRISY"

By the 1850s the Nativist movement had consolidated into a political party called the Native American Party or the American Party. It was better known, however, as the Know-Nothings, because members were instructed that when asked about the party's secret activities they should reply, "I know nothing." In the years leading up to the Civil War, the Know-Nothings became an influential political force whose candidates were elected mayors of Boston, Philadelphia, New York, Baltimore, Chicago, New Orleans, and Washington, D.C. They dominated state politics in all the New England states, as well as in Pennsylvania, Indiana, and California. But they did not limit themselves to politics—in cities and towns from Bath, Maine, to Galveston, Texas, Nativist mobs destroyed Catholic churches and institutions, and burned the homes of American Catholics. Occasionally German immigrants were targeted, but overwhelmingly Irish Catholics, the largest immigrant group in the United States at the time, were the most frequent victims of the Nativists.

To their credit, by and large the Democratic and Republican parties were not influenced by the anti-immigrant, anti-Catholic rhetoric of the Know-Nothings. In 1855, a rising Illinois Republican politician, Abraham Lincoln, wrote to his best friend Joshua Speed, "Our progress in degeneracy appears to me to be pretty rapid. As a nation, we began by declaring that 'all men are created equal.' We now practically read it 'all men are created equal, except Negroes.' When the Know-Nothings get control, it will read 'all men are created equal, except Negroes, and foreigners, and Catholics.' When it comes to this I should prefer emigrating to some country where they make no pretence of loving liberty—to Russia, for instance, where despotism can be taken pure, and without the base alloy of hypocrisy."

In New York City, Fernando Wood was mayor from 1854 to 1858. He was a refined Protestant gentleman from a good family who ran the city's Democratic machine and pandered shamelessly to the Irish, particularly by handing out patronage jobs in city government. Wood and his party hacks were quick to remind the Irish of the poverty and religious persecution they had suffered in Ireland and the hostility and discrimination they endured in America. But, they were told, Mayor Wood and the Democrats were their friends and defenders. To show that they were firmly on the side of the Irish, Wood and the New York Democrats spoke fervently of their support for Ireland's independence from England. Historian William L. Burton writes, "In the ruthless exploitation of the ethnic vote, [the Democrats] ignored housing, education, and poverty, choosing instead to stress

THIRD IRISH
REGIMENT

From Massachusetts, and First Irish Regiment for Nine Months' Service.

25 ABLE-BODIED MEN

Wanted to fill up the Company to be commanded by

CAPTAIN WILLIAMS,

Formerly of the MASS. 24th; now of the 55TH (IRISH) MASS. REG'T.

Come with us and our IRISH HERO,

CORCORAN

Let us carry the American Eagle over the Potomac, down like an avalanche through the land of Dixie, emulating

THE GLORY of the other IRISH REGIMENTS.

$150 Bounty

And all who Enlist will receive the STATE AID.

All Recruits to this Regiment, on signing the Muster Roll, will go at once into comfortable quarters, and receive full rations of the best the market affords. Apply immediately to

Captain WILLIAMS, or, Lieut. LEONARD!
No. 109 CAMBRIDGE STREET, BOSTON.

Herald Job Office, No. 1 Williams Court, Boston.

TO RECRUIT MORE IRISH TROOPS IN MASSACHUSETTS, THE PRINTER PUT THE TWO GREATEST INDUCEMENTS TO ENLIST—THE NAME OF THE HERO OF THE IRISH BRIGADE, COLONEL MICHAEL CORCORAN, AND THE PAYMENT OF A $150 BOUNTY—IN THE SAME POINT SIZE.

ethnic cohesion, Irish nationalism, and the need for alien Americans to stand together against antagonistic native-born Americans." Little wonder, then, that when naturalized Irishmen went to the polls in the 1850s and 1860s, most of them voted the Democratic ticket.

The Irish identified the Republicans as the party of the abolitionists, and the abolition of slavery, the Irish believed, was a direct threat to their economic status. Irish men and women took the jobs native-born Americans did not want—the most difficult, the most dangerous, the lowest paying. If all the slaves in the South were freed, the Irish feared that they would be competing against more than four million men and women who would work for even lower wages than themselves.

FLYING THE FLAG FROM THE STEEPLE

In the months leading up to the U.S. Civil War, no one could predict whether the Irish in New York would support the Union. The Irish had reason to be suspicious of a Republican administration. The editors of the *New York Times*, the leading Republican newspaper in the city at the time, had linked Catholicism—"popery," they called it—with slavery as two institutions "incompatible with the spirit of the age, and liberty and civilization." The editors went on to say that they looked forward to the "speedy destruction" of both.

When the Civil War broke out, James McMaster, editor of the *Freeman's Journal*, the leading Catholic newspaper in New York, wrote fire-breathing editorials criticizing the Lincoln administration as tyrranical. McMaster was no proponent of slavery; he mocked white Southerners who asserted that owning slaves was their God-given right. But McMaster believed in gradual emancipation, so newly freed slaves could be absorbed into the workforce without threatening the Irish.

Archbishop John Hughes supported the Union, but he dreaded the coming war. "It will be the most sanguinary if not ferocious war that ever dismayed humanity," he said.

Secretary of State William Seward had McMaster arrested for "editing a disloyal newspaper." He was locked up for six weeks in Fort Lafayette, on an island in New York Harbor, and his newspaper was banned from the U.S. postal system. McMaster was released, and his newspaper was permitted to be mailed again only after he took

EN ROUTE TO THE DOCK WHERE THEY
WOULD EMBARK FOR WASHINGTON,
D.C., TO BEGIN THEIR MILITARY
TRAINING, THE 69TH NEW YORK
STATE MILITIA MARCHED PAST ST.
PATRICK'S CATHEDRAL. THE BRICK
WALL HAD BEEN BUILT TO DEFEND
THE CHURCH FROM ANTI-CATHOLIC
RIOTERS.

an oath of loyalty to the United States and swore that any newspaper he published would "not be devoted to the overthrow of the Constitution and the Union."

Privately, Archbishop John Hughes (Pope Pius IX had elevated him to archbishop in 1850) expressed his low opinion of Lincoln and his cabinet, making an exception for his old friend William Seward, whom he regarded as "the only one in the cabinet of Mr. Lincoln fit to be at the helm." Hughes supported the Union, but he dreaded the coming war. "It will be the most sanguinary if not ferocious war that ever dismayed humanity," he said.

But once the Confederates fired on Fort Sumter in Charleston, South Carolina, on April 12, 1861, Hughes, like many other Irish New Yorkers, rallied to the cause of the Union. He ordered pastors to fly the Stars and Stripes from the steeple of every Catholic church in the archdiocese, and set the example by flying the flag from St. Patrick's Cathedral. When some New York priests objected to putting the flag on par with the cross, Hughes replied that if he had not made a public demonstration of his patriotism, "the press would have sounded the report that Catholics are disloyal, and no act of ours afterward could successfully vindicate us from the imputation."

Wood appeared on the stage with the Stars and Stripes draped over his shoulders like a shawl. He called on "every man, whatever had been his sympathies, to make one great phalanx in this controversy, to proceed to conquer a peace. I am with you in this contest. We know no party now."

In the months leading up to the Civil War, Fernando Wood (who had been re-elected mayor) spoke of declaring New York "an open city," essentially seceding from the Union so New Yorkers could still do business with the South, and Democratic New York could act independently of the state government in Republican Albany and the Lincoln Administration in Republican Washington, D.C. There was talk around town—and in Washington—that the mayor was crypto-Confederate, but keeping New York City out of a war just about everyone believed was coming was popular in some quarters, including among many of the Irish—an important segment of Wood's political base.

On April 15, 1861, the day after Fort Sumter surrendered, Mayor Wood issued a proclamation calling upon all inhabitants to behave as law-abiding American citizens, "irrespective of all other considerations and prejudices." Anti-Confederate feeling was sweeping the city, and Wood intended to ride the crest of it. The next day he called for a public rally. So no one could doubt his loyalty to the Union, Wood appeared on the stage with the Stars and Stripes draped over his shoulders like a shawl. He called on "every man, whatever had been his sympathies, to make one great phalanx in this controversy, to proceed to conquer a peace. I am with you in this contest. We know no party now." The throng—which included many Irish—roared its approval.

Wood busied himself starting regiments comprised of Tammany Hall Democrats. He proposed a special tax to equip New York City's troops, and when Colonel Robert Anderson, the hero of Fort Sumter, arrived in New York, Wood scarcely left his side, determined to bask in the patriotic glow of Anderson's reputation. Inspired by the words of their archbishop and excited by the actions of their mayor, the Irish lined up to volunteer for military duty—especially in the city's almost all-Irish 69th Infantry Regiment.

2

SONS OF ERIN:
The Commanders of the Irish Brigade

O n July 13, 1847, a large body of Irish political activists gathered at Conciliation Hall in Dublin. Most of the men in the chamber were supporters of Daniel O'Connell, "the Liberator," the Irishman credited with winning the repeal of the anti-Catholic penal laws in Ireland and the recognition of the political rights of the Irish. O'Connell went on to become the first Irish Catholic elected to the British Parliament and the first Irish Catholic Lord Mayor of Dublin since the Reformation. He was the darling of most Irish—but not all.

O'Connell was ambivalent on the subject of Irish independence, and he was openly opposed to revolution. The activists in the Young Ireland movement despised O'Connell as a toady of the British and a traitor to his homeland. O'Connell and his supporters knew this, so at the meeting in Conciliation Hall, O'Connell's supporters put forward what became known as the Peace Resolution, calling on all delegates to use only peaceful means to achieve their political goals. The resolution passed, but then a well-dressed, twenty-two-year-old man from Waterford took the floor. He was Thomas Francis Meagher, and he was a Young Irelander.

As he spoke, Meagher denounced the Peace Resolution. "There are times when arms alone suffice," he told the assembly, "and when political ameliorations call for a drop of blood, and many thousand drops of blood." Then he swept into the part of his speech that would become a classic of Irish nationalist oratory. "Abhor the sword? Stigmatize the sword? No, my lord, for at its blow, and in the quivering of its crimson light a giant nation sprang up from the waters of the Atlantic, and by its redeeming magic the fettered colony became a daring, free Republic." (He was referring, of course, to the United States, which had gone to war to win its independence from England.)

DANIEL O'CONNELL, SHOWN IN A PRINT CREATED AROUND 1873, USED A CAMPAIGN OF NON-VIOLENCE TO WIN CIVIL RIGHTS FOR CATHOLICS IN IRELAND. HE ONCE SAID, "THE ALTAR OF LIBERTY TOTTERS WHEN IT IS CEMENTED ONLY WITH BLOOD." YOUNG REVOLUTIONARIES SUCH AS THOMAS FRANCIS MEAGHER REJECTED O'CONNELL'S PACIFICISM AND CALLED FOR ARMED INSURRECTION AGAINST BRITAIN.

The speech strikes most contemporary readers as over-the-top, but in the 1840s, it was hailed as inspired. It became known as "the Sword Speech" and the orator was renamed "Meagher of the Sword."

When he finished his speech and returned to his seat, one of Daniel O'Connell's lieutenants rose and made a motion stating that no one who shared Meagher's views would be welcome in Conciliation Hall. At that, all the Young Irelanders rose and walked out.

IRELAND'S TROUBLES

Thomas Francis Meagher (pronounced "Mar") was born in 1823, in Waterford in southeastern Ireland. His family was well-off thanks to a prosperous commercial shipping business his grandfather had established about fifty years earlier. The Meaghers' money ensured that Thomas would enjoy privileges available to very few Irish boys. When he was about five or six years old, he was sent to a nearby convent where the Sisters of Charity taught him the basics of reading, writing, arithmetic, and the Catholic catechism. At age ten, he was enrolled at Clongowes Wood College, a Jesuit school in County Kildare. From Clongowes he went to Stonyhurst, the Jesuit college in Lancashire, England. The Meaghers were Catholic, and at the time, Stonyhurst was one of the few places in the British Isles where a Catholic could receive a university education—Catholics were barred from enrolling in the universities at Oxford and Cambridge.

While at Clongowes and Stonyhurst, Meagher began reading the history of Ireland. He knew the outline anecdotally from family and friends, but now he made a study of it, and he did not like what he read.

Ireland's troubles with England began late in the twelfth century when Adrian IV, the only Englishman ever elected pope, granted the title "Lord of Ireland" to King Henry II of England. Ireland was being torn apart by power struggles among the island's five kings and many noble families; Adrian hoped Henry could bring peace and order to the Irish.

On October 18, 1172, the first English troops disembarked in Ireland, led by Richard fitz Gilbert de Clare, Earl of Pembroke, better known as Strongbow. Meagher would describe him as "a royal pirate." Strongbow seized Waterford and Dublin, and the English barons who followed him carved out great estates for themselves on the island, but in the Middle Ages, the English never achieved a wholesale conquest of Ireland.

Ireland became much more important and attracted much more of the English king's attention after Henry VIII broke with Rome in 1534. In Dublin and the surrounding area known as the Pale, where the English exercised the most control, the inhabitants submitted to Henry's new church, but elsewhere in Ireland, the overwhelming majority of the nobles and the common people remained loyal to the Catholic faith. Henry and every English monarch who came after him feared that the Catholic Irish might ally themselves with Catholic Spain or Catholic France to break free from English rule, which perhaps could serve as a launching point for an invasion of England. And so, over the next century, England sent army after army into Ireland until it had complete authority over the country.

In the seventeenth century, England introduced a code of penal laws intended to humiliate, impoverish, and reduce to ignorance Ireland's nearly one million Catholics. Catholics could not hold political office, practice law, own weapons, or own a horse worth more than £5. Catholics could not operate schools nor send their children overseas to be educated. Catholic bishops were outlawed; any who were apprehended would be hanged, drawn, and quartered. A Catholic who owned land could not leave it all to his eldest son, but must divide it among all his children. Marriages performed by Catholic priests were invalid.

Most members of the Irish aristocracy and the merchant class could not imagine life without property and status, so they joined the Protestant Church. The Meaghers, however, remained Catholic, scraping along in County Tipperary until the 1760s, when Thomas's grandfather emigrated to Newfoundland where there were no restrictions on Irish Catholics. There, Grandfather Meagher founded the commercial shipping business that made his descendants rich.

Yet in spite of the privileges he enjoyed, Thomas Meagher deeply resented England's occupation of Ireland. After 300 years of English rule, the Irish were among the poorest, least educated people in Europe. "[The English] left us," Meagher said, "like blind and crippled children, in the dark."

THE REBELLION OF 1848

By the early 1840s, when Meagher was becoming active in Irish politics, England had repealed the penal laws, thanks to the campaigning of Daniel O'Connell. But there was another law the Irish wanted repealed—the Act of Union of 1800, which had abolished the Irish Parliament, granted the Irish a few token seats in the Parliament at Westminster, and effectively stripped any governance the Irish had of their own affairs. The Young Irelanders demanded the repeal as the first step toward Irish independence. Decades earlier, O'Connell, a consummate politician, would have found a way to draw the radicals into his own political organization, thereby neutralizing them. But in the 1840s, O'Connell was in his sixties and not the dynamic leader he had once been. He let himself be persuaded by his son John that the Young Irelanders must play no part in the Irish nationalist movement.

In 1847, six months after they had walked out of O'Connell's Repeal Association, the Young Irelanders formed the Irish Confederation, an organization that began with protest marches through the streets of Dublin, demanding repeal of the Act of Union. By June 1848, however, the Young Irelanders were plotting to overthrow English rule in Ireland. Meagher was sent to Munster, Ireland's southernmost province, to recruit men and collect money and arms for the uprising. In July, he was in Waterford, his hometown, where he gave an inflammatory speech from his hotel window. The authorities declared the speech seditious and Meagher was arrested and taken to Dublin, where he was released on bail.

As he waited for his trial to begin, Meagher continued his anti-English activities. He traveled back to Munster, where he addressed a crowd of 50,000 at Slievenamon outside the town of Clonmel. Returning to Dublin, he met with thirty other leaders of Young Ireland and began to plan their revolution. They did not realize that they had been infiltrated—one of their members was a government informer.

Meagher and two fellow leaders of the movement, William Smith O'Brien and John Blake Dillon, were given the task of beginning the revolution in Kilkenny, where the English garrison was small. Along the way to Kilkenny they harangued crowds, urging the men to join them. Very few did. The three Young Irelanders did not inspire confidence among the peasants and townspeople of County Kilkenny: They had no weapons to distribute to the recruits, no funds for an army, and no military experience. Furthermore, after years of famine, most of the peasants were in no condition—physically or psychologically—to wage a successful rebellion. It wasn't long before Meagher, Dillon, and Smith O'Brien became aware that the peasants were too sick, weak, and dispirited to fight. Meagher would recall later, "Hunger and disease, to the last extremity . . . had not only withered up the flesh and pierced the marrow in the bone . . . but worse than all—oh! Worse, a thousand times than death by the bayonet, or the gibbet—had eaten their way into the soul itself." Still, with the men they had, Meagher, Dillon, and Smith O'Brien pressed on. Only at the town of Carrick did they find people ready for revolution, but these men were so loud and unruly that the Young Irelanders could not organize them and were forced to march off without the men of Carrick.

Nonetheless, they tried to remain optimistic: In Dublin, Meagher, Dillon, and Smith O'Brien had been assured that in Kilkenny there were thousands of Young Irelanders ready to fight. When they arrived in Kilkenny town, they found that

THE SKIRMISH AT THE HOME OF WIDOW MARGARET MCCORMACK IN BALLINGARRY TOOK PLACE ON JULY 30, 1848. IT WAS THE ONLY "BATTLE" IN THOMAS FRANCIS MEAGHER'S FAILED ATTEMPT TO OVERTHROW ENGLISH RULE IN IRELAND.

membership in the local chapter ran to 1,700, and most of these were old men or boys. Only 600 men were strong enough to fight, and only about 200 had guns. To lead such a small, underarmed force against trained, veteran English troops would be madness, so Meagher and Dillon hurried off to Templederry, the parish of Father John Kenyon, an outspoken member of the Young Ireland movement. They expected the priest to help them find arms, funds, and more men for the uprising, but after hearing their description of the insurgents in Kilkenny, Father Kenyon said it would be best if the uprising were postponed until the Young Irelanders had a proper army. And so they returned to Kilkenny without troops, arms, or money.

THE SENTENCE

Father Kenyon was right; it would have been best if the would-be rebels at Kilkenny had dispersed to wait to fight another day, but Smith O'Brien and some of the insurgents were in the mood for rebellion. In the village of Ballingarry, they laid a trap for the local police. Someone leaked word of the ambush to the police, along with the absurd claim that 3,000 rebels had hidden themselves around the town. The police fled to the strongest building in Ballingarry—a stone house belonging to Widow Margaret McCormack.

As the police barricaded themselves inside, Smith O'Brien's men piled hay around the house and set it ablaze to smoke out the police. Suddenly, the front door opened and out walked Mrs. McCormack, prepared to negotiate a truce with Smith O'Brien. The widow and the revolutionary had barely begun to talk when the rebels started pelting the house with rocks. From the windows the police opened fire, killing one rebel and wounding another. The rebels returned fired for several minutes, until they ran out of ammunition. Just as Smith O'Brien was rallying his men to charge the house, a priest ran up, calling on the rebels to see sense and return to their homes. The rebels took the priest's advice, and the Revolution of 1848 came to an abrupt end minutes after it had begun.

Smith O'Brien, Meagher, and Dillon scattered into the countryside. English troops captured Smith O'Brien near Thurles, but Dillon managed to escape to France. Near Rathgannon, a priest found Meagher and suggested that he offer to surrender to the government on the condition that he be permitted to leave the country. Meagher agreed, but only if the English permitted all the insurgents to emigrate. George Villiers, the Lord Lieutenant of Ireland (Queen Victoria's official representative in the country), consented to the arrangement, but set a condition of his own—the rebels must all confess to high treason. Meagher rejected the offer, and was arrested.

At his trial, Meagher said that in the context of England's oppression of Ireland, "the treason of which I stand convicted loses all its guilt, is sanctified as a duty, will be ennobled as a sacrifice. . . . Pronounce, then, my lords, the sentence which the law directs; I am prepared to hear it. I trust I shall be prepared to meet its execution." He was convicted of high treason, and sentenced to be hanged, drawn, and quartered. The gruesome penalty had been abolished in England, but it was still on the books in Ireland, and some Irish feared that the English might try to discourage future uprisings by disemboweling Thomas Meagher and hacking his body into four pieces.

Of course, the English government, unwilling to see butchery committed in its name, intervened and commuted Meagher's sentence to exile for life at a penal colony in Van Diemen's Land, known today as Tasmania.

When Meagher, Smith O'Brien, and two other Young Irelanders arrived in Van Diemen's Land, the island had a population of approximately 65,000, about 30,000 of whom were convicts, and many of these were Irish. There was no prison such as one found in Europe, but probation stations where convicts were confined and put to work. After a period of years, a convict could earn a pass, which let him travel in and out of the station. Most highly valued among convicts was a ticket of leave, which gave the bearer freedom to travel anywhere he wished in Van Diemen's Land, as long as he swore not to try to escape. Meagher and the two Young Irelanders took the oath and received tickets of leave when they arrived on the island, but Smith O'Brien refused to promise he would not try to escape, so he was sent to a prison colony on Maria Island.

Meagher acquired a cottage and some land near the village of Ross, and hired a young Irishman to help him farm. Compared with typical forms of imprisonment, Meagher was exceptionally fortunate, but exile from home still stung, and the lack of friends of his own class and level of education depressed him (he was forbidden to live within 30 or 40 miles [48 or 64 km] of his fellow Young Irelanders). Then he received a letter from his fiancée in Ireland breaking off their engagement. She requested him to either return or burn her letter to him. The prospect of spending the rest of his life exiled became unbearable for Meagher; he began to think about escape.

In 1851, Meagher was twenty-eight years old and had been in exile for three years. That was also the year he completed his escape plans. Working with his father, who pledged to pay for the escape effort, Meagher found a ship's captain named Betts; in exchange for a payment of £600, Betts agreed to carry Meagher to a port in Brazil where he could catch another ship to America. Given that Meagher was in Van Diemen's Land, his father in Ireland, Betts in England, and their only method of communication was by mail, it took more than a year to confirm the arrangements.

COLONEL MICHAEL CORCORAN, THE POPULAR COMMANDER OF THE 69TH NEW YORK STATE MILITIA, WAS CAPTURED AT THE FIRST BATTLE

OF BULL RUN. WHILE IN PRISON HE WROTE, "ONE HALF OF MY HEART IS ERIN'S, AND THE OTHER HALF IS AMERICA'S."

In January 1852, Meagher walked to the Tamar River, where two fishermen waited for him. They rowed him to uninhabited Waterhouse Island, where he would rendezvous with Betts. Ten days Meagher waited, but Betts arrived at last and they set sail for Brazil, where Meagher disembarked at Pernambuco shortly before St. Patrick's Day. When an American ship, the *Acorn*, was ready to sail to New York, Meagher booked passage.

By the time he stepped ashore in New York City, Thomas Francis Meagher was already a celebrity. Irish newspapers in New York had covered Meagher's trial and conviction, and had kept his memory green during his years of exile. Early in 1852, two U.S. senators, James Shields of Illinois and William Seward of New York, urged their colleagues to pass a resolution expressing their sympathy for Meagher, Smith O'Brien, and other Irish patriots banished to Van Diemen's Land.

New York's thousands of Irish immigrants welcomed Meagher as a hero. Almost overnight his social calendar became crowded with invitations to receptions, assemblies, and dinners. He became a much-sought-after speaker. Irish militia companies named themselves after him. The Jesuits at St. John's College—later Fordham University—presented him with an honorary degree. President-elect Franklin Pierce invited Meagher to visit him at his home in Concord, New Hampshire. And an enterprising composer capitalized on the public's Meagher madness by publishing "The T.F. Meagher Polka."

Once the hoopla died down—and it took more than a year—Meagher began to build a life for himself in America. In 1855, he married Elizabeth Townsend, the daughter of a wealthy New York businessman, the ceremony being performed by Archbishop John Hughes in the chapel of his residence. In 1856, Meagher started a weekly paper, the *Irish News*, but as it did not provide enough income, he continued to travel, delivering speeches and lectures. That same year he was admitted to the New York bar.

Meagher's most famous case came in 1859 when Congressman Daniel Sickles hired Meagher as part of his defense team. Sickles had discovered that his wife, Teresa, was having an affair with Philip Barton Key (son of Francis Scott Key). When Sickles spotted Key loitering outside his Washington house, he grabbed a pistol, flung open the front door, and shot his wife's lover. Key was still alive, so Sickles walked over and with several more pistol shots, finished him off. Sickles had hoped that Meagher's celebrated oratory would turn the jury in his favor, but in the end, it was not Meagher but another of Sickles's attorneys, Edwin Stanton, who won his acquittal. Stanton argued that Sickles was innocent by reason of temporary insanity. It was not the first time such a defense had been offered in an American court, but it was the first time a jury accepted it.

SHARING THE SPOTLIGHT

Like many Irishmen in America in the years leading up to the Civil War, Meagher was sympathetic to the South. His lecture tours had taken him to the South, where he had been graciously received by members of the planter class. Furthermore, the South's longing for independence from the North was certain to strike a chord with men like Meagher who had worked for Ireland's independence from England. But after the bombardment of Fort Sumter, Meagher gave his allegiance to the Union. "My heart, my arm, my life—to the national cause!" he declared.

Then an advertisement appeared in the *New York Daily Tribune*: "Young Irishmen to arms! To arms young Irishmen! Irish Zouaves. One hundred young Irishmen—healthy, intelligent and active—wanted at once to form a Company under command of Thomas Francis Meagher." Within a week, Meagher, now a captain in the New York State Militia, had his company of Irish Zouaves, which the state rolled into the all-Irish 69th Regiment. In the 69th, Meagher shared the spotlight with another Irish hero, Colonel Michael Corcoran.

In 1861, the New York militia unit most popular with the Irish was the 69th Infantry Regiment commanded by Colonel Michael Corcoran. A tall, gaunt man, Corcoran was born in Carrowkeel, County Sligo, in 1827. His father had enlisted in the British Army and served in the West Indies. His mother was descended from Patrick Sarsfield, the young Earl of Lucan, who had fought for the Catholic Stuart king, James II, against the interloper William of Orange. After the Battle of the Boyne in 1690, when James's cause was lost, Sarsfield was among the Irish nobles and military men who joined their king in exile on the Continent.

The Corcorans were not wealthy but comfortable enough to provide Michael with an education. Thanks to his studies and his father's connections, nineteen-year-old Michael joined the Royal Irish Constabulary and was stationed in County Donegal. His enlistment coincided with the potato famine in which more than 1.5 million Irish would die of hunger and disease. The Constabulary was responsible for the orderly distribution of food to the starving, as well as guarding supply depots crammed with grain and cattle that were to be transported to England for sale. That so much food was leaving the country at such a time led the Irish nationalist John Mitchel to say, "The Almighty indeed sent the potato blight, but the English created the Famine."

The horrors of the Great Famine radicalized Corcoran—in 1848, he resigned from the Constabulary and joined the Ribbonmen, a secret society that terrorized landlords in rural Ireland. They burned barns, damaged farm equipment, and even maimed cattle—all to bring the sufferings of the Famine to the doorstep of the English landowners.

A PHOTO TAKEN IN 1861 SHOWS CAPTAIN THOMAS FRANCIS MEAGHER (PRONOUNCED "MAR"), THE FOUNDER OF THE IRISH BRIGADE, SEATED AMID MEMBERS OF THE 69TH NEW YORK STATE MILITIA. CAPTAIN MEAGHER WOULD BE COMMISSIONED A BRIGADIER GENERAL IN FEBRUARY 1862.

Someone informed the authorities that Corcoran was involved in these acts of sabotage, but someone else warned Corcoran that the police were after him. In 1849, twenty-two-year-old Michael Corcoran boarded a ship for America.

In New York, Corcoran supported himself by peddling oysters in the Bowery. Next he took a job as a clerk in the post office. Then he went to work for John Heaney (sometimes spelled Heeney), the owner of the Hibernian Hall on Prince Street, a tavern and social center for the Irish in Manhattan and the meeting place of the Ancient Order of Hibernians, a benevolent society dedicated to protecting the Irish and the Catholic Church against Nativists and other enemies. In 1851, Corcoran joined the 69th Regiment as a private. By 1858, Corcoran was the manager of the Hall and a captain in the militia. In his spare time, he had helped to found the New York chapter of the Fenian Brotherhood, a revolutionary society dedicated to the liberation of Ireland from English rule. And he had married Heaney's niece, Elizabeth Heaney.

THE QUARANTINE RIOT

In the 1850s, there was a quarantine station for sailors and immigrants at Seguine's Point on Staten Island in New York Harbor. At a time when there were no antibiotics and epidemics were commonplace, it was essential to isolate the ill from the general population of the city. The sick were kept at the quarantine station until they had recovered or died.

Understandably, Staten Islanders who lived near the station feared contagion, and were especially susceptible to rumors that the inmates were escaping and spreading disease. In September 1858, victims of yellow fever were being treated at the quarantine hospital. Yellow fever is spread by infected mosquitoes, but in the 1850s, no one knew that—all the people of Staten Island knew was that yellow fever was highly contagious and almost always fatal.

A few days after the yellow fever victims arrived at Seguine's Point, a large, armed mob stormed the quarantine station. The guards could not turn them back and sent word to Manhattan for reinforcements. The 69th Regiment was sent to put down the riot. By the time the troops arrived, the mob had shot and killed one hospital employee, had dragged many of the patients from their beds and beaten them, and had set fire to all of the station's buildings. Amid the chaos, Captain Corcoran kept his head: He dispersed the mob, protected the patients and hospital staff, put out the fires, and made the quarantine station secure. For his action during the Quarantine Riot, he was promoted to colonel.

In fall 1860, Queen Victoria's eldest son, Edward, Prince of Wales (the future King Edward VII), came to New York—the first visit to America by a member of the British Royal Family. To welcome the prince, the city organized a number of special entertainments, including a ball and grand military parade. All the colonels of all the city's militia regiments were invited to the ball in the prince's honor. Corcoran, the memories of the Famine still fresh in his mind, refused to go and sent a note that read, "I am not desirous of joining in the Festivity."

When Corcoran's superior officer ordered him to lead the men of the 69th in the military parade honoring the prince, Corcoran sent another note: "I could not in good conscience order out a regiment composed of Irish-born citizens to parade in honor of a sovereign under whose reign Ireland was made a desert and her sons forced into exile."

Many native-born Protestants and anti-immigrant newspaper editors saw in Corcoran and the 69th's disobedience a classic case of ingratitude and dual loyalties. The Irish would never assimilate into American society, the critics said, as long as their ethnic sensibilities trumped the demands that they act as good American citizens.

Colonel Corcoran was placed under arrest and informed that he would be tried before a court martial. Corcoran's stand became a cause célèbre in New York and across the country as Irish and non-Irish argued whether he was insubordinate or a man of principle. The question was never settled in court: The bombardment of Fort Sumter and Corcoran's call for all Irishmen to rally to the defense of the Union convinced the army to quash the colonel's trial, dismiss the charges, and reinstate him with the 69th.

Among the Irish in America, Corcoran was a hero who had risked prison rather than pay tribute to the Prince of Wales. The Irish of San Francisco sent him a massive medal cast of one pound (455 kg) of gold, and the Irish of Charleston, South Carolina, sent him a gold-tipped palmetto walking stick.

After the surrender of Fort Sumter to the Confederacy, President Abraham Lincoln called for 75,000 volunteers to defend the Union. Encouraged by Colonel Corcoran, Mayor Wood, and Archbishop Hughes—the three men who enjoyed the most influence over the Irish—Irish New Yorkers took the attack on Fort Sumter as an attack on their new homeland. The Irish militia units leapt to the Union's defense, and hundreds of Irishmen volunteered for service. Corcoran turned Hibernian Hall into a recruiting station for the 69th Regiment, which at the time had 245 men. Approximately 1,800 men lined up along Prince Street to enlist, and 3,000 more had written in, requesting to fight with the famous Colonel Corcoran.

WINSLOW HOMER PAINTED THIS SCENE IN A UNION ARMY CAMP. THE MEN ARE DRESSED IN THE COLORFUL UNIFORM OF THE ZOUAVES,

LIGHT INFANTRY DEVELOPED IN 1831 BY THE FRENCH ARMY FOR ACTION IN NORTH AFRICA. BY 1860 ZOUAVES WERE FASHIONABLE IN AMERICA—

THE UNION ARMY HAD ABOUT 70 ZOUAVE REGIMENTS AND THE CONFEDERACY ABOUT 25.

Most of these men were turned away—membership in the 69th Regiment was limited to 1,000. Among those who were accepted for service was Patrick Hughes, the archbishop's nephew.

On April 23, 1861, eleven days after the first shot was fired on Fort Sumter, Colonel Corcoran led the 69th through the streets of Manhattan's Lower East Side. On Great Jones Street they came to halt before the home of the Dalys: Charles was a prominent Irish-American judge, and his wife, Maria, had been asked to present the regiment with its new colors—an emerald green silk banner with a golden harp in the center, a golden sunburst above it, and a spray of golden shamrocks below. Running beneath the harp and shamrocks was a scroll bearing the regiment's motto in Gaelic: "*Riambh nar druid o sbairn lann*," or "They shall not retreat from the clash of spears."

The 69th turned south on Broadway, where the sidewalks were packed with cheering crowds, and well-wishers hung out of every window waving flags and handkerchiefs. The regiment headed to St. Patrick's Cathedral, where Archbishop Hughes said Mass for them, blessed them, and encouraged them to be courageous and chivalrous.

"Let the 69th Regiment know," he said, "that I shall be deeply afflicted if they should be less than brave in battle, less than humane and kind after the battle is over, and above all things, if by possibility, they should bring a tarnish upon their name, their country, or their religion."

Few of the enlisted men in the Irish Brigade had any military experience, but their officers were a different matter. Before emigrating to America, Captain John Gossen had served with the dashing 7th Hussars of Hungary, a regiment of Austria-Hungary's Imperial Army. Second Lieutenant William L.D. O'Grady had fought with Britain's Royal Marines. Surgeon Francis Reynolds had acquired battlefield medicine experience serving with the British Medical Staff during the Crimean War. And at least ten officers of the 69th were veterans of the Battalion of St. Patrick, 1,000 Irishmen who had volunteered to fight in defense of Pope Pius IX and the Papal States against Giuseppe Garibaldi.

From St. Patrick's Cathedral the 69th marched to Pier 4, where a steamship was waiting to take them to Washington, D.C. They docked at the capital on May 4 and marched to Georgetown College, where they were encamped. Seven hours a day several cadets from West Point drilled the Irish, transforming raw recruits into soldiers. On May 23, the 69th crossed the Potomac River into Virginia, which was Confederate territory; near the Aqueduct Bridge that spanned the Potomac, they built Fort Corcoran.

Archbishop Hughes had assigned Father Thomas Mooney to the 69th as chaplain. Mooney was an irrepressible, impulsive young man. As curate of St. Brigid's

Church in New York's East Village, Father Mooney had demonstrated a knack for saying the wrong thing to his parishioners, yet Archbishop Hughes had faith that eventually Mooney would mature. Now that they were in Virginia and a fight with the Confederates appeared imminent, the men of the 69th were in high spirits. Father Mooney, impressionable man that he was, shared their ebullience; when the men rolled a new cannon into place, Mooney, in a burst of enthusiasm, baptized it.

Not long afterward, Father Mooney received a letter from an angry Archbishop Hughes. "Your inauguration of a ceremony unknown to the Church [baptizing a cannon] was sufficiently bad, but your remarks on that occasion were worse." Unfortunately, what Father Mooney said at the baptism has not survived, but we do know that Hughes ordered him back to New York.

Meanwhile, the 69th, along with the approximately 35,000 other men of Brigadier General Irwin McDowell's army, waited for orders. Northern newspapers and Washington politicians were calling for McDowell to march on Richmond immediately and put a quick end to the rebellion. But McDowell had two problems: Overwhelmingly, his army was composed of recruits who had signed up for only ninety days of military service—once the ninety days were over, they were free to go home. Furthermore, few of these recruits had any battlefield experience, and McDowell was reluctant to lead them into a major engagement against the enemy. He brought his concerns to President Lincoln, who tried to reassure his general. "You are green, it is true," Lincoln said, "but [the Confederates] are green also. You are all green alike."

And so McDowell agreed to attack the armies of General Joseph E. Johnston and P.G.T. Beauregard, and the 69th prepared for its first battle.

3

LIKE A ROCK IN A WHIRLPOOL:
The Irish Brigade at Bull Run

The charge of a large Union force on a poorly defended Confederate position on Matthews Hill sent South Carolinians, under Brigadier General Barnard E. Bee Jr., and Georgians, under Colonel Francis Bartow, scattering in every direction. Amid the chaos, Bee pointed to nearby Henry House Hill, where Confederate General Thomas J. Jackson sat serenely on horseback. "There stands Jackson like a stone wall," Bee shouted. "Rally to the Virginians!" The fleeing regiments stormed up the hill, taking up new positions around the Henry family's white clapboard farmhouse.

It was about noon on a hot Sunday, July 21, 1861. While the South Carolinians, Georgians, and Virginians formed lines on the hilltop, Federal troops spent an hour resting and reforming their own lines for an attack. When Confederate snipers inside the Henry farmhouse began to pick off the men in blue, Captain Robert Bruce Ricketts of Pennsylvania ordered his artillery to shell the house. Confined to her bed in an upstairs bedroom lay Judith Carter Henry, an eighty-five-year-old widow. When the battle began, her son and daughter-in-law had begged her to evacuate to a safe place, but the elderly lady refused to abandon her home. During the bombardment, a Union shell blasted into her bedroom and tore off one of her feet; Judith Henry bled to death—she was the only civilian casualty of the Battle of Bull Run.

A gentle rise, about 700 yards (630 m) long, led up to the farmhouse where the Confederates were dug in. Brigade after brigade of Union troops charged up the slope, only to be driven back by heavy fire. Late in the afternoon, the 69th New York Regiment was ordered to prepare to go in. Many of the men shrugged off their packs and peeled off their sweat-soaked uniform coats. Most of them had never been in battle before; the roar of the artillery, the rattle of rifle fire, the dense clouds of smoke, and the screams of wounded men and horses unnerved many of these raw recruits. Fear put them on edge. When they spotted gray-clad troops moving through the woods on their flank, some of the Irishmen prepared to fire. Seeing the mistake, Captain James Haggerty spurred his horse, riding along the line, using his sword to slap lowered muskets upright before the men of the 69th New York fired on the men of the 13th New York. The North had not yet standardized its military uniforms, and the 13th New York was dressed in gray.

The 69th was commanded to lie flat in the grass and wait for orders. Meanwhile, Colonel William Tecumseh Sherman had his artillery rolled forward to shell the Confederates at closer range. Unfortunately, he failed to send in sufficient infantry to protect the gunners—the Confederates took advantage of Sherman's error, swarmed down the hill, and captured the guns. Sherman sent in the 2nd Wisconsin, then the 79th New York to recapture the artillery, but the Confederates drove back both regiments. Lying in the grass, the 69th had watched the failed assaults on Henry House Hill. Captain David Power Conyngham, a member of the 69th, described the scene. "Shell and round-shot ploughed the ranks," he wrote, "shattered the trees; thick volumes of smoke rose from the woods, and floated along the valleys."

When at last the order came to enter the fight, the Irish leapt up and charged the rise. "Batteries opened on them right and left," Conyngham wrote, "hurling grape into their very faces, while from the shelter of the woods a stream of lead was poured on them." One cannonball tore into Captain Thomas Meagher's horse. Seeing their hero fall, the Irish hesitated, but Meagher leapt to his feet and rallied the men. Colonel Michael Corcoran and Captain Haggerty joined the charge. As they surged forward, a Confederate bullet struck Haggerty through the heart, killing him instantly.

THE BALTIMORE RIOT

On April 14, 1861, after thirty-four hours of nonstop bombardment, Major Robert Anderson surrendered Fort Sumter in Charleston Harbor to the Confederacy. As part of the terms of the agreement, Anderson and his men would be permitted to return to the North via steamship, with the fort's flag in their possession. In the North, Anderson would be welcomed as a hero by cheering crowds, and his battered and torn flag venerated as a relic. But weeks earlier it was possible that Anderson might side with the Confederacy: He was a Kentuckian who had once owned slaves and was still pro-slavery, but he was also pro-Union, and in the end his Union sympathies outweighed all other considerations.

As Anderson and his men evacuated the fort, South Carolina governor Francis W. Pickens addressed the thousands of Charlestonians who had swarmed down to the waterfront to celebrate their victory. "The day has come," Pickens said, "the war

THE 6TH MASSACHUSETTS REGIMENT,
EN ROUTE TO WASHINGTON D.C.
TO PROTECT THE CAPITAL, WAS
ATTACKED BY ANGRY CROWDS AT
BALTIMORE'S NORTHERN RAILROAD
TERMINUS ON APRIL 14, 1861. AFTER
THE UNION TROOPS RESPONDED BY
FIRING INTO THE MOB, BALTIMORE
POLICE INTERVENED, ALLOWING
THEM TO BOARD A TRAIN AT THE
SOUTHERN TERMINUS, THEIR
ORIGINAL DESTINATION. FOUR
SOLDIERS AND TWELVE CITIZENS
WERE KILLED IN THE RIOT, AND
DOZENS MORE WERE WOUNDED.

is open, and we shall conquer or perish. . . . we have humbled the proud flag of the Stars and Stripes that never before was lowered to any nation on Earth."

When word of Major Anderson's surrender reached President Abraham Lincoln, he called for 75,000 volunteers to defend the Union and called for regiments to come immediately to Washington—the capital had very few troops to defend it. On April 19, the 6th Massachusetts Regiment arrived at Baltimore's northern railroad terminus; the train that would carry it to Washington waited at the southern terminus, at the other end of town. As the Union troops marched through the streets, angry crowds lined the sidewalks, jeering and cursing the Massachusetts regiment. Some hurled bricks and stones; the men of the 6th responded by firing into the mob.

Instead of dispersing, the mob attacked; the Massachusetts men pressed on, trying to reach the southern railway station, firing as they ran. Baltimore police intervened, placing themselves between the troops and the mob until the regiment was aboard the train, and the train safely on its way to Washington. Four soldiers and twelve civilians were killed in the riot, and dozens more were wounded.

> Winfield Scott, a native of Virginia, had held the office of commanding general for twenty years, but in 1861, he was seventy-five years old and so obese he could no longer mount a horse.

In the weeks that followed the surrender of Fort Sumter and the Baltimore riot, four more states seceded from the Union, including North Carolina, Tennessee, and Arkansas. On May 23, Virginia voters ratified their state's Act of Secession—now the Confederacy lay just across the Potomac River from Washington, D.C. The next day Lincoln sent troops to capture Alexandria, Virginia, a port city and a railroad hub. The Irish of the 69th were sent to occupy Arlington Heights, overlooking the Potomac.

The commanding general of the United States Army, Winfield Scott, began formulating a strategy to defeat the Confederacy. Scott, a native of Virginia, had held the office of commanding general for twenty years, but in 1861, he was seventy-five years old and so obese he could no longer mount a horse. The actual commander in the field was Brigadier General Irvin McDowell, an Ohio man, a graduate of West Point, and a veteran of the Mexican-American War. Although he had no experience commanding men in battle, he won this post thanks to the influence of his friend, Salmon Chase, secretary of the treasury.

On April 18, 1861, about fifty men from Kansas, calling themselves the Frontier Guards, moved into the White House to provide security for President Lincoln and his family. They had been organized by Senator James Lane of Kansas, who armed them with brand-new muskets and swords, but no uniforms—the situation in Washington was considered so urgent there had not been time to have the men fitted out with a uniform. The Lincolns gave the Frontier Guards the East Room as their barracks. John Hay, the president's twenty-three-year-old secretary, watched with amusement as the Guard spent some time in the evening "in an exceedingly rudimentary squad drill, under the light of the gorgeous gas chandeliers." Then the troops stretched out on the room's thick Brussels carpet, while sentries patrolled before the East Room door, each under strict orders to admit no one who did not know the password. Early the next morning when Lincoln came down from the family residence and tried to enter the East Room, a sentry barred his way because the president had not given the password. As more volunteers arrived in the capital, the city was sufficiently secure for the Frontier Guards to move to a regular barracks, but before they left, Lincoln thanked them "for their timely services in preventing . . . this capital from falling into the hands of the enemy."

For three months, troops from every part of the Union had poured into Washington, bringing a sense of security to the capital—and to the president and his family—that had been lacking during the first days of the war, when the city was virtually defenseless against a Confederate attack. By July 1861, approximately 35,000 men were encamped in Washington and its suburbs. Another 18,000 men under the command of General Robert Patterson of Pennsylvania had been sent to keep 11,000 Confederate troops under General Joseph E. Johnston bottled up in western Virginia's Shenandoah Valley and to prevent them from joining the Confederate force near the town of Manassas, Virginia, about 35 miles (56 km) from Washington. At Bunker Hill, Virginia, Patterson believed he had Johnston immobilized and sent dispatches to that effect back to Washington.

In the meantime, Congress was pressuring McDowell to strike the Confederates. On July 16, McDowell's troops set out for the tiny crossroads town of Manassas near a creek called Bull Run. Throughout the Civil War, the Confederacy tended to name battles after the nearest town, while the Union usually named the battle after a nearby stream. Consequently, the South refers to the battles of Manassas and Sharpsburg, while the North refers to the battles of Bull Run and Antietam.

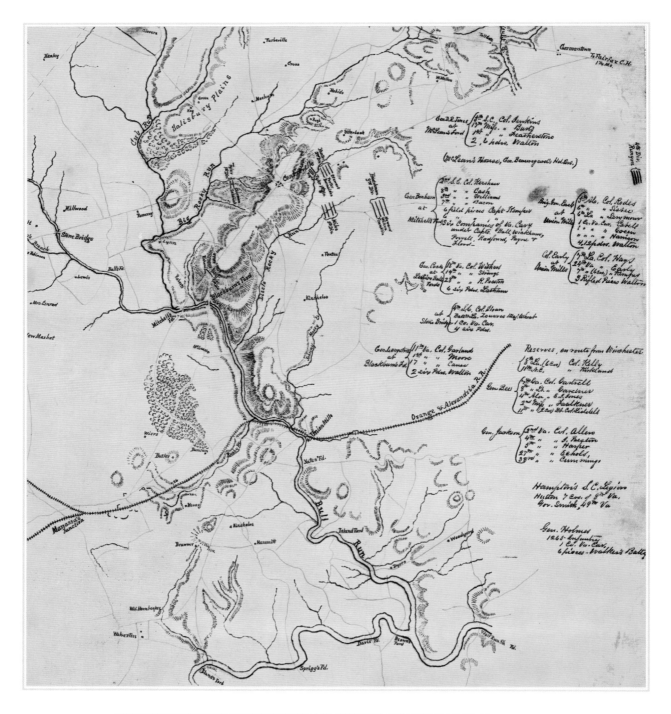

AN 1861 MAP SHOWS THE FIRST MANEUVERS OF THE BATTLE OF BULL RUN. NOTE THE STONE BRIDGE AREA ON THE UPPER LEFT OF THE MAP,
WHERE THE LOUISIANA TIGERS, A BATTALION UNDER MAJOR ROBERDEAU L. WHEAT, FOUGHT. THE TIGERS WERE A ZOUAVE BATTALION—LIKE
MANY OF MEAGHER'S FIGHTERS—AS NOTED BY THE CONFEDERATE TROOP LISTING ON THE MIDDLE RIGHT SIDE OF THE MAP.

Those days on the march reinforced McDowell's fears concerning his men. Almost all of them were undisciplined, untrained volunteers who could not even march properly. Time and again groups of men fell out of line to pick berries, fill their canteens, or scavenge chickens from Virginia farmyards. It took the army a day and a half to cover 12 miles (19 km).

As McDowell's men crept along, the Confederate army of about 22,000 under Brigadier General Pierre Gustave Toutant Beauregard was seizing the best terrain outside Manassas. Beauregard's family were members of Louisiana's wealthy, plantation aristocracy, so immersed in their French heritage that young Pierre did not begin to learn to speak English until he was twelve. At West Point, Beauregard was a classmate of Irvin McDowell. In April 1861, Beauregard commanded the bombardment of Fort Sumter, an event that made him the darling of the Confederacy, yet in terms of battlefield experience, he was as raw as McDowell was.

Beauregard took up his position on the southern side of Bull Run, placing his center at a spot where the banks stood 5 feet (1.5 m) high and the shoreline was thick with brush. On his left flank was a stone bridge across the stream—he sent half a brigade to hold the bridge. On his right flank was Mitchell's Ford, a shallow stretch of the stream that McDowell's army could wade across—Beauregard deployed approximately 11,000 men to the ford with orders to repulse the Union advance. When he was finished, Beauregard had a front 7 miles (11 km) long.

The first skirmish came on July 18, when a Union division under Brigadier General Daniel Tyler of Connecticut approached the stream and was met with heavy fire from snipers in the woods and artillery commanded by Brigadier General James Longstreet. Tyler retreated, but he brought back with him information that was useful to McDowell—Beauregard was defending the stream's prime crossing points.

That same day at Bunker Hill, General Johnston had received orders to bring his 11,000 men to Manassas to reinforce Beauregard. The next day the army escaped from Patterson—who had held back because he believed Johnston was in command of 26,000 men—boarded trains, and dashed across Virginia to Manassas.

"BULLY FOR US!"

Back in Washington, D.C., the mood among many civilians was positively lighthearted as they waited for word of a decisive Union victory. Some could not wait, and soon carriages filled with congressmen and other gentlemen in top hats and ladies in bonnets and brightly colored summer frocks rolled through the streets, heading for Manassas. Most of the spectators had brought picnic baskets and bottles of champagne so they could enjoy their midday meal while watching the battle.

Residents of nearby towns also came out. On a hill near Centreville behind the Union lines, a British war correspondent, William Howard Russell, stood amid a group of civilians. Beside him was a lady who had brought along her opera glasses so she could get a better view of the fighting. After one heavy artillery barrage she exclaimed, "That is splendid! Oh, my! Is it not first-rate? I guess we will be in Richmond this time tomorrow."

A Union officer rode up, waving his hat in jubilation. "We've whipped them on all points!" he shouted to the crowd. "We have taken all their batteries! They are retreating as fast as they can, and we are after them!" The civilians cheered, and the congressmen in the group congratulated one another, saying, "Bully for us! Bravo! Didn't I tell you so?"

The officer's report was accurate—Union troops had driven the Confederates from Matthews Hill and sent them running for the Warrenton Turnpike. But there the rout stopped, and the Confederates ran up Henry House Hill to join the Virginians led by the newly nicknamed Stonewall Jackson. But the Confederates on Matthews Hill represented only one tiny portion of the battle's 7-mile-long (11 km) front.

Defending the stone bridge was Captain Nathan "Shanks" Evans, a South Carolinian who acquired his nickname at West Point, where his fellow cadets mocked his exceptionally skinny legs. He was never able to shake the name. Evans was in command of the 4th South Carolina Infantry and was joined by Major Roberdeau L. Wheat, commander of a battalion known as the Louisiana Tigers. Wheat was a warrior by nature and physique—six foot three (191 cm), weighing 250 pounds (113 kg), he had volunteered to fight with William Walker in Nicaragua and Giuseppe Garibaldi in Italy. The Tigers were a Zouave battalion, inspired by the colorful infantry organized by the French in the 1830s to fight in North Africa. Zouaves were renowned for their flashy uniform that consisted of baggy blue-and-white striped pantaloons, a bright red cap, and a short royal blue jacket adorned with red braiding. In the late 1850s and early 1860s, there was a craze for Zouaves, whom civilians in the North and South considered dashing and gallant. In spite of their ludicrous uniforms, the Tigers were tough, strong men, most of them Irish stevedores who had worked on the docks of New Orleans. Together, Evans and Wheat had 1,000 men and two artillery pieces to defend the stone bridge.

Union Brigadier General Robert Shenck, the author of a book on poker, and Colonel William Tecumseh Sherman, who would become one of the most hated Union commanders in the South, made no effort to storm the bridge, but appeared

IN ADDITION TO HIS REGULATION UNION ARMY DRESS UNIFORM, THOMAS FRANCIS MEAGHER'S WARDROBE INCLUDED
FLAMBOYANT, NON-REGULATION UNIFORMS THAT HE DESIGNED HIMSELF, SUCH AS THE ONE SHOWN IN THIS PORTRAIT.
COLLECTION OF MICHAEL J. MCAFEE

AN AUGUST 3, 1861, ENGRAVING FROM *FRANK LESLIE'S ILLUSTRATED NEWSPAPER* SHOWS THE "GALLANT" 69TH NEW YORK STATE MILITIA ATTACKING A CONFEDERATE ARTILLERY BATTERY DURING THE FIRST BATTLE OF BULL RUN. THE IRISH WERE AMONG THE LAST UNION REGIMENTS TO LEAVE THE FIELD AT BULL RUN, AND IT IS THOUGHT THAT CAPTAIN MEAGHER MAY HAVE BEEN THE LAST MEMBER OF THE 69TH TO RETREAT.

to be reconnoitering the area. Evans and Wheat's men had barricaded themselves behind a rough wall of fallen trees that extended for a quarter mile (0.5 km) when Evans received a message from the Confederates' signal station that a Union force was moving toward his left flank. Evans took some of his South Carolinians, the Tigers, and two cannons and blocked the Union advance at a point across Sudley Road near the Sudley Church and the Carter family's farmhouse. Once the Yankees were in range, Evans ordered his artillery to open fire.

It was a valiant gesture, but Evans's force was outnumbered, and the situation became worse when Colonel Ambrose Burnside brought up his men; now the Confederates at Sudley Road were outnumbered three to one. By this time, Johnston and his men had arrived by train from western Virginia; Beauregard sent Johnston in to reinforce Evans. For the next hour, Yankees and Rebels struggled for control of the Sudley Road and Matthews Hill. Burnside's eight cannons pounded the summit of the hill: in twenty minutes, half of the men of the 8th Georgia were dead, wounded, or missing. During the fight, Jackson's Virginians arrived and dug in on Henry House Hill.

Shouting, "I ride to the sound of the guns!" General Johnston spurred his horse and galloped up Henry House Hill, with General Beauregard following behind him. At the summit, they found that Jackson had deployed his men under cover of the woods and rolled his thirteen artillery pieces into position. Johnston made his headquarters in the nearby Lewis farmhouse, while Beauregard remained with Jackson on the hilltop.

McDowell had ordered his gunners to roll up two Union howitzers and shell the hill, but the gunners' aim was terrible—the shells passed harmlessly over the Confederates' heads, crashing into the treetops behind them. Henry House Hill became the focus of the battle. One of the first regiments McDowell sent in was the 11th New York Fire Zouaves. Stripped down to their vivid red fireman shirts, the Zouaves were an impressive sight. The New Yorkers had just started up the hill when two companies of Virginia cavalry swept down, scattering them.

THE REBEL YELL

Late in the afternoon, McDowell sent in the Irish. Twice the men of the 69th New York tried to fight their way up Henry House Hill, but their progress was impeded by the bodies of the Union dead and wounded, and piles of equipment discarded by retreating Yankee troops.

Colonel Michael Corcoran was preparing the 69th for a third assault when he received orders to withdraw. It was just as well—more Confederate reinforcements were arriving on Henry House Hill, and two Union regiments, driven back by the

Confederates elsewhere on the field, suddenly appeared. They ran, every man for himself, through the neat lines of the 69th, breaking their formation and spreading consternation among the Irish.

Corcoran grabbed the Stars and Stripes from the color-bearer and, waving it vigorously, shouted orders to his men. No one could hear him—the roar of Confederate artillery and the panicky cries of the fleeing Yankees drowned out Corcoran's voice. Later, one of the men of the 69th, Private James McKay Rorty, would blame Colonel William Tecumseh Sherman for the rout at the bottom of Henry House Hill. According to Rorty, Sherman had "told the men to get away as fast as they could as the enemy's cavalry were coming." Rorty's account cannot be confirmed, but it may be a story born of bitterness—Rorty was taken prisoner by the Confederates at Bull Run. Several other men of the 69th were captured with him, including Colonel Corcoran, who at the time he was taken was still holding the flag.

Then two Virginia regiments commanded by Colonel Jubal Early and Lieutenant Colonel Jeb Stuart released a barrage of musket and artillery fire into the Union's right flank. Regiments from Maine and Vermont received the brunt of it, and quickly retreated across a creek known as Young's Branch. Under heavy fire, the Union's right collapsed. Seeing the Yankees in retreat, General Beauregard ordered a full-scale attack. The Confederates on Henry House Hill surged down the slope, shrieking like banshees—it was the first time Yankees had heard the rebel yell.

McDowell's army was in full flight, but at the bottom of the hill Captain Thomas Meagher was trying to rally his Irish Zouaves and the men of the 69th who had not fled the field. Swinging his sword over his head, Meagher pointed to the regiment's emerald green banner and cried, "Boys! Look at that flag—think of Ireland and Fontenoy!" Fontenoy was a battle in what is now Belgium, where, in 1745, an Irish brigade fighting for Louis XIV of France drove back the British, giving the French king victory.

There were not enough men to make a Fontenoy-inspired charge. Furthermore, the fight was now focused on the 69th regimental colors. After the Confederates had killed two color-bearers, John Keefe, a Zouave, had picked up the flag. Suddenly, a Rebel soldier ran up and tore the banner from its staff. Before he could get away, Keefe drew his revolver and shot the man dead, then snatched back the torn banner.

The sight of the entire Union army running off the field terrified the civilian spectators; they ran for their carriages. One civilian observer did not move fast enough: Congressman Albert Ely from Rochester, New York, was taken prisoner by the Confederates and held in Richmond for six months before he was released as part

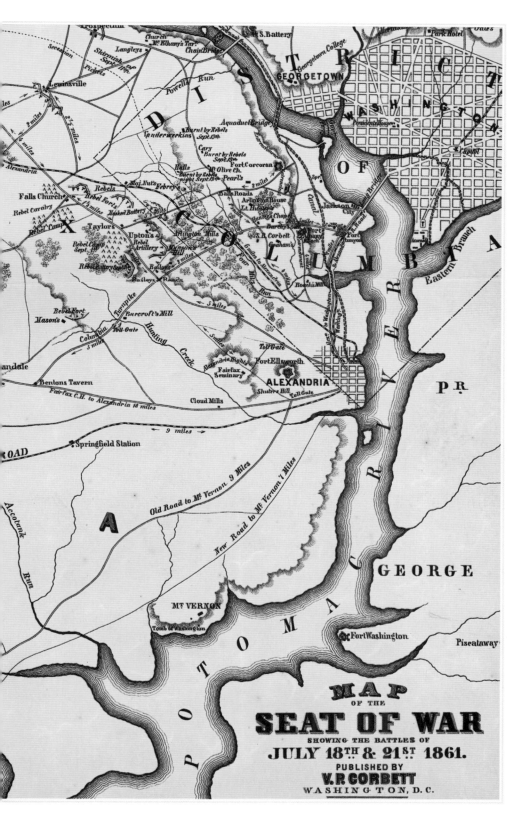

MAP
OF THE
SEAT OF WAR
SHOWING THE BATTLES OF
JULY 18TH & 21ST 1861.
PUBLISHED BY
V. P. CORBETT
WASHINGTON, D.C.

of a prisoner exchange. Colonel Michael Corcoran was also taken prisoner after he was shot in the leg and could not join the retreat from the battlefield. The Confederates held Corcoran for thirteen months until he was released in a prisoner exchange.

In their eagerness to escape the battlefield, the Union men jettisoned their equipment. Most significantly, McDowell's men left behind 27 cannons, 500 muskets, and 500,000 rounds of ammunition. The Union lost 470 killed, 1,071 wounded, and 1,793 missing. Confederate casualties were 387 dead, 1,582 wounded, and 13 missing. Of the 1,323 officers and men of the 69th, about 300 were killed, wounded, or missing at Bull Run.

The Irish were among the last Union regiments to leave the field at Bull Run, and it is thought that Captain Thomas Meagher may have been the last member of the 69th to retreat. The courage of the 69th at Henry House Hill, the tough fight it put up to save its regimental colors, and the distinction of being among the last Union troops to leave the battlefield won them praise even from Southern newspapers. The *Memphis Argus* assured its readers, "No southerner but feels that the Sixty-Ninth maintained the old reputation of Irish valor."

A STRANGE AND NEW POSITION

About 3:00 in the morning the 69th staggered into its camp at Arlington Heights. Shortly after sunrise McDowell's army entered Washington. Poet Walt Whitman, who was in the capital that day as a correspondent for the *Brooklyn Standard*, described the scene. "They come along in disorderly mobs, some in squads, stragglers, companies . . . queer-looking objects, strange eyes and faces, drench'd (the steady rain drizzles all day) and fearfully worn, hungry, haggard, blister'd in the feet . . . [Where] are the vaunts, and the proud boasts with which you went forth? Where are your banners and your bands of music?"

Beauregard's victory at Manassas set off wild rejoicing across the Confederacy. The day after the battle, July 22, as the Union army dragged itself up Pennsylvania Avenue, Confederate president Jefferson Davis promoted Pierre Beauregard to full general.

In the North, General Irvin McDowell experienced the cold comfort of knowing that his fears had been justified—the army was too green for a major battle. On July 25, General Winfield Scott relieved McDowell of his command. He was replaced by thirty-four-year-old George B. McClellan, an ambitious man who had taught engineering at West Point, had served as the United States' official observer during the Crimean War, and during the presidential campaign of 1860, had actively supported the Democrats' candidate, Stephen Douglas. Scott knew that McClellan had a genius for organization, and he hoped he would be a brilliant tactician too.

In the wake of the debacle at Bull Run, McClellan succeeded in reorganizing the Army of the Potomac and restoring confidence to its dispirited men. Ultimately, McClellan would prove to be an ineffectual commander: No matter how many men he had, no matter how well trained and well equipped they were, he imagined that the enemy had more men and more and better equipment.

Compounding the problem was McClellan's arrogance and sense of self-importance. The day after he was appointed general in chief, he wrote to his wife, Ellen, "I find myself in a new and strange position here—Presdt, Cabinet, Genl Scott & all deferring to me—by some strange operation of magic I seem to have become the power of the land. . . . I almost think that were I to win some small success now I could become Dictator or anything else that might please me—but nothing of that kind would please me—therefore I won't be Dictator. Admirable self-denial!" Furthermore, he had contempt for Lincoln, whom he referred to privately as "a gorilla" and "nothing more than a well-meaning baboon . . . ever unworthy of . . . his high position." The soldiers, who knew none of these things about McClellan, trusted, admired, and even revered him. Perhaps that is why Lincoln would tolerate him.

The same day McClellan received his command, the 69th Regiment left for home. The men had enlisted for ninety days, and on July 25 their ninety days of military service were up. Accounts of their courage at Bull Run had preceded them. When they arrived in New York, the Irish were welcomed by a cheering throng of well-wishers and a military parade that led them up Broadway. In the park across from City Hall, they were honored with a 69-gun salute.

About a month after the 69th's return home, Thomas Meagher held a benefit for the regiment's widows and orphans. While he appealed for funds, he also appealed for fresh recruits to sign on with the 69th for three years. The 69th would be the heart of Meagher's grander design—not just an Irish regiment, but an Irish brigade. The editors of the *Irish American* praised the idea as "a splendid object, and one that may well excite the enthusiasm of Irish-Americans, with whom the name of Meagher is now, more than ever, a word of talismanic power." Meagher opened a recruiting station on Broadway, where he called for "intelligent, active, steady young men—men of decent character, and with a proper sense of the duties and dangers of the service." Between September and November 1861, almost 3,000 men were accepted for service in Thomas Meagher's Irish Brigade.

4

ON TO RICHMOND:

The Irish Brigade during the Peninsula Campaign

A single company of Confederates, shielded by a dense clump of trees, kept a company of the Irish Brigade from advancing up Malvern Hill. While the Irish were pinned down by fierce fire from the trees, Captain David P. Conyngham observed the Rebel company's officer—a man he characterized as "a daring reckless boy"—stepping out from the protection of the trees to direct the defense. Turning to a sergeant named Driscoll, Conyngham said, "If that officer is not taken down, many of us will fall before we pass that clump."

"Leave that to me," Driscoll replied. Lying still, he waited for the officer to expose himself again. When he did, Driscoll fired, and the daring young Confederate fell. With their officer dead, the company of Rebels ran off and Conyngham's company advanced.

As the Irish drew up to the spot where the young man had fallen, Conyngham said, "Driscoll, see if that officer is dead—he was a brave fellow." Together they walked over to the place where the man lay face down on the ground. Sergeant Driscoll knelt and rolled over the body. The young officer looked Driscoll in the face, said, "Father," and then died. Sergeant Driscoll had shot and killed his own son.

"I will forever recollect the frantic grief of Driscoll," Conyngham wrote after the war, "it was harrowing to witness it."

When the order came for Conyngham and his company to charge, they left the grieving Driscoll beside the body of his son. But soon he appeared among them, his jacket off, firing his musket into the faces of the Confederates, charging the Rebel position alone. Moments later, Sergeant Driscoll was killed in a hail of Confederate fire.

OUTFITTING THE IRISH BRIGADE

By December 1861 the formation of the Irish Brigade was official. It comprised three New York infantry regiments—the 63rd, the 88th, and the famous 69th—as well as the 2nd Battalion New York Light Artillery. According to that tireless historian of the Irish Brigade, Joseph Bilby, most of the men selected as the Brigade's officers were veterans of Bull Run, and most of the recruits were Irish residents of New York City, although men enlisted from Brooklyn, Buffalo, Albany, and even as far away as Boston and Chicago. Shortly before Christmas, when the Brigade left New York for Virginia, it was about 2,000 men strong.

The state of New York issued the Brigade's uniform. The men wore a form-fitting, short jacket of dark blue wool that fell just below the waist. The coat buttons were stamped with the word "Excelsior!" the state motto. The trousers were sky-blue wool, held up by fabric suspenders, better known at the time as braces. Beneath their jackets the men wore a shirt of undyed wool flannel. For footwear, the Brigade was issued heavy-duty ankle-high leather shoes; the Irish called them "brogans," a Gaelic term for a shoe as opposed to a boot. For winter each man received a great coat of sky-blue wool; the coat was about knee-length, with a cape that fell to the elbows, and a stiff standing collar. Their hats, known as forage caps, were round and made of heavy broadcloth, with a squarish black enameled leather visor and a chinstrap. Army regulations forbade any insignia on the cap except the individual's company letter.

The state also issued to each man a canteen, a tin cup, a knife, fork, and spoon, a tin mess plate, a haversack for food, a knapsack for other supplies, a rubberized or gummed ground cloth to protect the soldier from the damp, and a heavy wool blanket.

Most of the Irish Brigade was armed with .69-caliber smoothbore muskets; some were issued British-made Enfield rifles. Although armies had been using smoothbore muskets since the seventeenth century, they were not satisfactory weapons. When fired, the lead ball ricocheted off the sides of the barrel. By the time the ball shot out of the mouth of the muzzle, its trajectory was entirely unpredictable. In addition to being inaccurate, the musket had a limited firing range of 80 to 100 yards (73 to 91 m). The barrel of a rifle, however, was engraved with a shallow spiral groove. When a lead ball was fired from a rifle, it spun down the barrel in a straight line, which gave a rifleman greater accuracy. Furthermore, a rifle had greater range—it could kill a man 300 yards (273 m) away. In spite of the rifle's superiority, most governments were unwilling to discard entire arsenals full of muskets and take on the expense of replacing them with rifles.

THE BREECHLOADER SHARPS RIFLE WAS MANUFACTURED IN HARTFORD, CONNECTICUT. ALTHOUGH IT WAS SIMPLER TO USE AND MORE
ACCURATE THAN SMOOTH-BORE MUSKETS, MOST UNION TROOPS—INCLUDING THE MEN OF THE IRISH BRIGADE—WERE ARMED WITH MUSKETS.
THE GOVERNMENT CONSIDERED IT TOO EXPENSIVE TO OUTFIT EVERY MAN WITH A NEW WEAPON, NO MATTER HOW SUPERIOR IT MAY BE.

President Lincoln, however, was fascinated by new weapons and eager to purchase them for the army. In June 1861, a salesman gave the president a demonstration of the new Union Repeating Gun, a prototype of the machine gun that could fire fifty bullets a minute. Lincoln was impressed and purchased the salesman's entire inventory—ten guns at $1,300 apiece.

Another weapon that won the president's approval was the breech-loading rifle, which eliminated the twelve-step process necessary to load and fire a musket. With a breech-loading rifle, a soldier inserted a cartridge into the rear of the gun barrel, took aim, and fired. It was that simple. Of the five regiments that composed the Irish Brigade, only the 28th Massachusetts was equipped by its state with breech-loading rifles; the rest of the Brigade, like most soldiers of the North and South, carried muskets.

The Irish were encamped at Camp California outside Alexandria, Virginia. At the time, they were under the command of Colonel Robert Nugent, a native of County Down, Ireland, currently living in New York City with his wife and children. Thomas Meagher remained in New York, waiting for Congress to commission him as a brigadier general. When the commission arrived, Meagher traveled to Camp California, where in early February 1862 the officers and men paid tribute to him with two dinner parties, the first a boisterous affair during which the enlisted men torched an enormous bonfire in Meagher's honor, and the second a formal dinner, with music supplied by the band of the 2nd New Jersey Infantry.

All that winter the troops drilled and trained; General in Chief George McClellan wanted no repeat of the disorder and lack of discipline displayed at Bull Run. Camp life was tedious, and the weather dreadful. A member of Meagher's staff, Lieutenant James B. Turner, wrote that life that winter was "damp, dull, disagreeable; the rain is pouring, the sky is overcast and gloomy, the earth beneath your feet is a vast, treacherous, terrible sea of muddy matter, consisting of two-thirds clay and one-third water."

Some of the officers and men had military experience, most either from service in the British army or with the Battalion of St. Patrick, which had fought for Pope Pius IX in Italy. There were professional men in the ranks, as well as Fenians, Irish nationalists who looked upon America's Civil War as excellent experience for a future war to liberate Ireland from the English. But most of the men of the Irish Brigade were laborers—strong, tough, combative, short on the social niceties, but courageous, and as it turned out, utterly dependable in battle.

AT THE BATTLE OF FAIR OAKS, GENERAL THOMAS FRANCIS MEAGHER, SHOWN IN THIS CURRIER & IVES LITHOGRAPH, ABOUT 1862,

EMPLOYED HIS FAVORITE TACTIC: FIRING A ROUND OF BUCK-AND-BALL INTO THE ENEMY RANKS, FOLLOWED BY A BAYONET CHARGE.

THE GENERAL'S PLAN

On January 27, 1862, Lincoln issued President's General War Order No. 1, commanding the army and the navy to move against the Confederacy on February 22—George Washington's birthday. Four days later, he issued President's Special War Order No. 1, ordering an attack on the Confederate supply lines near Manassas, Virginia. After reading the president's special order, McClellan came to the White House to suggest an alternate plan.

McClellan's strategy was to transport the entire Army of the Potomac by steamship down Chesapeake Bay to the town of Urbanna on the Rappahannock River. From there it would attack and capture Richmond, capital of the Confederacy. Lincoln considered McClellan's strategy excessively ambitious, but the general assured the president that his plan to seize Richmond would deliver "the most brilliant results." To crush the rebellion so soon after the Southern states had seceded and bring the war to a swift end was tempting: In the end, Lincoln gave his approval.

In the armada of transport ships collected to carry the army to the Virginia Peninsula, the Irish Brigade was assigned two steamships, the *Ocean Queen* and the *Columbia*. Before it embarked, Secretary of War Edwin Stanton reorganized the Army of the Potomac into four army corps—the Irish were assigned to the 2nd Corps under Brigadier General Israel B. Richardson, a Vermont man who had settled on a farm in Michigan. During the Mexican War, Richardson had proved so ferocious in battle that he acquired the nickname "Fighting Dick."

By now the Irish Brigade had all been equipped with .69-caliber smoothbore muskets. It was General Meagher's preferred weapon because it was deadly at close range, especially when loaded with buck-and-ball, cartridges that contained a .64-caliber lead ball and three .30-caliber buckshot pellets. Meagher envisioned his Brigade attacking the enemy head-on, discharging a deadly volley of buck-and-ball, then charging in with bayonets.

The plan McClellan had presented to Lincoln called for a quick march from Urbanna 40 miles (64 km) west to Richmond. If the army were lucky, it would surprise the Confederates and seize the city; otherwise, it would use its 100 cannons to pound Richmond into submission. The Federal troops, numbering more than 100,000, had gotten as far as Yorktown, about 30 miles (48 km) from Urbanna, where a Confederate force of 13,000 led by Major General John B. Magruder spooked the always overcautious McClellan. Although he had an enormous army, McClellan was convinced that he was outnumbered, that Yorktown was defended by 100,000 men, so, rather than attack he besieged Yorktown.

The Irish Brigade was assigned to construction duty, building corduroy roads—"paving" dirt tracks with freshly cut trees. Corduroy roads made for a bumpy ride in a wagon, and uncertain going on foot, but they were preferable to slogging through deep mud. It was while building the roads that the Brigade suffered its first casualty—a tree fell on Private Patrick Casey, killing him.

Unlike most sieges in history, the siege of Yorktown in April 1862 was almost pleasant. Captain James B. Turner described the Union camp for readers of the *Irish American* newspaper. Federal troops were "encamped in the most delightful manner possible," he said. "Many tents have between them ornaments and devices of various kinds, harps and shamrocks preponderating." Furthermore, the streets through the camp were adorned with arches of evergreen boughs. It was a festive siege.

There was not much shooting. Occasionally, a Confederate sniper shot at a Yankee, and everyday Confederate artillery fired off a few rounds in an effort to bring down McClellan's observation hot air balloon. The artillery shells always missed their mark, and the only excitement came when the rope snapped and the balloon drifted off in the direction of Richmond, with Brigadier General Fitz John Porter in the basket. But by releasing the valve he let out enough hot air to land safely 3 miles (4.8 km) from the Union camp.

On May 5, McClellan was ready to begin shelling Yorktown. His earthwork batteries were complete and his artillery was in place, but that night the Confederates anticipated him, releasing a barrage of artillery. George Thomas Stevens, a surgeon of the 77th Regiment of New York Volunteers, wrote, "From one end of the line to the other the shells and shot poured into our camps, and the arches of fire that marked the courses of the shells, with flame spouting from the mouths of the guns, created a magnificent pyrotechnic display."

The next morning orderlies reported that the Confederate batteries in Yorktown were deserted. Under the cover of the artillery, Magruder had led his 13,000 men out of the siege. McClellan was free to proceed to Richmond.

FIRST BLOOD

General Joseph E. Johnston pulled his troops back to Williamsburg, and McClellan followed. Outside Virginia's colonial capital, McClellan's new Army of the Potomac saw its first action. It was a bloody beginning: The Union lost more than 2,200 men, killed, wounded, or missing, and the Confederates lost more than 1,600. There were two especially memorable moments during the May 5 battle. The first occurred when Major General D.H. Hill and Brigadier General Jubal Early led their men

DURING THE NEW YORK CITY DRAFT RIOTS OF JULY 1863, COLONEL ROBERT NUGENT, SHOWN IN A PHOTOGRAPH TAKEN BETWEEN 1860 AND 1870, COMMANDED THE TROOPS THAT ATTEMPTED TO RESTORE ORDER. THE NEARLY ALL-IRISH MOB REGARDED NUGENT AS A TRAITOR, AND RETALIATED BY LOOTING, THEN BURNING, HIS HOUSE.

THE UNION ARTILLERY AT YORKTOWN IS SHOWN IN THIS PHOTOGRAPH. THE APRIL 1862 SIEGE OF YORKTOWN INVOLVED LITTLE SHOOTING AND AN ALMOST PLEASANT ATMOSPHERE. "MANY TENTS HAVE BETWEEN THEM ORNAMENTS AND DEVICES OF VARIOUS KINDS, HARPS AND SHAMROCKS PREPONDERATING," CAPTAIN JAMES TURNER WROTE IN THE IRISH AMERICAN NEWSPAPER.

out of the woods to attack Union troops commanded by Brigadier General Winfield Scott Hancock. The Confederates had barely begun their attack when they realized that they had misgauged the enemy—Hancock's men outnumbered the Rebels. As Hill and Early pulled their men back, Hancock ordered a bayonet charge. In the bloodbath that ensued, the Confederates lost about 800 men to the Union's 100.

The second unforgettable moment at the Battle of Williamsburg occurred at a Union battery. Confederates had captured it, and one-armed Brigadier General Phil Kearny was determined to take it back. Swinging his sword over his head with his only good arm he led a charge, crying, "Don't flinch, boys! They're shooting at me, not at you!"

The Confederates abandoned Williamsburg, McClellan declared himself victorious, and the army advanced on Richmond.

At White House Landing, the army reached the house where George Washington had courted Martha Custis. Tacked to the door of the historic home was a note that read, "Northern soldiers who profess to reverence Washington, forebear to desecrate the home of his first married life, the property of his wife, now owned by her descendants." The note was signed, "A grand-daughter of Mrs. Washington." That lady was Mary Custis Lee, the wife of General Robert E. Lee.

McClellan set up his tent on the front lawn, refusing to occupy the venerable house. Then he posted guards to prevent the men from breaking in and pilfering historic artifacts. Finally, he extended his protection to Mrs. Lee, sending her through the Union lines with a safe conduct and an escort of Federal troops.

THE SPIRES OF RICHMOND

On May 24, the Union army could see the church spires of Richmond. In the city, the government and civilians were in a state of panic. The gold from the Confederate treasury and documents from the Confederate archives were packed, loaded into train cars, and ready to be shipped south at the first sign that McClellan would attack the city. The Confederate Congress evacuated, as did the First Lady of the Confederacy, Varina Davis, with her four children; her husband, President Jefferson Davis, remained in Richmond. The Richmond garrison braced itself for the attack it expected would come at any moment, but once again McClellan stopped in his tracks. He wired Washington that he was outnumbered and needed 40,000 more men before he could begin his assault on Richmond. In fact, McClellan had General Johnston, the Confederate commander, outnumbered three to two.

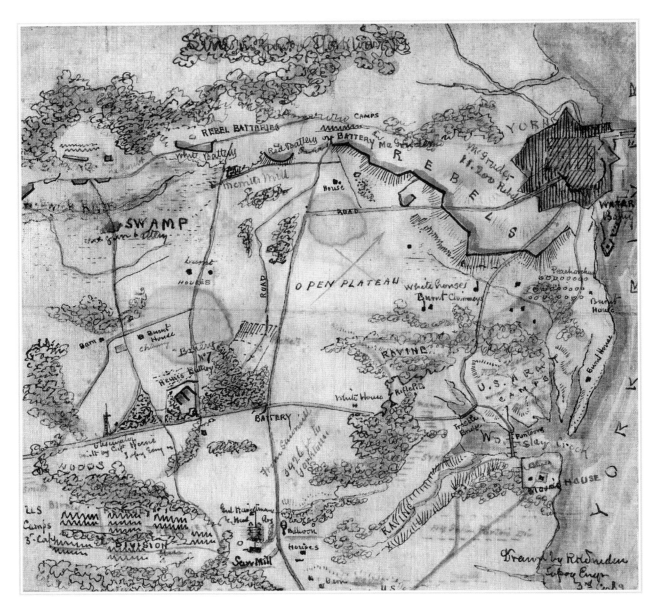

THE MAP, CREATED BY ROBERT KNOX SNEDEN, SHOWS THE POSITIONS OF THE UNION AND CONFEDERATE ARMIES WEST OF YORKTOWN,
AS THE SIEGE OF THE CITY GOT UNDERWAY. THE IRISH BRIGADE WAS CONSIGNED TO BUILDING ROADS AS PART OF THE SIEGE.

In Washington, Secretary of War Edwin Stanton read McClellan's demand for more troops and lost his temper. "If he had a million men," Stanton said, "he would swear the enemy had two million, and then he would sit down in the mud and yell for three."

The 40,000 men McClellan wanted were occupied elsewhere. General Irvin McDowell was in Virginia's Shenandoah Valley, fighting Stonewall Jackson. Perhaps "chasing" is the correct term, for Jackson drove his men hard, typically demanding that they cover 25 miles (40 km) in a day. In four weeks Jackson had collected a vast amount of supplies from the valley's prosperous farms and inflicted 7,000 casualties on McDowell's army. Then, unexpectedly, he turned his army east and hurried to reinforce Richmond.

"FIXED BAYONETS AND A SWEEPING FIRE"

On May 31, at a place the Union called Fair Oaks and the Confederates, Seven Pines, the armies of Johnston and McClellan clashed. Days earlier McClellan had sent about 40,000 of his men across the Chickahominy River. On the night of May 30, a torrential rainstorm had so flooded the river that most of the bridges were swept away—and McClellan's army was divided. Johnston, seeing an opportunity, planned to attack the stranded Union troops on the south side of the river.

Johnston's strategy called for two Confederate forces to attack the Union flanks simultaneously, followed by a third force driving into the Union's center. But at dawn on May 31, the force under General Longstreet marched off in the wrong direction. When Longstreet encountered General Benjamin Huger, who was to attack the Union's flank, he made matters worse by giving Huger orders not to attack as planned but to wait and support the attack on the Union center. Now Longstreet had not only taken his own men out of the battle, but Huger's men too. It was not until 1:00 in the afternoon that all the commanders finally sorted out the confusion and everyone was at last in their assigned position for the attack—five hours later than initially planned.

Confusion reigned even after the battle began. For unknown reasons, the Confederate commanders held back thousands of men from the fight—Longstreet sent in only 12,500 of the 29,500 he had under his command.

On June 1, the second day of battle, the 69th and 88th regiments of the Irish Brigade were concealed in the woods. As they stepped out from the cover of the trees and into an open field, they took heavy fire from the Confederates. Captain James McMahon, one of General Meagher's aides, led the men of the 88th to a small farmhouse nearby, which shielded them from enemy fire. Better still, McMahon found that the house was ideally situated, enabling the 88th "to pour in a withering fire on the enemy's flank, compelling them to fall back," as David P. Conyngham recalled.

Elsewhere on the battlefield, the Confederates were taking a beating, with General Daniel Sickles driving Confederates out of the safety of the woods and five regiments commanded by General Hooker scattering the enemy. Some of the Confederates regrouped in front of General Richardson's 2nd Corps for a massed attack. "The Irish Brigade met them," Conyngham tells us, "with fixed bayonets and a sweeping fire, hurling their lines before them."

The Confederates lost more than 6,100 men, the Union more than 5,000, 100 of whom were members of the Irish Brigade. During the fight, a piece of shrapnel struck General Johnston in the chest. He survived, but the wound was sufficiently severe that he was obliged to resign his command.

Jefferson Davis had ridden out from Richmond to witness the battle. After visiting Johnston in his tent, the president returned to the capital. Along the way, he informed his chief military officer, who had accompanied him to Seven Pines, that he was to take command of the Army of Northern Virginia. That chief military advisor was General Robert E. Lee.

The next day, Lee called on President Davis to discuss his plans. He would build new defenses around Richmond and leave a garrison to defend the city while, with the bulk of his army, driving McClellan from the peninsula. He had time—for two weeks McClellan had sat on the banks of the Chickahominy with approximately 60,000 troops, fretting that Lee had him outnumbered, but still convinced that shortly he would roll his 100 artillery guns into position above Richmond and force the city to surrender. How he planned to achieve that goal without moving his army to the Confederate capital he did not explain.

McClellan waited for the 40,000 men of McDowell's army, but Lincoln sent only 15,000—the rest he kept in Washington to defend the city from a possible Confederate attack. McClellan was stung by what he perceived as lack of support from his commander in chief. If the Peninsula Campaign failed, he said, "the responsibility cannot be thrown on my shoulders."

JEB STUART'S RIDE

Robert E. Lee was the polar opposite of George B. McClellan. He did not complain to President Davis that compared with the enemy his numbers were insufficient (although they were), nor did he protest that the Yankees were better equipped (which was also true), nor did he refuse to take action until all his demands were met. Instead, with the Army of the Potomac within sight of Richmond, Lee resolved to take the initiative and attack McClellan. But first he sent Brigadier General Jeb (short for James Ewell Brown) Stuart on a daring reconnaissance mission. The twenty-nine-year-old Stuart was a cavalryman par excellence, and he played up the part with his dashing costume: red-lined gray cape, bright yellow sash, and a peacock plume in his hat, which he wore at a rakish angle. Stuart led his 1,200 cavalrymen in a full circle 150 miles (240 km) around McClellan's army—a feat they accomplished in three days, during which time they harassed the Yankee army by chopping down telegraph poles, burning outlying camps, and capturing 170 Yankee prisoners and 300 horses and mules. According to historian Geoffrey C. Ward, they "slowed only to accept bouquets and kisses from admiring women."

McClellan sent his own cavalry troop to intercept Lee's cavalry and capture Stuart. The commander of the Union cavalry was Brigadier General Philip St. George Cooke—Jeb Stuart's father-in-law. Halfway through the ride, Stuart found his way blocked by the still-flooded Chickahominy River. His men threw a rough log bridge over the river, raced across, then set fire to the bridge, leaving Cooke and his men angry, frustrated, and stranded on the other side.

Stuart returned with the location of the various divisions of McClellan's army. This was useful information for Lee, but for the men in the field, the significance of Stuart's ride was much larger—it was a tremendous boost to their morale. Stuart's biographer, John W. Thomason, writes that after the ride, "the Southern trooper was confirmed in his opinion that he could outride, outfight and outdare anything the Yankee nation might put on four legs."

Lee's strategy was to drive McClellan away from Richmond and then from the Virginia Peninsula. Based on Stuart's report, Lee decided to attack the Union force near Mechanicsville on the north side of the Chickahominy River, commanded by General Fitz John Porter. McClellan's army was still divided by the Chickahominy, and Porter's command was the smaller of the two forces. Lee planned to leave 22,000 men on the south side to fight off McClellan's main force; meanwhile, Stonewall Jackson would attack Porter's flank while A.P. Hill and the bulk of Lee's army crossed the river and attacked Porter's center.

Lee chose the morning of June 26 for his attack; Jackson would strike first, then Hill would cross the river. But in what remains one of the most perplexing mysteries of the Civil War, the immortal Stonewall Jackson never attacked that day. Hill waited until afternoon before finally, on his own initiative, he led his 16,000 men

Capt. Russell. Phot.

ON MAY 3, 1863, THE YANKEES
AVENGED THEMSELVES AT MARYE'S
HEIGHTS, WHERE THOUSANDS HAD
FALLEN DURING THE 1862 BATTLE
OF FREDERICKSBURG. THE UNION
STORMED UP THE SLOPE AND
SWEPT THE CONFEDERATES FROM
THE STONE WALL. PHOTOGRAPHER
ANDREW J. RUSSELL TOOK THIS SHOT
OF CONFEDERATE CASUALTIES AT
THE WALL.

against Porter. Union resistance collapsed almost immediately, but their retreat was deceptive. A mile (1.6 km) back the Federals were dug in above Beaver Dam Creek. A.P. Hill ordered his men forward, where they were met with a deadly barrage of artillery and musket fire. By nightfall, when the fighting stopped, Hill had lost approximately 1,400 men to the Yankees' 400. That same night McClellan pulled his men back from Beaver Dam Creek to Gaines' Mill, which he considered more defensible.

The next day, Lee attacked again. It was a day full of confusion: This time, Stonewall Jackson led his men into the fight, but when they were less than a mile (1.6 km) from where A.P. Hill was battling Porter again, Jackson brought his troops to a halt, apparently uncertain what to do next. While Jackson hesitated, Lee sent in Longstreet to reinforce Hill, and one of Jackson's commanders, acting without orders, led his division to support Hill. Then Lee sent in John B. Hood and his Texans, who succeeded in breaking Porter's line.

Some of the Yankees began to flee the battlefield; near the Chickahominy they ran into the 69th. Meagher, outraged at the sight of men running from a fight, ordered a company of the Irish to fix bayonets and sent them, under the command of Colonel Robert Nugent, to stop the fugitives. Once the Irish had turned them back, all the brigades of the 2nd Corps moved to the front. The reinforcements did not give the Union a clear victory, but it did prevent what could have degenerated into a rout.

That night McClellan ordered his army to pull back across the Chickahominy, with the Irish of the 69th and the 88th performing rear guard duty. Encamped in his new location, McClellan wrote of the battle to Lincoln, "If we have lost the day we have yet preserved our honor & no one need blush for the Army of the Potomac. I have lost this battle because my force was too small. I again repeat that I am not responsible. . . . In addition to what I have already said I only wish to say to the President that I think he is wrong, in regarding me as ungenerous when I said that my force was too weak. I merely reiterated a truth, which today has been too plainly proved. I should have gained this battle with (10,000) ten thousand fresh men. If at this instant I could dispose of (10,000) ten thousand fresh men I could gain the victory tomorrow." In fact, McClellan had kept 60,000 to 70,000 troops in reserve.

After the Battle of Gaines' Mill, McClellan began his retreat from the peninsula.

THE HUNGRY IRISH

On June 28, McClellan's army retreated toward the James River. He withdrew the divisions he left outside Richmond, and sent men to his supply depot at the White House to carry off everything that could be packed into a wagon, and destroy whatever could not. His new base would be at Harrison's Landing on the James, where McClellan would occupy Berkeley Plantation, the birthplace of the late President William Henry Harrison.

On June 29, three Confederate brigades under John B. Magruder attacked the Union rear guard at Savage's Station. Lee's original order had been for Magruder to swing around McClellan's army and cut off its path of retreat while Longstreet and A.P. Hill attacked the rear guard. But Longstreet and Hill got lost in the backcountry roads, so Magruder attacked alone. Nonetheless, he so frightened the retreating Yankees that they abandoned piles of equipment, as well as 2,500 wounded men in field hospitals.

The next day, June 30, outside the town of Glendale, Lee ordered another attack on the Federals, sending in seven divisions against the four of McClellan's rear guard. This time Longstreet and Hill were on hand, but the other Confederate commanders bungled their orders. Nonetheless, Longstreet and Hill almost broke through the Union lines—only determined counterattacks by Generals Hooker and Kearny saved the Army of the Potomac from what might have been disaster. That day the Union lost 3,000 men, but the Confederates lost 3,500.

After a week of frustration, watching his carefully conceived strategies come to nothing, General Lee adopted a tactic that Civil War historian William C. Davis has described as "an almost utter lack of finesse." The Army of the Potomac had seized the high ground—Malvern Hill. Lee brought up eight divisions and 200 cannons—each one aimed at the summit of the hill.

The Confederate artillery fired round after round, but it did not clear the Federals from the hilltop. In fact, the Union guns succeeded in knocking out many of the Confederate batteries. Then Union sharpshooters moved forward, attacking the brigade led by Brigadier General Lewis Armistead. The Confederates drove back the sharpshooters, just as Magruder arrived on the scene with his men. Believing that Armistead had the Yankees on the run, Magruder hurried into the battle, charging up Malvern Hill. Union artillery at the summit cut down the charging Confederates by the hundreds.

McClellan had not sent in the Irish Brigade, and as evening came on, the Irish were waiting for a mutton dinner—they had captured some stray sheep and sent them to the Brigade's cooks. At seven o'clock, before the meal arrived, orders came to reinforce General Porter's position on Malvern Hill. The hungry Irish went into battle, with the 69th in the lead, followed by the 88th, and with the 63rd and 29th Massachusetts covering the rear. According to Conyngham, at the front, the 69th

ALL ALONG THE SIDES AND SUMMIT
OF MALVERN HILL—THE BATTLE
DEPICTED IN THIS 1862 IMAGE—LAY
"THE DEAD AND THE DYING OF THE
IRISH BRIGADE," HISTORIAN DAVID
CONYINGHAM WROTE. THE IRISH
BRIGADE LOST 188 MEMBERS IN THIS
BITTERSWEET UNION VICTORY.

fired "murderous volley after volley into the enemy," reloading and firing again so quickly that their guns became clogged, too hot to the touch, and had to be discarded; they took up fresh weapons from the dead and wounded.

It was dark now, and on the battlefield, men of both North and South could see a lantern moving about—a dangerous thing in the midst of a fight. It was one of the 69th chaplains, Father Thomas Ouellet. Wearing his purple stole, he went from one wounded man to the next, asking, "Are you Catholic? And do you wish absolution?" One badly wounded soldier replied, "No, but I would like to die in the faith of any man who has the courage to come and see me in such a place as this."

The Confederates made one final charge, attacking the 69th head-on while Confederate snipers, concealed in the woods and nearby house, picked off the Irish. The men of the 88th joined the fight, and in spite of the withering Union fire, some of the Confederates reached the summit. Now the fighting was hand-to-hand, as the men used their muskets as clubs and their bayonets as daggers. Finally, as darkness descended on the hill, the Confederates gave up the fight. McClellan had a victory, the Army of the Potomac was saved, but as Conyngham recalled, all around the summit and sides of Malvern Hill lay "the dead and the dying of the Irish Brigade." The Brigade's casualties were 188 men at Malvern Hill.

Among the heroes of Malvern Hill was seventeen-year-old Private Peter Rafferty of the 69th New York. At Malvern Hill he was struck in the thigh, but refused to leave the field and kept fighting. He was hit twice more—one bullet shattered his jaw, and another struck his tongue. Even so, Rafferty continued to fight. He was taken prisoner by the Confederates and confined in the Libby Prison in Richmond. After seven days of battle, the city was inundated with wounded—doctors had no time to spare for prisoners of war. After days of lying in the prison untreated, Rafferty was nursed at last by the Sisters of Charity, who left their convent to tend the men no one else would care for. After sixty-five days in prison, Rafferty was released as part of a prisoner exchange. For his bravery at Malvern Hill, he was awarded the Medal of Honor.

GARRYOWEN: THE MARCHING SONG OF THE IRISH BRIGADE

Like the rest of the Irish Brigade, Rafferty most likely would have sung "Garryowen," the marching song of the Irish Brigade.

Garryowen (*Garrai Eoin* in Gaelic) means "Owen garden." It is a suburb of Limerick. For reasons unknown, in the late eighteenth century the neighborhood became the inspiration for a drinking song sung in Limerick gentlemen's clubs. The 5th Royal Irish Lancers adopted the song as their marching song, and other Irish regiments of the British Army took it up, too, including the Royal Irish Fusiliers and the Irish Regiment of Canada.

Before the Civil War, the virtually all-Irish 69th New York State Militia marched to "Garryowen." It is said that General George Armstrong Custer heard an Irish soldier singing "Garryowen" and liked the galloping rhythm of the tune so much that after the war he made it the official song of the 7th Cavalry. There is a tradition that in 1876 "Garryowen" was played at the Battle of the Little Bighorn, where Custer and his men were massacred by Sioux, Cheyenne, and Arapaho warriors.

Let Bacchus' sons be not dismayed
But join with me, each jovial blade
Come, drink and sing and lend your aid
To help me with the chorus:

Chorus:
Instead of spa, we'll drink brown ale
And pay the reckoning on the nail;
No man for debt shall go to jail
From Garryowen in glory.

We'll beat the bailiffs out of fun,
We'll make the mayor and sheriffs run
We are the boys no man dares dun
If he regards a whole skin.

Our hearts so stout have got no fame
For soon 'tis known from whence we came
Where'er we go they fear the name
Of Garryowen in glory.

5

THE BLOODIEST DAY:
The Irish Brigade at Antietam

The Sunken Road was an ideal defensive position. Running along the crest of a hill, it was about 4 or 5 feet (1.2 to 1.5 m) deep and several hundred yards long—long enough to provide protective cover for approximately 2,300 Confederate soldiers under the command of General Daniel Harvey Hill, the brother-in-law of Stonewall Jackson. At about 10:30 on the morning of September 17, 1862, some of Hill's troops saw 1,000 Union soldiers emerge from a field of tall corn, but the Confederates were not overly concerned. Already that morning they had mown down half of the 1st Delaware commanded by Brigadier General Max Weber; when Weber's men fell back, they left behind 450 men dead or wounded. Colonel Dwight Morris rushed forward with his Connecticut brigade, but they were forced to retreat, too, after suffering 156 casualties.

Now Major General Israel Richardson, commander of the 2nd Corps, sent the Irish Brigade against the Confederates hunkered down in the Sunken Road. Keeping out of sight of Hill's men, the Irish waded across Antietam Creek, followed a lane near the Roulette Farm, and then entered the field of flourishing corn. When they emerged from the corn, they stood on the edge of 100 yards (91 m) of open ground; at the opposite side of the field, obstructing their advance on the Confederate position at the Sunken Road, stood a chest-high split-rail fence. Brigadier General Thomas Meagher called for volunteers to dash across the field and dismantle the fence. Eighty men ran forward and at least half of them were cut down by Confederate fire, but the survivors managed to take the fence apart.

As the Irish waited for the order to advance, the Catholic chaplains, Father William Corby, C.S.C., and Father Thomas Ouellet, S.J., spurred their horses forward. Riding along the formation, the priests blessed the Irish Brigade.

Four flag-bearers stood in the front ranks. One carried the Stars and Stripes and three carried the Irish Brigade's green banner. Meagher had ordered his men to load their muskets with buck-and-ball, cartridges that contained a .64-caliber lead ball and the three larger-than-usual buckshot pellets of .30 caliber. In close fighting, a volley of buck-and-ball was especially deadly, the equivalent of a shotgun blast. Meagher planned to decimate the Confederates with such a volley, then charge in with bayonets and sweep Hill and his men from the Sunken Road. But as they ran up the ridge toward the road, the Confederates released a blast of minie ball fire. Among the fallen were the three men who carried the green-and-gold banners of the Irish Brigade. But Meagher would not call for a retreat. "Boys!" he shouted. "Raise the colors and follow me!"

Captain James McGee of New York took a banner from the hands of a wounded color-bearer and advanced. A Confederate minie ball cut clean through the flagstaff, and the banner fell to the ground. As McGee bent down to retrieve it, a bullet passed through his cap. Tempting fate a third time, he lifted the colors on its short staff, and charged forward, waving the green banner in defiance. But in their exposed position, the Irish could not withstand the Confederates' firepower; with the rest of his comrades, McGee retreated, the green banner wrapped around his shoulders so it would not fall again.

THE DITHERING GENERAL

General George McClellan, commander of the Army of the Potomac, feared that General Robert E. Lee would lead his Army of Northern Virginia against Washington or Baltimore. McClellan's instincts were correct—Lee did intend to lead his men north, but to the important Union railway hub at Harrisburg, Pennsylvania. This invasion of the North had been planned by General Lee and endorsed on September 7, 1862, by the president of the Confederacy, Jefferson Davis. "We are driven to protect our own country," Davis said, "by transferring the seat of war to that of an enemy who pursues us with a relentless and apparently aimless hostility." Early in September, Lee led 40,000 men across the Potomac River and into Maryland. One boy who watched them as they marched past described the Confederates as "a most ragged, lean and hungry set of wolves. Yet there was a dash about them that the northern men lacked."

Lee's Maryland Campaign, as it came to be known, was ambitious: First, he wanted to separate Maryland from the Union and bring it into the sphere of the

ALEXANDER GARDNER, A COLLEAGUE OF THE RENOWNED NEW YORK PHOTOGRAPHER MATHEW BRADY, TOOK THIS GROUP SHOT AT HARRISON'S LANDING, VIRGINIA, IN JULY 1862. THE MAN SEATED AT THE FAR RIGHT IS FATHER WILLIAM CORBY, CSC, A PROFESSOR FROM THE COLLEGE OF NOTRE DAME IN SOUTH BEND, INDIANA, WHO BECAME A CHAPLAIN OF THE IRISH BRIGADE.

Confederacy; second, virtually every battle of the Civil War to date had been fought in Virginia—Lee and Davis wanted the North to experience the pain, destruction, and disruption of war on their own turf, beginning in the prosperous state of Pennsylvania; finally, Lee hoped that a string of Confederate victories would convince Northern voters in the midterm election of 1862 to send to Congress men who were willing to recognize the independence of the Confederacy and make peace.

Once in Maryland, Lee sent half of his army under Stonewall Jackson to capture Harpers Ferry, the gateway to the rich farms of Virginia's Shenandoah Valley and a vital communications link, which was still in Union hands. Meanwhile, Lee continued marching north. McClellan, ever the cautious commander, followed Lee at a distance, uncertain what to do. In fairness to McClellan, however, he did not know that Lee had divided his force and was vulnerable.

Then on September 13, in a field where Confederates had camped the night before, a Union corporal found three cigars wrapped in a sheet of paper, which bore Lee's plans for the campaign. McClellan was euphoric. "Here is a paper," he told his aides, "with which, if I cannot whip Bobbie Lee, I will be willing to go home." Then he sent a telegram to President Abraham Lincoln. "I have all the plans of the rebels," he wrote, "and will catch them in their own trap if my men are equal to the emergency." Now McClellan knew that Lee had about 18,000 men to McClellan's approximately 95,000, yet rather than attack boldly, McClellan, always reluctant to commit his men to battle, still hesitated.

The Confederates took up position atop a long ridge east of the town of Sharpsburg, Maryland, a prosperous little town that thrived on the produce of the surrounding farms, a few local industries, and the traffic of the Chesapeake and Ohio Canal. At the bottom of the hill meandered a stream, Antietam Creek. The men of the North, who crossed the creek to reach the Confederates, would call the battle Antietam, while the Confederates, who had arrayed themselves outside the town, called the battle Sharpsburg.

On September 15, McClellan and his vast army arrived at Antietam. Major General James Longstreet of Georgia described the appearance of the "Federals," as he called them: "The number increased, and larger and larger grew the field of blue until it seemed to stretch as far as the eye could see." Surveying the scene, McClellan declared, "By George, this is a magnificent field, and if we win this fight it will cover all our errors and misfortunes forever!"

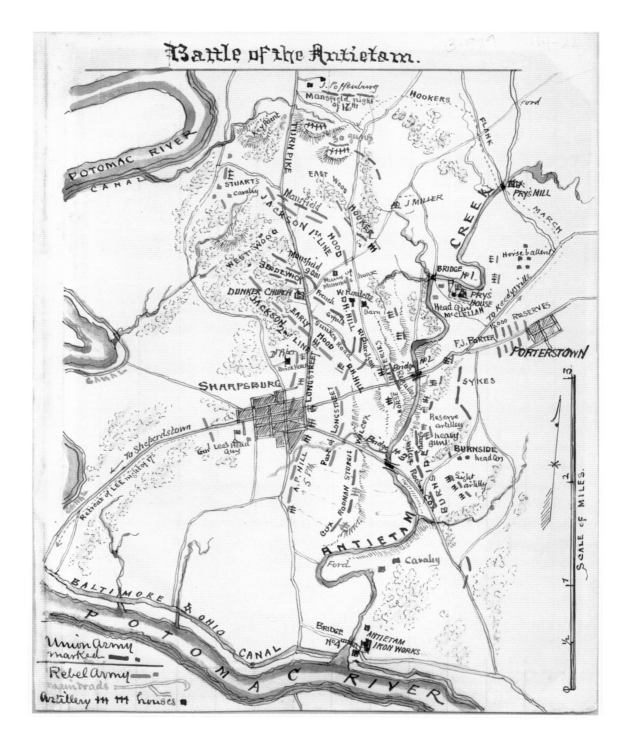

FOUGHT IN THE FARMLAND OUTSIDE THE TOWN OF SHARPSBURG, MARYLAND, THE BATTLE OF ANTIETAM WOULD BE THE BLOODIEST

SINGLE DAY OF THE CIVIL WAR, WITH 22,720 MEN FROM THE NORTH AND SOUTH KILLED, WOUNDED, OR MISSING.

THE MAP, CREATED BY ROBERT KNOX SNEDEN IN THE 1860s, SHOWS THE THREE MAIN BATTLES THAT RAGED ON SEPTEMBER 17. 1862:

AT THE DUNKER CHURCH, IN THE SUNKEN ROAD, AND AROUND THE BRIDGE LABELED #3.

But once again, McClellan put off the fight. Neither on the 15th nor on the 16th did he send in his men to overwhelm Lee's army, outnumbered almost four to one. And while McClellan dithered, Confederate couriers recalled Stonewall Jackson, who returned, doubling the size of Lee's army.

THE FIRST PHASE OF BATTLE

The Battle of Antietam was really three battles. The first took place along the Hagerstown Turnpike near the Dunker Church, a modest whitewashed meetinghouse of a German pacifist sect. The second battle raged along the Sunken Road. The third battle took place at a graceful stone bridge that spanned Antietam Creek.

The fighting began at six in the morning, when Major General Joseph Hooker of Massachusetts ordered his cannons to fire on the rise where Stonewall Jackson had set up his artillery. Under the cover of artillery fire, the Union troops, with bayonets fixed, charged the Confederate position. Confederate artillery returned fire, and Confederate infantry, concealed in two dense clumps of trees near the Dunker Church, opened fire. The Confederate artillery and rifles mowed down the men of the 12th Massachusetts Volunteer Infantry—within minutes, 224 of the 334 infantrymen fell, dead or wounded.

But the Union troops kept coming, loading and firing as they charged. Bit by bit the Confederate ranks broke up until they were in full flight, running for the cover of the woods. At that moment Jackson sent in his reserves—the Texas Brigade, commanded by General John Bell Hood. This counterattack by fresh troops spooked the Union men, who turned and ran into a nearby cornfield. Union artillery stood arrayed along the edge of the field, and Union reinforcements stood ready. The Union gunners shortened the fuses of their artillery shells so that seconds after being fired from the cannon they would explode in the faces of the advancing Confederates. As the Texans charged into the corn, the Union batteries and Union infantry opened fire. Of the approximately 850 Texans who charged into the cornfield, about 550 were killed there.

But the Confederates poured heavy fire into the Union ranks too. The Union officers ordered three regiments to pull back. Covering their retreat were the men of the 90th Pennsylvania Volunteer Infantry. They lost 98 men before they fell back, moving slowly and in good order. In defiance of the enemy, their color-bearer walked backward, waving the regimental banner.

For four hours, the armies fought back and forth across the now-leveled cornfield. At about nine in the morning, a Confederate sharpshooter wounded General Hooker in the foot; he tried to remain at the front, but Hooker lost so much blood from the wound that he became lightheaded. He was taken to a field hospital for treatment. Near the cornfield, Captain Oliver Wendell Holmes Jr., of the 20th Massachusetts Volunteer Infantry—known as the Harvard Regiment, because almost all of its officers were Harvard graduates—was trying to rally his men against a surprise attack on their rear. Suddenly a bullet pierced his neck, barely missing Holmes's jugular vein. He slumped to the ground. When he opened his eyes he saw his regiment's chaplain bending over him. "You're a Christian, aren't you?" the chaplain asked. Holmes nodded. "Well, then, that's all right!" the chaplain cried as he ran off with the rest of the retreating troops.

About noon a wagon pulled up to the edge of the cornfield. A small, dark-haired woman climbed down, and went looking for an Army surgeon; she introduced herself as Clara Barton, presented him with her wagon full of medical supplies, and offered her services as a nurse. The surgeons put her to work immediately. She tended the wounded and the dying, brought them water, and cooked for them in the kitchen of a neighboring farmhouse. Meanwhile, bullets and artillery shells were still whizzing over the cornfield. As Barton was cradling a wounded man, offering him a drink of water, she felt a tug at her sleeve. Barton described the moment: "A ball . . . passed between my body and the right arm which supported him, cutting through his chest from shoulder to shoulder. There was no more to be done for him and I left him to his rest. I have never mended that hole in my sleeve."

By ten a.m., 8,000 men were killed or wounded in the cornfield and around the Dunker Church. Now the battle shifted 600 yards (540 m) south of the church to the Sunken Road.

"THIS SCENE OF TUMULT"

The Sunken Road linked the neighborhood's farms with the gristmill on Antietam Creek. Almost 200 years of travel and natural erosion had combined to create a track 4 to 5 feet (1.2 to 1.5 m) below ground level. General Hill had recognized it as a natural rifle pit, and had crammed about 2,300 men into the road.

Arrayed against the Confederates were 5,700 mostly inexperienced Union troops led by Brigadier General William H. French, a Texan who, when his state seceded, offered his services to the Union. They advanced on the Sunken Road across the fields and through the orchard of the Mumma and Roulette families. Hill recalled that they marched "with all the precision of a parade day."

Perhaps thinking of Bunker Hill and "the whites of their eyes," Colonel F.M. Parker of the 30th North Carolina Infantry had told his men to hold their fire until they could see clearly the cartridge boxes that hung from the Union troops' belts.

THE IRISH BRIGADE DRIVE THE REBELS OUT OF THE CORNFIELD NEAR THE DUNKER CHURCH IN THIS 1862 PENCIL DRAWING BY IRISH-BORN ARTIST ARTHUR LUMLEY. DURING THE FIGHT, GENERAL JOSEPH HOOKER WAS WOUNDED IN THE FOOT AND CAPTAIN OLIVER WENDELL HOLMES, JR. WAS SHOT THROUGH THE THROAT. BY 10 A.M., 8,000 MEN HAD BEEN KILLED OR WOUNDED IN THE CORNFIELD.

ALEXANDER GARDINER WAS ONE OF SEVERAL PHOTOGRAPHERS WHO RECORDED GRAPHIC SCENES OF THE
ANTIETAM BATTLEFIELD. THIS PHOTO SHOWS DOZENS OF CONFEDERATE DEAD PILED ATOP ONE ANOTHER IN
THE SUNKEN ROAD. THE 1,000-MAN IRISH BRIGADE WOULD LOSE MORE THAN HALF ITS MEN AT ANTIETAM,
MOST OF THEM FIGHTING AT THE SUNKEN ROAD.

"Aim at these," Parker instructed his men. And they did. The first volley "brought down the enemy," Parker said, "as grain falls before a reaper."

"The effect was appalling," Colonel John B. Gordon of Georgia reported. "The entire front line, with few exceptions, went down in the consuming blast." Within five minutes the Union suffered 450 casualties.

Men from New York and Pennsylvania regiments charged the Sunken Road and almost achieved their goal before they were killed or driven off by the withering Confederate fire. In spite of the carnage, General French sent in one brigade after another. Albert Richardson, a reporter for the *New York Tribune*, described the scene: "On the great field were riderless horses and scattering men, clouds of dirt from solid shot and exploding shells, long dark lines of infantry swaying to and fro, with columns of smoke rising from their muskets, red flashes and white puffs from the batteries—with the sun shining brightly on all this scene of tumult."

The 132nd Pennsylvania Infantry Regiment was full of raw recruits, waiting anxiously in the yard of the Roulette farm for the order to charge the Sunken Road. As they waited, a Confederate shell smashed into the Roulettes' beehives and the regiment was attacked by swarms of angry bees.

"CLEAR THE WAY!"

The Confederates' left flank had suffered heavy casualties that morning around the Dunker Church and the cornfield. The Sunken Road was the Confederate center; if it gave way, McClellan believed he would be able to send in his troops to smash Lee's right flank. General Lee was aware of the importance of the road, too, and to underscore its significance, he rode over to speak with one of the commanders at the trench, Colonel Gordon. His orders, Lee said, were to hold the Sunken Road. "We will be here," Gordon replied, "'til the sun goes down or our victory is won."

For most of the morning it appeared that Gordon would keep his promise to Lee. The well-protected Confederates in the Sunken Road had repulsed every Union brigade sent against it. Now they would face the Irish Brigade. General Meagher had ordered his brigade to march to the crest of a ridge above the Sunken Road, fire two volleys into the Confederates below, then make a bayonet charge that would dislodge the defenders from the trench. The Irish had just reached the crest when they were surprised by a charge of North Carolina, Georgia, and Alabama troops. The massed guns of the Confederates cut down dozens of Irish—within the first minutes of engaging the enemy, the 69th New

IRONICALLY, THE BATTLE OF ANTIETAM BEGAN AROUND THE DUNKER CHURCH, THE MEETINGHOUSE OF A PACIFIST SECT. THEN IT MOVED TO A NEARBY CORNFIELD AND THE SUNKEN ROAD BEFORE CULMINATING AT A STONE BRIDGE OVER ANTIETAM CREEK, AS SHOWN IN THIS MAP BY MAPMAKER ROBERT KNOX SNEDEN, MADE IN SEPTEMBER 1862 FOR UNION GENERAL SAMUEL P. HEINTZELMAN.

ANTIETAM. Maryland. Sept 1862. Made for Maj Gen Heintzelman USA by

S Keedy

KEEDYSVILLE
Union Hospitals

Nicodemus

School

US Signal Statin
Telegraph to Washington

Gerling Keedy

School

rs of
LAN
House
Orchard
Reserve
R. Fry Farm
HUMPHRIES

WOODS

wagons

US Signal
Mountain
Station

Headqrs
Signal corps
Regular
Battery

PORTERSTOWN

Porter Head qurs

Potoms Train
To Harpers Ferry

Fitz John
PORTER
Reserve Artillery
Regular
Battery
Burnside
Signal statin

Reserves

US
Signal corps
Porter's headqrs
Burnsides
headqrs

Gen SYKES

CROOK
Gen
BURNSIDE

Sumner

MORELL
of
Porter

13.819 men

STURGIS

WILCOX

BROOK

Ravine

ANTIETAM

Position
for men
16 Sept
Brainhall Battery
RICHARDSON

of COX (infantry)

To Rohersville

CREEK

Rebel line
16
Sept
Rev S Adams

Barns Brid
No 4

OHIO
CANAL

Stone
BRIDGE No 4
MILL

ANTIETAM IRON WORKS

CANAL

Sneden del

RIVE

York and the 63rd New York lost about 60 percent of their men. Captain Joseph O'Neill of Company A saw all his men killed or wounded in just two volleys from the Sunken Road.

Amid the chaos, Lieutenant Colonel Patrick Kelly of the 88th New York kept his head. Kelly, forty years old, was an immigrant from County Galway, Ireland, a tall, handsome man with a long, thick beard. As the Confederates charged out of the Sunken Road and the 69th and 63rd New York fell back, Kelly raced forward with his men, ordering them to fire into the Confederates' flank. Now it was the men of the South who retreated.

The Irish Brigade pressed forward, finally reaching the top of the slope. Below, in the Sunken Road, the Confederates were waiting. As the first Irish troops crested the rise, the Confederates opened fire. Chanting their battle cry, "Faugh-a-Ballagh!" or "Clear the way!" the Irish surged forward. Another blast from the Confederates decimated the Irish ranks, and once again the 88th New York came to the rescue.

> The living fought among the wounded, the dying, and the dead—
> no Confederate soldier dared expose himself to the Irish fire
> by climbing out of the Sunken Road to carry a wounded man
> to the field hospitals.

A safe distance away, General McClellan and his staff watched the Irish assault on the Sunken Road. Hearing the Confederate volleys and seeing the green banners fall, a young lieutenant lamented, "The day is lost, General! The Irish fly!" The general was sullen and silent for several moments, then he exclaimed, "No! Their flags are up! They are charging!" Meanwhile, Meagher cried to his men, "We shall give them a few more volleys, boys, and then the bayonet!"

The Irish were not the only casualties. The blasts of buck-and-ball tore into the Confederates packed densely into the trench. The living fought among the wounded, the dying, and the dead—no one dared expose himself to the Irish fire by climbing out of the Sunken Road to carry a wounded man to the field hospitals.

THE DEATH OF A CELEBRITY

While the New York regiments battled the Confederates at almost point-blank range, Colonel Joseph Barnes had led the 29th Massachusetts to a hollow where his men were as well protected as the Confederates in their trench. From their position the men of the 29th could see clearly the Confederate reserves, waiting in a cornfield, far out of range of the Irish muskets at the Sunken Road. But the 29th had been armed with Enfield rifles, which could hit the Confederates in the cornfield. Major Charles Chipman gave the order to open fire: Shocked and confused, certain that they were in a safe place, the reserves saw dozens of their comrades cut down by the Enfield rifles.

Back at the Sunken Road, Meagher was ready for his bayonet charge. "Raise the colors, boys!" he cried. "Follow me! Charge bayonets!" With a roar the Irish charged down the slope, but once again the fire from the Sunken Road was too intense—the 69th fell back. At that moment some Confederates climbed out of the trench and attempted a counterattack. The 69th swung around and killed or wounded almost every attacker.

Captain Patrick Clooney was still commanding his men of the 88th, directing their fire into the road, when a bullet smashed his knee. He fell, then pulled himself back on his feet, using a regimental banner as a crutch. He refused to be taken to a field hospital, and as he stood among his men he was struck twice more—in the chest and the head—and fell down dead. Clooney was a celebrity among the Irish Brigade: Before enlisting to fight for the Union, he had volunteered to fight for Pope Pius IX in the Battalion of St. Patrick, 1,000 Irishmen who went to Italy to fight in defense of the pope and the Papal States against Giuseppe Garibaldi and his effort to forge a united Italy.

In the Sunken Road, Colonel Gordon still held the line as he had promised General Lee, this in spite of four wounds in his arms and legs. Then a fifth Union bullet struck Gordon in the face. His cap flew off, and he pitched forward, falling face-first into it. His blood flowed freely into the cap, and he would have drowned in it had it not been for another bullet that pierced the cap and let the blood drain out.

BATTLEFIELD RUMORS

While the Irish were battling the Confederates, General John C. Caldwell led his 61st and 64th New York and 5th New Hampshire regiments forward, but not very far forward. He positioned his men at the bottom of the rise, out of the line of Confederate fire. The tremendous casualties suffered by the brigades that had preceded him to the Sunken Road unnerved Caldwell; he would not give the order for his men to advance in support of the Irish Brigade. Meagher, relieved to see Caldwell's troops, whom he believed were his reinforcements, was confused when they did not enter the battle. He saw among Caldwell's regiments a man he knew, Colonel Francis Barlow, and rode down to him. "For God's sake, Barlow," Meagher said, "come up and help!" "I am truly sorry, General," Barlow replied, "but my orders are to remain here. I must wait for new orders from General Caldwell."

Since the aftermath of the Battle of Antietam, there has been a lingering question about exactly where General Caldwell was during this crisis. Some veterans of the battle claimed that they saw him ride away from his troops and take refuge in a field—behind a tall haystack. But Caldwell was not the only subject of rumors that day. Immediately after his confrontation with Colonel Barlow, Meagher was riding back up the slope toward the 88th New York when he fell off his horse and was carried off the field. According to this version of the story, Meagher was found to be drunk. Another version claims that his horse was shot, went down, and narrowly missed crushing Meagher. Whatever the truth may be, Meagher was carried off to the field hospital and missed the rest of the battle.

In spite of their casualties, the Irish Brigade did not retreat from the crest above the Sunken Road, and so Confederate casualties mounted. Hill and Gordon's men no longer felt invulnerable in the trench; they felt pinned down. Little by little, men began to climb out of the Sunken Road and race for the cover of the cornfield. Some of them made it—those who were not picked off by the 29th Massachusetts' sharpshooters.

Then General Israel Richardson arrived at the scene. Seeing Caldwell's regiments standing by idly as the Irish fought virtually alone, he demanded to know where General Caldwell was to be found. No one knew. "God damn the field officers!" Richardson shouted. Then he ordered Barlow to advance in support of the Irish Brigade; Richardson would lead Caldwell's 5th New Hampshire regiment.

The appearance of Richardson and Barlow on the crest was timely—the Irish Brigade was at a fraction of its original strength and running so low on ammunition that the men scavenged among the pockets and cartridge boxes of the dead and the wounded. The Brigade's officers believed that if the Confederates mounted one more assault, the Irish ranks would break or be obliterated.

Richardson ordered his troops to load and fix bayonets, then he sent Colonel Barnes to the 29th Massachusetts with instructions to prepare to charge. Two Irish color-bearers ran toward the Sunken Road, waving the green banners defiantly. A company of Confederates accepted the challenge, leaping out of the trench to capture the flags, until they heard the cheers of the 29th Massachusetts charging out of the hollow. Crying, "For Ireland and St. Patrick!" Captain John Joyce rallied the remnant of the Irish Brigade for one last assault on the Sunken Road.

Faced with fresh troops and Irishmen out for vengeance, most of the Confederates scrambled out of the Sunken Road and fled. A few stood their ground—they were either killed or taken prisoner. Farther down the trench, a large number of Confederates still held their position. Barlow ordered his men to fire into their flank, then took the survivors prisoner.

"WHAT THE HELL ARE YOU DOING?"

Now that the Confederates had been driven from the Sunken Road—which Union troops took to calling the Bloody Lane—the Irish Brigade was assigned to picket duty at the cornfield, some 200 yards (180 m) from the road. The focus of the battle, which had begun at the Dunkers Church and then moved to the Sunken Road, shifted again, to the 12-foot-wide (3.6 m) stone bridge over Antietam Creek on Lee's right flank.

Since approximately 9:30 that morning, Major General Ambrose Burnside had been probing the Confederate defenses on the opposite side of the narrow stone bridge, while also sending out scouts to find a place where his army of about 12,500 men could avoid the bottleneck of the bridge and ford the creek en masse. Facing him was Brigadier General Robert Toombs, with about 500 men, mostly Georgians, and two batteries of artillery. Toombs had the advantage of being on high ground in a rock quarry and enjoying the cover of dense woods. At 11 a.m., Burnside still had not crossed the creek, and McClellan was getting impatient. He sent a rider to Burnside with orders to move. With no other choice, Burnside ordered two regiments, the 2nd Maryland and the 6th New Hampshire, to cross the bridge. When they had gotten within 50 yards (45 m) of the Confederate lines, Toombs's men in the woods opened fire, decimating the men from Maryland and New Hampshire, forcing them to retreat. Meanwhile, scouts reported that at Snavely's Ford, about 2 miles (3.2 km) from the bridge, they had discovered a crossing place for the army. Brigadier General Isaac Rodman took about 2,100 men to the ford, intending to attack Toombs on the flank and from the rear, while Burnside prepared for an assault across the stone bridge.

Burnside ordered a barrage of artillery to clear the Confederate batteries off the hilltop. His plan was to send the 2nd Maryland and 6th New Hampshire over the bridge, while the rest of 9th Corps covered them with massed rifle fire.

The Marylanders, led by Lieutenant Colonel Jacob Duryea, led the way, but long before they reached the bridge, the Georgians hidden in the woods and the artillery at the quarry—which the Union guns had failed to eliminate—cut through the charging ranks. The Marylanders' surgeon, Dr. Theodore Dimon, wrote that Colonel Duryea, who was running several steps ahead of the troops, turned around and saw dozens of men dropping to the ground, dead or wounded, and dozens more hesitating to move forward. "What the hell are you doing there?" Duryea shouted. "Straighten that line there! Forward!" Incredibly, the Marylanders did as ordered and surged toward the bridge, but the Confederate fire was too deadly; the regiment scattered and ran for cover. In that charge, the 2nd Maryland lost 44 percent of its

ON OCTOBER 4, 1862, PRESIDENT ABRAHAM LINCOLN VISITED GENERAL GEORGE McCLELLAN—WHO WAS STILL AT ANTIETAM—

TO LEARN WHY HE HAD FAILED TO PURSUE AND CRUSH LEE'S DEFEATED AND RETREATING ARMY OF NORTHERN VIRGINIA.

THE NEXT MONTH, HE WOULD RELIEVE McCLELLAN OF COMMAND.

strength. An unknown member of Major General Fitz John Porter's staff sent a message to McClellan's headquarters that Burnside had tried to send a regiment across the bridge, but "they were driven back like sheep by enemy's artillery."

Burnside refused to give up. He called for two fresh regiments to try to cross the bridge. Brigadier Edward Ferrero was given command of the assault and permitted his choice of regiments. Ferrero was unique among the commanders at Antietam—he had been on the faculty of West Point, but instead of teaching tactics, he had taught dancing and other social graces to the future officers of the U.S. Army. For this offensive, however, Ferrero did not want gentlemen, he wanted battle-hardened veterans, so he selected two of the toughest regiments at Antietam, the 51st New York and the 51st Pennsylvania.

As Ferrero assembled his force of about 670 men, the Union artillery and infantry laid down covering fire. The New Yorkers and Pennsylvanians charged the bridge, 300 yards (273 m) away, but once again withering Confederate fire kept them from their goal. The two regiments took cover behind a wooden fence and a stone wall, where they returned fire. And then the Union troops noticed something—the Confederates were not firing as often. Furthermore, they could see men in twos and threes leaving their positions and racing up the slope to the artillery batteries. It could only mean one thing—the Confederates were almost out of ammunition.

Eager to exploit the first break 9th Corps had had all day, Colonel Robert Potter of the 51st New York leapt up and with his color-bearer ran toward the bridge. All the New Yorkers and Pennsylvanians followed, while the remaining Confederates in the woods fled for the safety of the quarry. Lieutenant Colonel William Holmes of the 2nd Georgia drew his sword and rallied a few men to meet the Union onslaught: Holmes and almost all the men with him were killed in the hail of Union bullets. It had cost 550 Union lives, as opposed to 120 Confederates, but Burnside had captured the bridge. Shortly thereafter, Rodman arrived with his force. And there they stayed, on the far side of the bridge, resting and waiting for fresh supplies of ammunition, for most of the men were out of cartridges.

Seeing the Georgians in full flight and the masses of Burnside's troops assembling, General Lee feared that they would attack and drive him and what remained of his army all the way to the Potomac. But then Lee saw a column of troops approaching, led by a mounted officer wearing a blood-red shirt. It was Major General A.P. Hill with 3,000 Confederates that Stonewall Jackson had left behind as a garrison at Harpers Ferry. Inspired by Hill, the Confederates rallied and charged into Burnside's flank, but the fight was brief. After such a bloody day, both sides appeared to have lost heart. When Burnside pulled his men back to the stone bridge, the Confederates did not pursue. As the sun set, the fighting at Antietam petered out.

McClellan could claim Antietam as a Union victory—Lee's invasion of the North had been stopped cold. But McClellan did not take the next step—attacking and smashing the Army of Northern Virginia. The next day President Lincoln sent McClellan a congratulatory telegram, with this order: "Destroy the rebel army if possible." It was possible, but McClellan did not move against Lee. No matter how large his force or how well supplied his men, McClellan always imagined that the enemy was larger and even better provisioned. Even after the Battle of Antietam, when it was clear that he had the upper hand, he dawdled, fearful as ever of losing more troops or suffering an unexpected defeat.

On October 1, Lincoln traveled to Sharpsburg to consult with his general, and returned believing that McClellan would hunt down Lee and destroy his army. Lincoln wrote, "I came back thinking he would move at once. But when I got home he began to argue why he ought not to move. I peremptorily ordered him to advance. It was nineteen days before he put a man over the [Potomac] River and nine days longer before he got his army across, and then he stopped again." Lee retreated through the Blue Ridge Mountains, and McClellan followed, but at such a distance that Lee was in no danger. Angry and frustrated, on November 5, 1862, Lincoln relieved McClellan of command.

Protocol demanded that such an order be delivered in person, so Secretary of War Edwin Stanton assigned the unpleasant duty to his assistant, Brigadier General Catharinus P. Buckingham, the highest-ranking officer at the War Department. Buckingham said that he was "thunderstruck" when he learned that the president had relieved McClellan of command, but Stanton had no doubt that McClellan must go. "[Stanton] had not only no confidence in McClellan's military skill," Buckingham wrote later, "but he very much doubted his patriotism, and even his loyalty."

Traveling by special train, Buckingham arrived at the army's camp in the midst of a blizzard. His orders were to call upon General Burnside first and offer him command of the army. Then, with Burnside, he would bring the president's order to McClellan. It was about 11 p.m. when Buckingham and Burnside entered McClellan's tent; they found the general writing a letter to his wife, Ellen. McClellan was cordial, and if he was surprised to have an officer from the War Department visit him so late at night he did not show it. As kindly and courteously as possible, Buckingham handed the envelope containing the order to McClellan.

After Buckingham and Burnside left, McClellan returned to his letter. "Of course I was much surprised," he wrote, "but as I read the order in the presence of Gen. Buckingham I am sure that not the slightest expression of feeling was visible on my face, which he watched closely. They shall not have that triumph. They have made a great mistake. Alas for my poor country! . . . Our consolation must be that we have tried to do what was right; if we have failed it was not our fault."

A MORAL CRUSADE

Antietam was the bloodiest single-day battle of the Civil War and the deadliest day in American military history. On D-Day 1944, the United States lost about 6,600 men, but at Antietam the combined losses of the North and the South were approximately 22,720 killed, wounded, or missing. As for the 1,000 men of the Irish Brigade, they suffered 540 casualties, almost all of these at the Sunken Road. The day before the Irish went into battle, 120 new recruits had arrived; 75 of these newcomers were killed or wounded at Antietam.

At the Sunken Road, the Irish Brigade accomplished what two previous Union brigades had failed to do—withstand the Confederates' fire, ultimately drive them from the trench, and give possession of the center of the battlefield to the Army of the Potomac. The Irish Brigade turned the tide at Antietam. By driving off the Confederates, it all but ensured a Union victory. The Irish had been building a reputation as tenacious fighters; at Antietam they cinched it.

And the victory the Irish helped win resonated in unexpected ways for the rest of the war. Lincoln needed success on the battlefield so he could publish his Emancipation Proclamation from a position of strength. The Proclamation destroyed any hope the Confederacy had of gaining international recognition and support. The war was now as much a fight for freedom as to restore the Union, and Great Britain, which had been an enemy of slavery for decades, and France would not send their troops to preserve slavery. Lincoln had shifted the emphasis of the war from a constitutional crisis over secession to a moral crusade for human freedom.

6

"OUR FIGHTERS ARE DEAD":
The Irish Brigade at Fredericksburg

The town of Fredericksburg, Virginia, stood on a gentle incline that sloped down to the Rappahannock River. Behind the town rose a series of ridges, including Prospect Hill, Telegraph Hill, and Marye's Heights. During the last weeks of November and the first weeks of December, General Robert E. Lee had occupied the high ground, carefully putting his men and artillery into place. The Army of the Potomac, led by General Ambrose Burnside, was massed on the other side of the Rappahannock. Earlier in the war, the bridges across the river had been destroyed; to attack Lee, Burnside would need pontoon bridges.

A rumor went around the camp of the Irish Brigade that Burnside planned to have them assault the ridges above Fredericksburg. One anxious Irish private sought out one of the Brigade's chaplains, Father William Corby (before the war, Father Corby had taught at a small Catholic men's college in Indiana called Notre Dame).

"Father," the young man said, "they are going to lead us over in front of those guns which we have seen them placing, unhindered, for the past three weeks."

"Do not trouble yourself," the priest replied, "your generals know better than that."

THE EMANCIPATION PROCLAMATION

Abraham Lincoln never joined any religious denomination. He was never baptized. Yet he had read and reread the King James Version of the Bible until its concepts shaped his conscience just as its cadences shaped his writing. As the Civil War dragged on, Lincoln was turning more and more often to the Bible—for comfort certainly, but also to try to discern the will of God amid all the bloodshed and devastation. He had been debating with himself and his cabinet about emancipating the slaves, and when Lee invaded Maryland, the president made a private vow: If Lee was driven out of the North, Lincoln would take it as a sign from heaven and free the slaves.

By the President of the United States of America:

A Proclamation.

Whereas, on the twenty-second day of September, in the year of our Lord one thousand eight hundred and sixty-two, a proclamation was issued by the President of the United States, containing, among other things, the following, to wit:

"That on the first day of January, in the year of our Lord one thousand eight hundred and sixty-three, all persons held as slaves within any State or designated part of a State, the people whereof shall then be in rebellion against the United States, shall be then, thenceforward, and forever free; and the Executive Government of the United States, including the military and naval authority thereof, will recognize and maintain the freedom of such persons, and will do no act or acts to repress such persons, or any of them, in any efforts they may make for their actual freedom.

"That the Executive will, on the first day

THIS IS ONE OF THE 15 SOUVENIR COPIES OF THE EMANCIPATION PROCLAMATION—ALL OF WHICH WERE SIGNED BY ABRAHAM LINCOLN. THE ORIGINAL DOCUMENT, WHICH HE SIGNED ON NEW YEAR'S DAY 1863, IS PRESERVED AT THE NATIONAL ARCHIVES IN WASHINGTON, D.C. THE EMANCIPATION OF THE SLAVES OUTRAGED MOST IRISH IMMIGRANTS, WHO FEARED THEY WOULD BE COMPETING WITH THE NEW FREEDMEN FOR JOBS.

NATIONAL ARCHIVES

After McClellan's victory at Antietam and Lee's withdrawal back into Virginia, Lincoln believed that "God had decided the question in favor of the slaves." On September 22, Lincoln announced that he would publish an Emancipation Proclamation on January 1, 1863. In this document, Lincoln freed all the slaves living in the Confederacy, but not the slaves in territory occupied by the Union army or in the border states of Maryland, Tennessee, and Missouri (he did not want to antagonize the citizens of those states, many of whom were not entirely loyal to the Union). But among the four million slaves in the South, the Emancipation Proclamation gave them confidence that when the war was over, if the Union won, they would be free. It also inspired thousands of slaves not to wait but to run away from their masters and seek protection with the Union army.

In Richmond, Jefferson Davis damned the Proclamation as the "most execrable measure recorded in the history of guilty man." In London, the publisher of the *Spectator* observed, "The [United States] government liberates the enemy's slaves as it would the enemy's cattle, simply to weaken them in the coming conflict." The *Spectator* had a point: As more and more slaves ran away, there would be fewer to work the plantations, food supplies would dwindle, and the economy of the South would be weakened, perhaps even collapse. Nonetheless, there was jubilation among many Northerners that the institution of slavery in America was on its deathbed.

The Emancipation Proclamation also changed the character of the war. Previously, North and South fought over a legal question: The South insisted that the states had the right to secede; the North insisted that the Union must be preserved. With his Emancipation Proclamation, Lincoln had transformed the war into a moral crusade. As Julia Ward Howe expressed it in "The Battle Hymn of the Republic," "As He [Jesus Christ] died to make men holy, let us die to make men free."

The Irish in the Union army did not find Howe's lyric inspiring, nor were they enthusiastic about the emancipation of the slaves—their old fear that someday they must compete with the freemen for jobs was coming true. As a result, where once the Irish Brigade had to turn men away, now it would be difficult to find fresh recruits.

With McClellan gone, Lincoln needed a new commander of the Army of the Potomac. He chose Ambrose Burnside. In fact, this was the third time Lincoln offered Burnside the command. Burnside had been a successful general at the battles of Roanoke Island and Fort Macon in Virginia and at New Bern in North Carolina, so he was likely to appeal to the troops and the American public. Burnside was well known to be a friend of McClellan, which would make McClellan's friends in the government likely to support his appointment. But Burnside hesitated. He believed he did not have the level of experience necessary to command such a large army—that was why he turned down the president twice before. But this time was different—if he declined again, Lincoln would probably turn to Joseph Hooker, and Burnside loathed Hooker. So Burnside accepted Lincoln's offer.

It took seventeen days for the War Department to deliver the pontoon boats Burnside needed to get his army across the Rappahannock. While the Yankees waited, they watched Lee's army of 75,000 take up defensive positions on all the ridges above Fredericksburg. Burnside had an army of approximately 120,000 men, yet he was at a disadvantage because Lee had seized the high ground.

Lee sent a message to the citizens of Fredericksburg, urging them to evacuate before the battle began and they found themselves trapped between the two armies. It was December, and the snow lay deep. Major Robert Stiles, a Confederate artilleryman, witnessed the exodus. "I never saw a more pitiful procession than they made trudging through the deep snow, after the warning was given and as the hour drew near," he wrote in his memoir, *Four Years Under Marse Robert*. "I saw little children tugging along with their doll babies—some bigger than they were—but holding their feet up carefully above the snow, and women so old and feeble that they could carry nothing and could barely hobble themselves. . . . Where they were going we could not tell, and I doubt if they could."

Burnside selected the locations for four pontoon bridges—two at the northern end of town, one at the southern end of Fredericksburg, and the third, a mile (1.6 km) downstream at a place called Deep Run. On December 10, 1862, under the cover of night, Burnside's engineers transported their material for the bridges to the river. On December 11, 1,600 Mississippians under the command of Brigadier General William Barksdale moved into the abandoned houses and stores of Fredericksburg, especially those close to the river. From windows and doors and cellars, sharpshooters and snipers picked off the Union engineers and their work crews who were trying to throw the bridges across the Rappahannock. To cover the bridge builders, the 7th Michigan and the 19th Massachusetts Volunteers were sent down to the riverbank. Even so, construction of the pontoons made slow progress. Only at Deep Run, which had escaped the Confederates' notice, were the engineers able to build a bridge unimpeded.

On December 12, to clear out the Mississippians, Union gunners directed heavy artillery fire at the buildings along the riverbank where most of the sharpshooters had taken refuge. For two hours, 150 cannons blasted away at the empty town, leveling some houses, setting fire to others, but still the snipers did not retreat. Using the

CONFEDERATE SNIPERS HOLED UP IN THE RUINED BUILDINGS OF FREDERICKSBURG HINDERED THE CONSTRUCTION OF PONTOON BRIDGES ACROSS THE RAPPAHANNOCK RIVER. SOME IMPATIENT UNION TROOPS USED THE PONTOONS AS BOATS, ROWED ACROSS THE RIVER, AND TRIED TO DRIVE THE SNIPERS FROM THEIR POSITIONS IN THIS NATIONAL PARK SERVICE IMAGE.

pontoons as boats, some Union troops rowed across the Rappahannock, attacked, and succeeded in driving out the Mississippi sharpshooters. Finally, the Yankee engineers could complete their bridges. As Burnside began to move his men across the Rappahannock, Lee could see where the Union general planned to attack. He called in the troops that he had stationed at fording places about 12 miles (19 km) from Fredericksburg (in case Burnside decided to cross there), and waited for Burnside's next move.

THE FIRST ASSAULT

At sunrise on December 13, the Confederates looked down on approximately 100,000 men in blue, waiting for the order to attack: They would be led by Major General Edwin Sumner of Massachusetts, a man so tough that his men believed a musket ball once struck his skull and bounced off, and General William Franklin of Pennsylvania, an engineer who before the war had supervised the construction of the dome of the U.S. Capitol. Sumner's 57,000 troops stood ready to storm General James Longstreet's 41,000 men on Marye's Heights. Franklin would send his 51,000 men against Stonewall Jackson's 39,000 men on Prospect Hill. When a Confederate major fretted about the lopsided numbers, Jackson reassured him, "Major, my men may sometimes fail to take a position, but to defend one, never. I am glad the Yankees are coming!"

Burnside's plan for the battle was simple and suicidal: Sumner would send a single division—12,000 men—up Marye's Heights while Franklin would send a single division against Jackson on Prospect Hill. Burnside believed that if he could capture these two high points and turn the artillery batteries up there against Lee, the Confederate line would crumble.

The first assault was made on Prospect Hill, with a division led by Brigadier General George Meade and Brigadier General John Gibbon, both of Pennsylvania. Before the war, Meade had directed the construction of lighthouses along the coasts of New Jersey and Florida; Gibbon had taught artillery tactics at West Point where he wrote *The Artillerist's Manual*, a book used by the gunners of the North and the South. At 8:30 in the morning, Meade and Gibbon led their division against the center of Stonewall Jackson's line. They got about half a mile (0.8 km) from the crest of the hill when the combined fire of Confederate muskets and cannons immobilized them. For the next two hours every man in the division sought cover from the deadly hail of musket balls and exploding shell fragments. It took a barrage of Union artillery on Jackson's guns before Meade and Gibbon had an opportunity to advance.

29 Batteries of 147 guns

11 batteries Col Tompkins

2d Corps STAFFORD HEIGHTS

Song street lost 3.415 men

PLAN of Battle on 13th Decr

From Plan of Topog Engineers 3rd Army Corps

PLAN of THE BATTLE of FRE

The 2nd and 9th Corps were the Right Grand Division under SUMNER. The 1st and 6th Corps were the Left Gra

Genl Franklin USA Commanded all the forces after Crossing the River. He had 6

Union Army - 1.284 Killed - 9.600 wounded

Rebel Army - 608 " 4.116 "

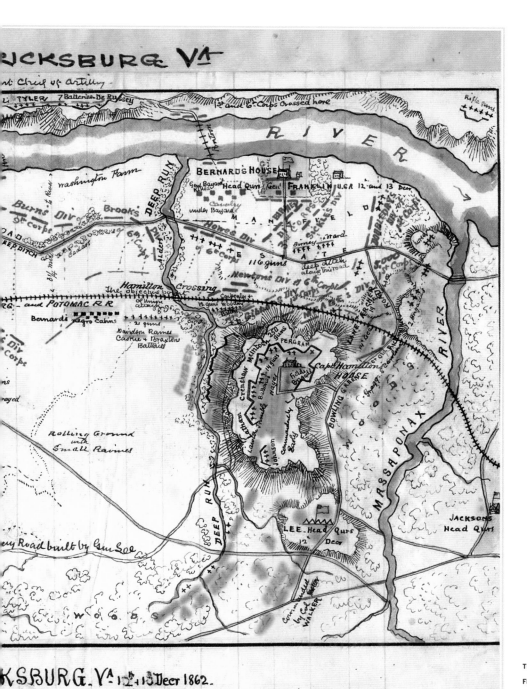

ICKSBURG VA

rt Chief of Artillery

L. TYLER 7 Batteries De Russey

3rd and 6th Corps crossed here

Rifle guns

R I V E R

Bernards House

Gen Bayard Head Qurs Gen FRANKLIN U.S.A. 12 and 13 Decr

Cavalry under Bayard

Washington Farm

DEEP RUN

Brook's

Burns Div or corps

ROAD

EEP DITCH

Howe's Div 6th Corps

116 guns

deep ditch along this road

5.000 1st Corps

Hamilton Crossing
the objective point

RG — and POTOMAC R.R

Meade's Div of 6th Corps

Bernards negro Cabins

21 guns

Davidson Raines Castles + Brayton Batteries

220 guns

PERGRAM

Crenshaw McIntosh 14 guns

Capt Hamilton

HORSE

BOWLING GREEN

Rolling Ground with Small Ravines

DEEP RUN

MASSAPONAX RIVER

Road built by Gen Lee

LEE. Head Qurs
12

Decr

JACKSONS
Head Qurs

KSBURG. VA 12th + 13th Decr 1862.

e under FRANKLIN. The 3rd and 5th Corps were the Centre Division under HOOKER. 11th Corps were Re

— only 16.000 to 18.000 men were engaged in Battle. Of these only 8.000 at any one

g missing or prisoners. TOTAL = 12.653.
" " TOTAL = 5.377

1994 89 39

THIS MAP OF THE BATTLE OF
FREDERICKSBURG WAS DRAWN BY
ROBERT KNOX SNEDEN OF NEW YORK,
A LANDSCAPE PAINTER WHO BECAME
A UNION ARMY MAPMAKER DURING
THE CIVIL WAR. THE MAPS AND
PAINTINGS HE PRODUCED DURING
THE WAR ARE AMERICA'S LARGEST
COLLECTION OF SOLDIER ART.
VIRGINIA HISTORICAL SOCIETY

The Union division charged, cutting through a brigade commanded by Brigadier General Maxcy Gregg of South Carolina, a handsome lawyer-turned-soldier. The Confederates, thinking their guns had pounded Meade and Gibbon to dust, panicked and abandoned their positions. In the fighting, Gregg was killed. But then Jackson ordered a counterattack and Meade, Gibbon, and their men ran back down Prospect Hill.

The assault on Prospect Hill cost the Union more than 4,800 casualties—including a severely wounded General Gibbon—while the Confederates lost approximately 3,400 men. General Franklin did not attempt another attack on Prospect Hill, but sat out the remainder of the battle. Meade and Gibbon had broken through Stonewall Jackson's line, but only briefly. Nonetheless, it was the only Union achievement of the day.

WITHERING FIRE

Two days earlier, at four in the morning on December 11, the Irish Brigade was roused and ordered to the Rappahannock River. As it marched by the camp of the 14th Brooklyn, their fellow New Yorkers cheered, and the 14th's band struck up an Irish drinking song popular with Irish troops, "Garryowen." General Meagher looked splendid in a uniform of his own design: a tailored dark green jacket embroidered with silver stars, with black knots at the shoulders. Across his chest he had draped a yellow silk sash.

The 1,200 men of the Irish Brigade believed they were marching into battle, but they did not get far—December 11 was the day the army engineers were trying, without success, to build their bridges across the Rappahannock. The Irish did not cross to the battered, deserted town of Fredericksburg until the morning of December 12. There they spent the day, waiting for further orders, which came at last shortly after sunrise on December 13. Before they marched out of Fredericksburg, General Thomas Meagher had each man slip a sprig of green boxwood into his hatband—a debonair gesture to identify the Irish Brigade.

The division that would attack Marye's Heights had been selected from the 2nd Corps, commanded by Brigadier General William H. French of Maryland. In the 1850s, French had been Stonewall Jackson's superior officer, and the two men had not gotten along. At the summit of the hill was Longstreet's artillery, each cannon placed for best advantage. Anything that tried to cross the 800 yards (720 m) of open ground below Marye's Heights would be within easy range of Longstreet's guns. Furthermore, at the base of the hill was another sunken road, like the one at Antietam, and a stone wall, about 500 yards (450 m) long. Longstreet had sent Georgians to the wall and filled the ground behind it with South Carolina infantry.

GENERAL JAMES LONGSTREET PLACED HIS ARTILLERY AT THE SUMMIT OF MARYE'S HEIGHTS. "OUR ARTILLERY, BEING IN POSITION,

OPENED FIRE AS SOON AS THE MASSES [OF UNION TROOPS] BECAME DENSE ENOUGH TO WARRANT IT," LONGSTREET WROTE.

"THIS FIRE WAS VERY DESTRUCTIVE AND DEMORALIZING IN ITS EFFECTS."

According to orders, Sumner was not to move out until he had been informed that Franklin's attack on Jackson had been successful. When eleven o'clock came and Sumner still had not received any news, he ordered his division commanders to prepare to attack.

About noon, Sumner's division marched out of the ruins of Fredericksburg. Brigadier General Nathan Kimball of Indiana led the first assault on the Confederate position. They were within 125 yards (114 m) of the stone wall when the Rebels opened fire. Minie balls and artillery shells swept through the Union ranks; within minutes hundreds of men in blue lay dead or dying on the slope of the hill. Kimball was struck in the thigh and carried to the rear.

But the Union troops attacked again, and again, and again, and each time they were met by withering fire—just as Longstreet had planned. That afternoon Longstreet virtually destroyed French and Winfield Scott Hancock's brigades and Oliver O. Howard and Samuel D. Sturgis's divisions. Joseph Hooker rode to Burnside's headquarters, where he maintained that further assaults on Marye's Heights would be a "useless waste of life." In spite of the horrific casualties, Burnside refused to back down; instead, he ordered Hooker to prepare to send in his division.

"WHAT A PITY!"

Two hundred yards (180 m) outside of Fredericksburg, the Irish Brigade found its way blocked by a canal. There was a rickety wooden bridge across, and it seemed to take an eternity for the 1,200 men to cross. Once they were assembled on the other side, Meagher got them into battle formation again. He ordered all officers to dismount and go ahead on foot. As for Meagher, he had been wounded in the knee and was compelled to retire, but he would retreat no farther than just outside Fredericksburg, where he had a clear view of his Irishmen.

After watching the slaughter of French and Hancock's brigades, it was the turn of the Irish. By chance, they were directed to attack the part of the stone wall defended by the 24th Georgia Infantry, a regiment filled with Irishmen. "What a pity!" one of the Georgian Irish cried. "Here comes Meagher's fellows." As the Union Irish Brigade advanced, a roar of Irish Confederate musket fire tore through their ranks. "Companies and regiments seemed to evaporate," wrote historian George C. Rable of the scene.

Years later, recalling that afternoon before Marye's Heights, Captain John H. Donovan of the Irish Brigade said, "It was impossible for human nature to withstand this, and yet we were left there all afternoon unrelieved." Major James Cavanaugh rallied the Irish. "Blaze away and stand it, boys!" he cried. Cavanaugh got within 50 yards (45 m) of the stone wall before he went down with a bullet through his thigh.

As Private William McCarter of the Irish Brigade raised his arm to fire his rifle, a musket ball struck him in the armpit. Blood soaked his shirt and pants; woozy from the loss of blood, he collapsed on the field. A moment later, the man standing nearest McCarter was shot and killed. He fell across McCarter, pinning him to the ground but also shielding him—the dead man's body absorbed bullets that otherwise would have hit and almost certainly killed William McCarter.

As the Union Irish Brigade advanced, a roar of Irish Confederate musket fire tore through their ranks.

Captain John O'Neill fell, the bullet puncturing a lung before lodging by his spine. An exploding shell crippled Color Sergeant William H. Tyrrell. No longer able to stand, he went down on his one good knee, gripping the regimental colors until five musket balls tore into him and he toppled over, dead.

General Meagher had borrowed a horse and ridden up to make the attack with his men. In the face of the terrible slaughter, he did not call for a retreat, but massed his brigade together into two lines and shouted the order, "Load, and fire at will!" The Irish behind the stone wall and the Irish on the slope released barrage after barrage into each other's faces. A shell fragment struck Meagher in the leg, throwing him from his horse. For the second time that day, he was carried off the battlefield.

To escape the deadly Confederate fire, some of the Irish took refuge behind a small brick house on the slope. Others piled up wooden fence posts and, lying flat on the ground, hoped this pathetic barricade would protect them. But there were men still on their feet, cursing the Rebels as they fired.

The valor of the Irish Brigade deeply moved Confederate General George Pickett. After the battle he wrote to his fiancée, "Your soldier's heart almost stood still as he watched those sons of Erin fearlessly rush to their deaths. The brilliant assault on Marye's Heights of their Irish Brigade was beyond description. We forgot they were fighting us and cheer after cheer at their fearlessness went up all along our lines."

THE BAYONET CHARGE

In spite of the casualties, Burnside ordered yet another assault on Marye's Heights. Lee worried that perhaps the Georgians at the stone wall were becoming weary, that under the stress of these repeated attacks, their line might break. To reinforce the

ARTIST FREDERICK CARADA PAINTED THE UNION ATTACK ON MARYE'S HEIGHTS. GENERAL AMBROSE BURNSIDE ORDERED MORE THAN A DOZEN ASSAULTS ON THE HEIGHTS, BUT THE CONFEDERATES REPULSED ALL OF THEM. IN FIVE HOURS, THE UNION WOULD LOSE 7,000 MEN AT MARYE'S HEIGHTS, THE CONFEDERATES 5,000. THE IRISH BRIGADE WOULD LOSE 545 MEN KILLED, WOUNDED, OR MISSING— ALMOST 50 PERCENT OF ITS STRENGTH.

Georgians, Longstreet sent in the brigade of South Carolinians. Now there were so many Confederate troops massed behind the wall that they stood several men deep. Longstreet took advantage of the situation by ordering rotating lines of fire. The men at the wall would fire, then step back to reload. The next row of men would step up to the wall and fire, then step back to reload, and so forth, creating a relentless storm of musket fire.

A soldier from the 19th Massachusetts recalled picking his way among dead and wounded Yankees as he advanced on the wall; it was difficult to keep his footing because "the grass was slippery with their blood."

In obedience to Burnside's orders, General Couch sent in another division—it got no closer than 100 yards (91 m), then was obliged to fall back. Burnside sent in Hooker's division. Hooker led his men into Fredericksburg, where he conferred with other commanders who had led assaults on the Heights. Convinced that another attack was futile, Hooker and his men stayed put in the town.

When Brigadier General Andrew A. Humphreys's turn came to lead his brigade up the hill, he decided to try a different strategy. Humphreys was a Pennsylvania man, a veteran of the Seminole Wars, a strict disciplinarian with his troops, but also a man of great bravery. Shouting "Officers to the front!" he ordered a bayonet charge. As the Pennsylvanians surged forward, wounded men on the ground called on them to stop; some grabbed the trouser legs of the charging men. As a result, for a few moments the line wavered, but ultimately the Pennsylvanians swept toward the stone wall. They were within 50 yards (45 m) of it when four ranks of Confederates raised their muskets and fired. One of the Confederates at the wall that day described the charge: "The first line melted but the second came steadily on, over the dead and dying of the former charges, to share the same fate. Ye gods! It is no longer a battle, it is a butchery!"

Humphreys's charge failed, and left another 1,000 casualties at the wall.

The final assault came at sunset, led by Colonel Rush Hawkins, a New York City lawyer. Hawkins tried to flank the Confederates, but the Rebels saw what he was doing and shifted their position slightly to meet him. Union General Robert Ransom, who witnessed Hawkins's attack, said the Confederates' withering fire sent the men "actually howling back to their beaten comrades in the town."

It was dark when the Union commanders gave up. There would be no more assaults on Marye's Heights.

That night, Burnside considered still further attacks on the Confederate positions, but his commanders flat out refused to spill any more blood at

Fredericksburg. The Union army stayed in camp, collecting its wounded and burying its dead. Lee stayed where he was, too, waiting to see whether Burnside would launch another assault. But on December 16, the Confederates awoke to find Burnside and his army gone—they had pulled back to Falmouth, Virginia, where the general made winter camp.

The Confederacy was jubilant. The *Richmond Examiner* proclaimed the Battle of Fredericksburg "a stunning defeat to the invader, a splendid victory to the defender of the sacred soil."

In the North, news of the defeat and the terrible casualties plunged the nation into grief and the president into one of his spells of depression. Burnside tried to shift the blame from himself, saying he could have whipped Lee at Fredericksburg if the pontoons from the War Department had arrived on time. To salvage his military reputation, Burnside began planning a new campaign in the Fredericksburg area. Unknown to the general, two of his subordinate officers paid a call to Lincoln, informing him of Burnside's intentions and assuring the president that the campaign was doomed. Lincoln wired Burnside, instructing him to make no move deeper into Virginia. Stung by what he took to be Lincoln's lack of confidence in him, Burnside resigned; Lincoln refused to accept the resignation and permitted Burnside to proceed with his campaign.

On January 20, 1863, the Army of the Potomac set out once again for the neighborhood of Fredericksburg. That night it began to rain; within hours, the shower had become a downpour—and it continued for four days. The roads were transformed into a thick gumbo of mud so deep that wagons, cannons, horses, mules, and men became stuck in the mire. Burnside called off "The Mud March," as his campaign came to be known.

Within days of the debacle, General Hooker told a newspaper reporter that Burnside was incompetent. Burnside responded by dismissing Hooker and seven senior officers he considered insubordinate. Then he traveled to the White House, where he told Lincoln that he must either confirm Burnside's general order dismissing the eight officers, or he must accept Burnside's resignation. Lincoln accepted the general's resignation.

SQUANDERING IRISH LIVES

In five hours the Union lost 7,000 men at Marye's Heights; Longstreet lost 1,700 defending it. In total, the Union casualties at Fredericksburg were over 13,000 killed, wounded, or missing. The Confederates lost approximately 5,000.

"Our musketry alone killed and wounded at least 5,000," General Longstreet recorded later, "and these, with the slaughter by the artillery, left over 7,000 killed and wounded before the foot of Marye's Hill. The dead were piled sometimes three deep, and when morning broke, the spectacle that we saw upon the battlefield was one of the most distressing I ever witnessed. The charges had been desperate and bloody, but utterly hopeless. I thought, as I saw the Federals come again and again to their death, that they deserved success if courage and daring could entitle soldiers to victory."

Of the 1,200 men of the Irish Brigade who marched out of the ruins of Fredericksburg to assault Marye's Heights, 545 were killed, wounded, or missing—in other words, the Irish lost almost 50 percent of their strength. The Battle of Fredericksburg was the Irish Brigade's bloodiest day—it lost more men at Marye's Heights than at any other battle of the Civil War. Captain William J. Nagle of the Irish Brigade wrote to his father, "Oh! It was a terrible day. The destruction of life has been fearful, and nothing gained. . . . Irish blood and Irish bones cover that terrible field to-day. . . . We are slaughtered like sheep, and no result but defeat." The *Irish American* newspaper reprinted Nagle's letter in its December 27, 1862, edition. The idea of slaughter was repeated by one of the Brigade's chaplains, Father William Corby. In his memoirs he stated, "[T]he place into which Meagher's brigade was sent was simply a slaughter pen with absolutely no protection for our ranks. . . . Needless to say, our brigade was cut to pieces."

Back home the Irish began to wonder whether the Irish Brigade suffered such high casualties because the Union commanders were at heart anti-Irish and did not mind squandering the lives of Irish soldiers. After Fredericksburg, Boston's Irish newspaper, the *Boston Pilot*, lamented, "We did not cause this war, [but] vast numbers of our people have perished in it . . . the Irish spirit for the war is dead! . . . Our fighters are dead."

Such suspicions were not limited to the Irish. Joseph B. Polley, a Texan who had fought at Fredericksburg, wrote to his sweetheart at home, "To assault [Marye's Heights] was a desperate undertaking, and it would seem that the calculating, death-fearing, simon-pure Yankees shrank from it. . . . Foreigners, though, were plentiful in the Federal army, and the loss of a few thousand more or less would break no Yankee hearts; therefore, I imagine, Meagher's Irish Brigade was selected for the sacrifice."

On January 16, 1863, a little more than a month after the battle, at St. Patrick's Cathedral in New York City, one of the Brigade's chaplains, Father Ouellet, sang a Solemn High Requiem Mass for the repose of the souls of the fallen men of the Irish Brigade. The clergy of the cathedral assisted him, and a military band joined the cathedral's organ and choir to supply the music for the Mass. In the congregation were General Meagher and his wife; Colonel Robert Nugent, who had been wounded at Fredericksburg; and several other wounded officers from the Irish Brigade. In the center aisle before the high altar, draped in black and flanked by six tall candles, stood the catafalque, an empty coffin that represented all of the men of the Irish Brigade who had been killed at Fredericksburg and earlier engagements.

In 1861, when the Irish Brigade had marched through the streets of New York, Meagher commanded 2,250 men. After Fredericksburg, 600 were left. The men of the 116th Pennsylvania and the 28th Massachusetts, who had been assigned to the Irish Brigade, raised the number to 1,058 enlisted men and 139 officers. The 28th Massachusetts was not composed of Irishmen—in fact, they were all Yankee Protestants, all descended from the English families who had settled Massachusetts in the seventeenth century. Nonetheless, they and the Irish got on well together, and the soldiers of the 28th described themselves as "honorary Irishmen." But the combination of the death toll at Fredericksburg and Lincoln's signing of the Emancipation Proclamation dampened Irish enthusiasm for the war. To Meagher's dismay, in the first months of 1863, the Irish Brigade received no new recruits to replace the men lost at Marye's Heights.

7

"WHAT WILL THE COUNTRY SAY?":
The Irish Brigade at Chancellorsville

General Ambrose Burnside's officers had barely cleaned the muck off their mud-soaked uniforms before they deluged President Lincoln and Secretary of War Edwin Stanton with angry telegrams and letters damning Burnside's incompetence and howling for his resignation. Burnside's ineptitude was not the only problem—after Fredericksburg, the American public and the Army of the Potomac were depressed and demoralized. In the army, the dejection was made worse by what the men endured on a daily basis: maggoty hardtack and putrid salt pork, epidemics of dysentery and scurvy, and field hospitals so ill equipped that patients lying in their cots got frostbite because no one remembered to order stoves. On top of all these troubles, the men were not being paid regularly—many had not been paid in months. Unlike the Confederacy, which was short of cash, short of food, short of everything, the Union had more than it needed to prosecute the war: Army warehouses were stuffed with fresh meat, fruit, vegetables, medicine, and other supplies, but an inept bureaucracy failed to deliver them to the soldiers.

On January 26, 1863, Lincoln relieved Burnside of command and appointed in his place General Joseph Hooker of Massachusetts. Hooker, forty-nine years old, was brash, a loudmouth, full of bombast and full of himself. However, during the Peninsula Campaign of 1862, he had proved that he was a steady commander in the midst of battle. Lincoln hoped that in Hooker he had found at last an aggressive commander who would bring an end to the war.

About this time, the Lincolns held a reception at the White House. One of the guests, Henry Raymond, the editor of the *New York Times*, drew the president aside for a quiet word. The *Times'* correspondent with the Army of the Potomac had passed along to his editor some hard things General Hooker had said about Lincoln and his administration, specifically that the administration was full of "imbeciles" and that the civilian government ought to be replaced by a dictator. Leaning close to Raymond's ear so that he could not be overheard, Lincoln replied, "That is all true—Hooker does talk badly; but the trouble is, he is stronger with the country today than any other man."

Not long after the White House reception, Lincoln wrote candidly to his new commander. "Only those generals who gain successes," he said, "can set up dictators. What I now ask of you is military success, and I will risk the dictatorship."

Lincoln's frankness touched a chord in Joe Hooker. For weeks he kept the letter in his pocket, showing it to friends and saying, "He talks to me like a father. . . . I shall not answer this letter until I have won him a great victory."

A NEW COMMANDER AND A NEW STRATEGY

The Army of the Potomac had made winter camp in Stafford County, Virginia. During those long, idle months the men had grown undisciplined and sloppy. Hooker began with sweeping changes in camp life. Sanitation in the camp was dreadful—Hooker ordered the men to dig fresh latrines and scrub clean the wooden huts in which they spent the winter. He had fresh onions and potatoes delivered to the camp twice a week, and freshly baked bread came four times a week. As the men's diet improved, the number of cases of scurvy, dysentery, and other diseases dropped. Nonetheless, Hooker also resupplied the hospital—and he ordered stoves to heat the wards.

The men had become listless and shoddy—Hooker ordered daily calisthenics and close-order drills, as well as frequent parades. Burnside had favored massive divisions; Hooker broke up the divisions into seven corps, which would be easier to maneuver on the battlefield. Inspired by the superlative cavalry commanded by Confederate Major General Jeb Stuart, Hooker created a distinct cavalry corps.

Hooker and his army were fortunate: They may have been ill supplied during the winter of 1862–63, but at least there were supplies to be had. Three miles (4.8 km) away, Lee and his Army of Northern Virginia were short on rations, shoes, socks, shirts, blankets, overcoats, and fodder for the horses. Meat was so scarce it was reduced to 4 ounces (112 g) of bacon per man per day. By Lee's order, the men foraged daily for edible roots because virtually no vegetables were available. Two years into the war, the Confederacy's resources were running dangerously low. Unlike the North, the southern states did not have a host of textile mills and factories to manufacture the uniforms, boots, weapons, and ammunition the army needed, nor could the plantations produce enough food to feed the civilian population and the troops too. Lee was even short on manpower—his army was less than half the size of Hooker's—60,000 Confederates to 130,000 Federals.

EDWIN FORBES, AN ARTIST EMPLOYED BY *FRANK LESLIE'S ILLUSTRATED NEWSPAPER*, DREW THIS SKETCH OF THE STEEPLECHASE RACE SPONSORED BY THE IRISH BRIGADE AS PART OF ITS CELEBRATION OF ST. PATRICK'S DAY, 1863. AFTER THE WAR GENERAL WILLIAM TECUMSEH SHERMAN COLLECTED AS MANY OF FORBES'S SKETCHES AS HE COULD FIND AND PRESENTED THEM TO THE FEDERAL GOVERNMENT.

By the time spring arrived in Virginia, the Army of the Potomac was in fine shape, while the Army of Northern Virginia was still miserable. As March 17 approached, Hooker decided that the entire army would join the Irish Brigade in celebrating St. Patrick's Day. The Irish erected an outdoor chapel of evergreen boughs where their chaplains would celebrate Mass. A second arbor of evergreens was raised before headquarters. On the saint's day, long wooden tables were set up by the arbor, piled high with food. One table bore a large wooden tub, painted green, which, according to historian Stephen Sears, was "filled with a near-lethal punch containing eight baskets of champagne, ten gallons of rum, and twenty-two gallons of Irish whiskey."

After Mass had been said, the party started. There were horse races and boxing matches, and the men lined up to try to climb a greased pole (tacked to the top was $50 in cash and a fifteen-day pass). The steeplechase, over a homemade obstacle course, generated the most excitement that day: Before it was over several riders had suffered broken bones, and one man and two horses were killed. All day long an endless stream of fresh food and more alcohol fueled the festivities so that at nightfall, as Sears put it, "no one went home hungry or sober."

About three weeks later, on April 5, President Lincoln, with his wife, Mary, their ten-year-old son Tad, and three guests, arrived at the camp to review the army. The party traveled by steamboat to Aquia Landing, where Hooker had a special train waiting, its cars draped with bunting. At the camp, the Lincoln family and their guests were greeted by Hooker and his officers.

The next day, the Lincolns and their guests, Hooker, and the general's staff took their places on the reviewing stand to see the 10,000 men of the cavalry corps pass in parade. Across the Rappahannock River, many Confederates had come out of their camp and climbed to high ground so they could watch the pageantry too. Cantering to the music of their bands, the cavalry rode by, splendid in dark blue uniforms. Two days later, the infantry turned out for the First Family—75,000 men marched by, with the precision drill of one New York infantry regiment, Duryée's Zouaves, especially delighting the president.

Lincoln spent a happy week with his army, and had time to sit down with his commanders to discuss the military situation. General McClellan's plan to capture Richmond was no longer practical. "There is no eligible route for us into Richmond," Lincoln wrote in his notes. "Hence our prime object is the enemies' army in front of us."

Hooker's plan was to keep a corps of infantry near Fredericksburg, on Lee's right flank, while his 10,000 cavalrymen and three corps of infantry would cross the

Rappahannock at Kelly's Ford and threaten Lee's left flank. They would take up position at a crossroads village called Chancellorsville.

STONEWALL JACKSON'S SURPRISE ATTACK

Through the reconnaissance missions of Stuart's cavalry, Lee was aware that Hooker's men were on the move. On April 29, Lee ordered his commanders to prepare for action.

Stonewall Jackson's wife, Anna, and their five-month-old daughter, Julia, were visiting at the time. This was the first time the general had seen his youngest child, so it had been an especially poignant and happy few days for the Jackson family. With the Yankees advancing, Jackson arranged for Anna and Julia to return home, and then he turned his attention to the coming battle.

It was the understanding of Hooker's commanders that they would attack Lee, overwhelming him with their superior numbers. But once he was on Lee's side of the Rappahannock, Hooker did not order an attack, but sent out his engineers to fell trees and build breastworks. He decided to wait for Lee to attack him. Why Hooker changed his strategy is unknown; historian William C. Davis suggests that as the battle approached, Hooker lost his nerve. Nonetheless, the defenses Hooker erected hastily at Chancellorsville were impressive: Anchored at one end by the Rappahannock, the fortification made it impossible for Lee to attack Hooker's left flank, he would have to send his Army of Northern Virginia against Hooker's center or right flank.

In a meeting with Lee, Stonewall Jackson revealed his plan to swing his men around in a wide circle to attack Hooker's right. Lee asked how many men Jackson would take, and Jackson replied that he would take his entire corps—approximately 29,000 men—leaving Lee with about 31,000 men. Furthermore, Jackson would take more than 100 cannons, too. With the Union and Confederate lines scarcely more than 3 miles (4.8 km) apart, concealing the movement of so many men and so much artillery would be difficult if not impossible. And sure enough, on the morning of May 2, 1863, as Jackson set out with his corps from Guiney Station, Union troops stationed near Hazel Grove, a small hill southwest of Chancellorsville, spotted them and passed the word to their commander, General Daniel Sickles, who passed the message along to Hooker. Unfortunately, Hooker misread what Jackson was doing—Hooker thought Lee was in retreat, and Jackson's force was the vanguard of the Confederate army.

Hooker ordered Sickles to send two divisions to attack the "retreating" Confederates. Instead of running from the Yankees, some Confederate detachments skirmished with the Federals, while Jackson focused on his task of getting his army and his guns in place to attack Hooker's right flank.

About 5:15 in the afternoon, the Union troops stationed on the right flank of their army were surprised to see a large number of deer, foxes, and other wildlife scampering out of the woods. A moment later a horde of Confederates, shrieking the rebel yell, burst out of the cover of the trees. The 153rd Pennsylvania and the 54th New York were at the outer edge of the Union flank—Jackson's corps steamrolled them. Taken by surprise, thousands of Union troops ran down the road that led to the large brick house that was the home of the Chancellor family; here Hooker had set up his headquarters.

In spite of the fear and chaos in the Union ranks, Jackson did not manage to roll up Hooker's right flank. Some Union brigades dug in and fought, which slowed the Confederate advance. The condition of Jackson's men was also a factor—they had marched 15 miles (24 km) before going into battle, and after the initial charge many of the Rebels hadn't the energy to keep the momentum of their attack going. After nightfall, Jackson's men pulled back to reform, which gave the Yankees time to regroup. In spite of possessing the element of surprise, Jackson's attack on Hooker's right had failed.

ABANDONING THE HIGH GROUND

On May 2, the Irish Brigade held been held in reserve, but on the morning of May 3, it was ordered to the front, where Jackson had renewed his attack. The Irish lined up near the Chancellor house; as Major St. Clair Mulholland exchanged a good morning with Major John Lynch, a Confederate artillery shell came screaming toward the brigade. It struck Lynch. In his memoirs, Mulholland wrote that Major Lynch was reduced to "an unrecognizable mass of quivering flesh and bones." Confederate artillery killed ten more of the Irish Brigade before the order was given to move to the edge of the nearby woods and lie flat on the ground. Even so, the deadly hail of Confederate shells killed and wounded many of the Irish where they lay. A shell decapitated one orderly as he rode by; the terrified horse galloped away, but the headless body remained in the saddle for 50 yards (45 m) before falling to the ground at last.

Jackson's men, their strength restored by a good night's rest, pressed the attack ferociously on the Union right. Jackson's men may have had spirit, but Hooker had numbers—76,000 troops squared off against Jackson's 29,000. The rest of Lee's army was divided, with Stuart's men west of Chancellorsville and Lee's occupying the eastern and southern outskirts of the town—these two bodies of the Confederate army were separated by a distance of about 2 miles (3.2 km).

En. Hookers Head Quarters at the Chancellorsville
May 1st 1863. Edwin Forbes,

THE CHANCELLOR FAMILY'S RED BRICK HOUSE WITH ITS LARGE TWO-STORY FRONT PORCH BECAME HEADQUARTERS
FOR UNION GENERAL JOSEPH HOOKER. AT ONE POINT, HOOKER WAS STRUCK UNCONSCIOUS WHILE LEANING AGAINST
ONE OF THE COLUMNS ON THE FRONT PORCH AFTER IT WAS SHATTERED BY A CONFEDERATE SHELL.
UNFORTUNATELY FOR THE CHANCELLOR FAMILY, THE HOUSE DID NOT SURVIVE THE BATTLE.

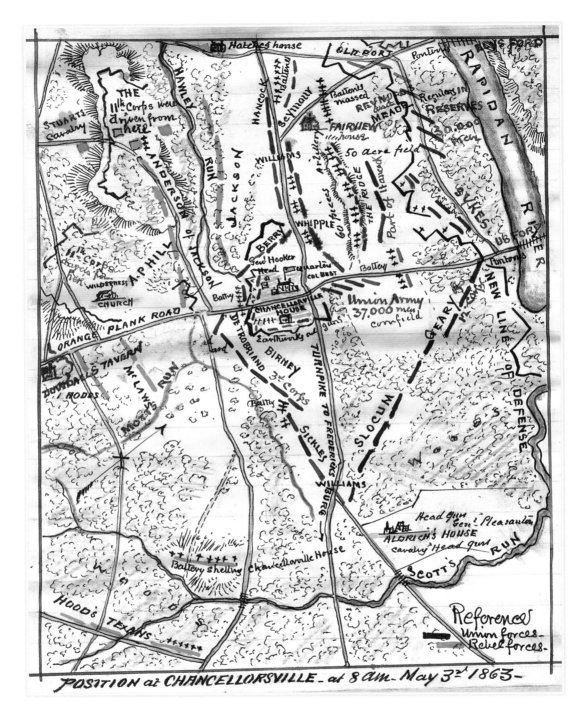

POSITION at CHANCELLORSVILLE - at 8 am - May 3rd 1863 -

IN THIS MAP, ROBERT KNOX SNEDEN SHOWS THE POSITION OF THE ARMIES AT CHANCELLORSVILLE AT 8 IN THE MORNING OF MAY 3, 1863.

ALSO VISIBLE ON THE MAP IS THE CHANCELLOR FAMILY'S HOUSE. CONFEDERATE ARTILLERY KILLED NEARLY ALL THE GUNNERS

OF THE 5TH MAINE BATTERY, POSITIONED IN THE CHANCELLORS' YARD. THE IRISH BRIGADE HELPED THE SURVIVORS KEEP

THE MAINE GUNS FROM FALLING INTO ENEMY HANDS.

VIRGINIA HISTORICAL SOCIETY

Sickles still occupied the high ground at Hazel Grove, a vantage point that gave the Union artillery a clear, unobstructed field of fire. Sickles could have softened up the Confederate lines with his guns, then Hooker could have sent his men smashing into Jackson's force, then Stuart's, and finally into Lee's command. But Hooker had not recovered his nerve; he remained behind his breastworks. Incredibly, he even ordered Sickles to abandon Hazel Grove. Once the Union gunners pulled out, the Confederates moved in. "There has rarely been a more gratuitous gift of a battlefield," wrote a gleeful Colonel E. Porter Alexander of Georgia. Acting swiftly, his men rolled their guns to the summit of Hazel Grove and trained them on the Union lines.

Confederate regiments stormed the Union defenses, while Confederate artillery bombarded the Union troops. It was not yet ten in the morning, and already thousands of men lay dead and wounded. Seeing the Confederate brigades under Major General Henry Heth beginning to waver, Stuart sent in reinforcements, but some of the troops, horrified by the carnage they were witnessing, hesitated to join the fight.

At the Chancellor house, Hooker stood leaning against one of the columns on the front porch. A Confederate shell shattered the column, a piece of which struck Hooker. The general fell to the ground, unconscious. When he came to, he was dazed, but for a time he insisted on staying where he was to supervise the battle. It was with some effort that his staff convinced Hooker to retire to a tent at the rear and summon his senior subordinate, Major General Darius Couch. A New Yorker who had been educated at West Point, Couch had trained as a naturalist and once led a Smithsonian Institution–sponsored scientific expedition into northern Mexico. From his cot, Hooker told Couch, "I turn the command of the army over to you. You will withdraw it and place it in the position designated on this map."

As Couch emerged from the tent with the map clutched in his hand, a small group of officers crowded around him. "We shall have some fighting now!" exclaimed Colonel N.H. Davis. Instead, to the shock and frustration of the officers, Couch issued orders for retreat.

THE REAR GUARD OF THE REAR GUARD

As the Federals pulled back, Fairview Heights, high ground even closer to the Union lines than Hazel Grove, was vacated. Colonel Alexander rushed twenty-six cannons to the Heights; the retreating Yankees were about 750 yards (683 m) away— in essence, Alexander's guns would be firing at point-blank range. "We deployed on the plateau & opened on the fugitives, infantry, artillery, wagons—everything—swarming about the Chancellorsville house & down the broad road leading thence to the river," Alexander wrote later.

The Chancellor family's house had become a field hospital—fourteen-year-old Sue Chancellor recalled, "Our piano served as an amputating table." Sue and her family and some neighbors—sixteen civilians in all—had taken shelter in the basement. Now, as Alexander's guns pounded the house and yard, a member of Hooker's staff ran down the basement stairs to order them out—the house had caught fire. As the Chancellors and their friends raced after the retreating Union troops, they passed piles of amputated limbs, and row upon row of corpses, covered with canvas.

Although the Union army was in retreat, the fighting had not lessened at all. The Confederates kept advancing, and the Federals kept firing as they withdrew toward the river. In the midst of the carnage was General Couch, calmly directing the retreat personally. Two bullets grazed him and twice his horse was shot from under him, but he never lost his composure.

There were a handful of cannons, perhaps sixteen in all, in the area around the burning Chancellor house. They were outgunned by the Confederates on Fairview Heights and by another Confederate battery on Plank Road, which ran below the Heights. But the Union gunners kept firing, hoping to provide some cover to the retreat. Lieutenant Francis Seeley had six Napoleons, or 12-pound field guns, but only enough men alive to work four of them. He ordered the guns loaded with canister shot, then waited as Confederate infantry advanced on him. When the Rebels were 350 yards (319 m) away, Seeley gave the command, "Fire!" Hundreds of small lead balls raked through the Confederate lines, sending the survivors running for cover.

Confederate artillery killed virtually all the gunners of the 5th Maine Battery, who had taken up position in the Chancellors' yard. As the surviving Maine gunners bolted to catch up with the retreating Union army, some men of the Irish Brigade ran to the Maine guns and by sheer brute strength rolled them out of the yard and toward the Union army, thereby saving them from falling into enemy hands. Meanwhile, other members of the Irish Brigade covered the men dragging away the Maine artillery. These Irish were "following the brigade tradition," writes Joseph Bilby, "of being the rear guard of the rear guard."

Even with the Union troops in retreat, the Confederates kept up their attack, following them and firing on them from the cover of the forest. Some artillery crews turned the guns on the forest, releasing, according to Captain D.P. Conyngham, "such a fierce, destructive fire on them of grape and canister, that

light, 12 Pdr Napoleon Gun, Brass,
Rappahannock

ARTIST EDWIN FORBES SKETCHED THIS II2-POUND BRASS NAPOLEON GUN, POSSIBLY ONE OF THE GUNS USED
TO COVER THE UNION ARMY'S RETREAT FROM CHANCELLORSVILLE.

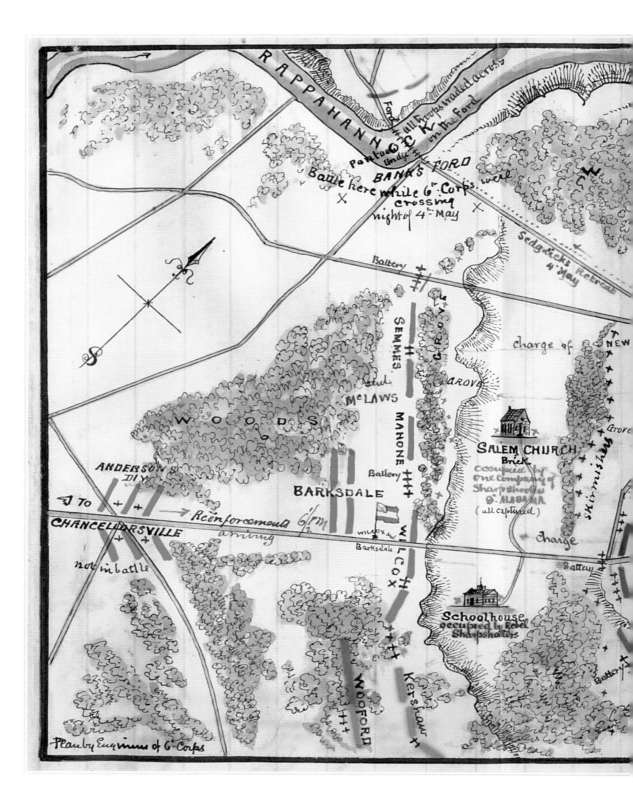

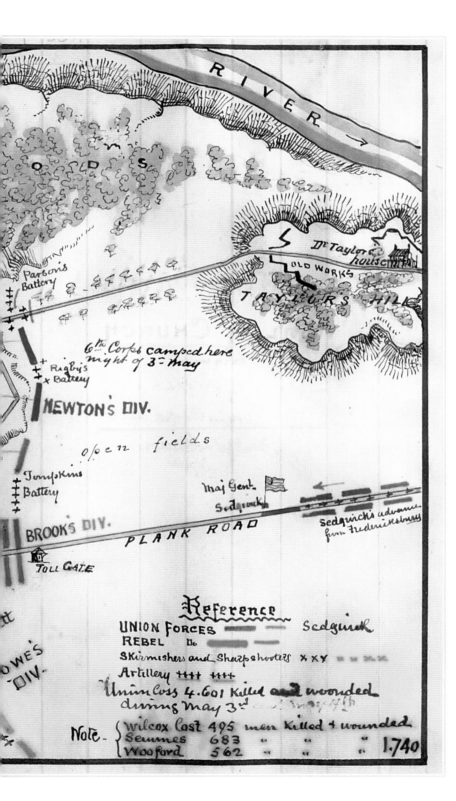

THE DATE ON THIS MAP IS IN ERROR:
THE FIGHTING AROUND SALEM
CHURCH DURING THE BATTLE
OF CHANCELLORSVILLE TOOK PLACE
ON MAY 4, 1863.
VIRGINIA HISTORICAL SOCIETY

[the Confederates] were literally mowed down in hundreds. A dense, sulphurous fog of smoke obscured the plain, while high above the shouts and cheers of the combatants rose the volcanic din of artillery."

RETURN TO MARYE'S HEIGHTS

As Hooker's men retreated, pursued by Jackson's men, a courier galloped up to General Lee with alarming news: In an effort to link up with Hooker, Major General John Sedgwick with an army of 30,000 Union troops had attacked Fredericksburg, about 7 miles (11.2 km) east of Chancellorsville. The sudden appearance of 30,000 fresh troops might inspire Hooker to abandon his retreat and turn back to fight Lee again.

Marye's Heights, where the Irish Brigade and so many other Union brigades had suffered so many casualties, was now occupied by 9,000 Rebels and fifty-six cannons, all under the command of General Jubal Early. On May 3, Sedgwick ordered an assault on the Heights. Twice the Confederates drove back the Union assaults—just as they had in December 1862. But the third time the Yankees attacked, they leapt over the infamous stone wall, surged up the slope of Marye's Heights, and drove the Confederates from their positions.

The Confederates regrouped on another rise nearby, where they used the Salem Church and a schoolhouse as little fortresses. Sedgwick pursued the Confederates, hitting them so hard that they abandoned the church and the school—but only temporarily. Suddenly, the Confederates turned and attacked the Yankees, pushing them back. This seesaw fight at Salem Church took the lives of 500 Union and 600 Confederate troops.

That night, General Lee devised a plan to destroy Sedgwick's army by having three divisions attack him simultaneously on three fronts. Lee would command the attack personally. It was a complicated maneuver, and two of Lee's commanders, Jubal Early and Major General Lafayette McLaws, misunderstood what they were supposed to do. They wasted the entire morning as each waited for the other to move out first. The third commander, Major General William Anderson, also failed to advance on Sedgwick— he was waiting for fresh men to relieve his own worn-out troops. The attack, which Lee had scheduled for dawn, did not take place until six in the evening.

In the gathering twilight, Jubal Early attacked as directed and pushed back the Yankees. Anderson and his men, however, rather than attacking the part of the Union line assigned to them, drifted off toward Early's position. McLaws's men lost their way in the woods. With nightfall the botched attack came to an abrupt halt. Under the cover of darkness, Sedgwick led his 30,000 men back across the Rappahannock to reunite with Hooker and the main body of the Army of the Potomac.

On the morning of May 7 General Hooker issued a statement to the Army of the Potomac: "The major-general commanding tenders to this army his congratulations on its achievements of the last seven days. If it has not accomplished all that was expected, the reasons are well known to the army. It is sufficient to say they were of a character not to be foreseen or prevented by human sagacity or resource." Certainly on the Union side there was a dearth of human sagacity—digging in behind defensive works rather than attacking Lee, removing the Union guns from Hazel Grove. In addition to the approximately 14,000 men he lost at Chancellorsville, Hooker left behind for the Confederates 14 pieces of artillery, 20,000 muskets, and 31,000 knapsacks crammed with rations and other supplies.

Lee also congratulated his troops: "The conduct of the troops cannot be too highly praised. Attacking largely superior numbers in entrenched positions, their heroic courage overcame every obstacle of nature and art, and achieved a triumph most honorable to our arms. To the skillful and efficient management of the artillery the successful issue of the contest is in great measure due."

"LET US CROSS OVER THE RIVER, AND REST UNDER THE SHADE OF THE TREES"

Twice in less than five months, first at Fredericksburg and now at Chancellorsville, Lee scored stunning victories against Union armies that vastly outnumbered his own. But the victory at Chancellorsville was bittersweet. After dark on May 2, Stonewall Jackson and his staff rode out on a reconnaissance mission. After seeing that Hooker had taken a defensive position, Jackson turned back. He had just reached the Confederate lines on the Old Mountain Road where the 18th North Carolina was stationed. There were reports of Union cavalry in the area, and the North Carolinians were on edge. Seeing horses approaching, they opened fire. "Cease fire!" Jackson's staff shouted. "You are firing into your own men!" Major John Barry, who was in command of the North Carolina troops, declared that it was a Yankee trick. "Pour it into them, boys!" he cried.

Several members of Jackson's staff fell dead, and Jackson was struck by three bullets, two in the left arm and one in the palm of his right hand. Jackson's frightened horse bolted off the road, crashing into the underbrush, pursued by a mounted officer who at last managed to catch the reins and bring Jackson's horse to a halt.

Jackson dismounted and attempted to walk to a field hospital, but his wounds were severe and he was weak from loss of blood. His staff found a stretcher and began to carry him to the hospital, but their way led them within range of the Union

PHOTOGRAPHER MATHEW BRADY STAGED THIS PHOTO OF A UNION SOLDIER OFFERING WATER
TO A WOUNDED COMRADE AFTER THE BATTLE OF CHANCELLORSVILLE.

guns. One of the stretcher-bearers was shot and killed, but another staffer caught the stretcher before it fell to the ground. Further along, however, another stretcher-bearer tripped and Jackson was dumped onto the ground. When Jackson reached the field hospital at last, Dr. Hunter McGuire, medical director of the 2nd Corps, examined the wounds: The musket balls had shattered the bones in Jackson's upper and lower left arm—Dr. McGuire saw no alternative but amputation.

After the operation, Jackson asked to be taken to the plantation of an acquaintance, Thomas Coleman Chandler's plantation in Guiney Station, Virginia. It was about 24 miles (38.4 km) away, but that is where Jackson wished to recuperate. A work detail was sent ahead to fill in ruts and potholes and smooth the road. A mattress was laid inside the ambulance for Jackson, and he was accompanied by Dr. McGuire, the Rev. Beverly T. Lacy, a chaplain, and other members of his staff. Chandler invited Jackson to stay in the plantation house, but the general preferred the privacy of the estate office building, a small white clapboard house nearby.

Jackson and his party arrived on May 4, and for the next two days, Dr. McGuire saw signs that the general was improving—the amputation wound appeared to be healing, Jackson slept soundly through the night, and he had a good appetite, although the doctor limited Jackson's diet to light meals, such as bread and tea.

On May 7, Jackson's condition suddenly became grave: He had contracted pneumonia, and in his weakened physical condition, McGuire feared the general would not survive. Jackson's staff sent for his wife, Anna. Telegraph messages and newspapers spread the word across the Confederacy that General Jackson's condition was very grave. Throughout the South, clergymen led their congregations in prayer, beseeching God to spare the life of Stonewall Jackson.

During his last three days, Jackson was often nauseous and in pain; he drifted between periods of lucidity and delirium. On May 10, Dr. McGuire informed Anna Jackson that her husband would die within a few hours. She brought him the news herself. "Very good," he said, "very good. It is all right." Anna sent for their daughter, Julia, so Jackson could kiss the baby good-bye, then she took a seat in a chair beside her husband's bed and waited for the end. It came at about 3:30 in the afternoon. In a clear voice Jackson said, "Let us cross over the river, and rest under the shade of the trees." A few moments later, Stonewall Jackson was dead.

MEAGHER RESIGNS

At Chancellorsville, the Irish Brigade had lost 92 men—a modest number compared with their casualties at Antietam and Fredericksburg. But the Brigade's strength was dwindling—it was down to only a few hundred men. Repeatedly General Meagher had written to Secretary of War Stanton requesting permission to travel to the North to recruit fresh volunteers, or at least to grant leave to the surviving men of the Irish Brigade. Inexplicably, Stanton never replied to Meagher's requests; he never even acknowledged receipt of Meagher's letters.

On May 8, 1863, stung, angry, and frustrated by the inaction of the War Department, which he thought seemed pleased to let the Irish Brigade be annihilated bit by bit in each successive battle, Meagher resigned his command "of this poor vestige and relic of the Irish Brigade," as he put it. On May 20, Stanton accepted Meagher's resignation.

The War Department's mistreatment of the Irish Brigade and its swift acceptance of Meagher's resignation infuriated the Irish in the North. "The War Department have not only inflicted upon [Meagher] and his brave Brigade an unmerited and outrageous injustice," wrote the editors of the *Irish American* newspaper, "but they have done the National cause an irreparable injury by their neglect and ill-treatment of a body of representative citizens, whose valor on every battlefield elicited the generous encomiums of the foes against whom they fought."

Not everyone responded with outrage. A reporter for one Yankee newspaper claimed that Meagher's "habitual drunkenness accounts for the prompt acceptance of [his] resignation." Even some within the Irish community were happy to see Meagher go—they regarded him as a callous butcher who had led hundreds of his men to their deaths. But Father William Corby, one of the Irish Brigade's chaplains, answered that argument. "Gen. Meagher and his Brigade simply obeyed the orders of superior officers, and went in at the time and place assigned them," he wrote. "Had Gen. Meagher disobeyed such legitimate orders, he would have been liable to be cashiered, and thus have disgraced himself and his race for all time."

As for Meagher's officers, fifty-nine commissioned officers and twenty-nine noncommissioned officers presented him with testimonials of their appreciation. The commissioned officers thanked him for bringing to his command "that courage and devotedness which has made the Brigade historical, and by word and example, cheering us on, when fatigue and dangers beset our path." The noncommissioned officers lamented their "mournful duty" to bid him farewell. But they recalled with joy and pride "that devoted band of Irishmen that rallied at your call around the Green Flag of our native land, and who are here now to evince their sincere and heartfelt sorrow at the loss of an indomitable leader, a brave companion, and a stern patriot."

But the sorrow the Irish Brigade felt at the loss of Meagher was insignificant to the losses suffered at Chancellorsville by American families North and South: Approximately 14,000 Union troops and 10,000 Confederate troops were killed, wounded, or missing. When the casualty report reached President Lincoln, the color drained from his face. With trembling hands he passed the telegram to two friends who were visiting him at the time, Dr. Anson Henry, Lincoln's personal physician, and Noah Brooks, a young newspaperman from Sacramento, California. Coming only five months after the Union lost approximately 13,000 men at Fredericksburg, the casualty report from Chancellorsville was a calamity. As Henry and Brooks read the telegram, Lincoln paced the room, saying, "My God! My God! What will the country say?"

THE TURNING POINT:
The Irish Brigade at Gettysburg

It was almost noon on July 2, 1863, and the 530 men of the Irish Brigade were resting on the eastern slope of Cemetery Ridge above the small town of Gettysburg. They could hear the fire of muskets and artillery at Little Round Top, but the Irish were being held in reserve. Then General Winfield Scott Hancock rode up and joined Colonel Patrick Kelly, Colonel John Burns, and General John C. Caldwell, who were observing the fight. For an hour the officers watched the battle; then, as the Confederates drove back the Union men, Hancock said, "Caldwell, get your division ready."

As the four brigades of Caldwell's division went into formation, the Irish Brigade found itself standing before a large boulder. One of the Brigade's chaplains, Father William Corby, climbed on top of the rock and called for the men's attention. They were about to go into battle, there was no time for him to hear the confession of every man of the Brigade individually, he explained, but in such an emergency, the Catholic Church permitted a priest to grant general absolution. He instructed them to recall their sins, beg God's pardon, and recite silently the Act of Contrition, just as they would if they were in a confessional. Then Father Corby drew from a pocket of his black frock coat a violet stole. As he draped it around his neck, the men of the Irish Brigade—Catholics and non-Catholics alike—removed their caps and knelt on the grass. Raising his right hand, he made the sign of the cross over the Brigade as he recited the words of absolution: "May our Lord Jesus Christ absolve you, and I, by His authority, absolve you from every bond of excommunication and interdict, insofar as it lies within my power and you require; therefore, I absolve you from your sins, in the Name of the Father, and of the Son, and of the Holy Ghost. Amen."

A member of the Irish Brigade, Major St. Clair Mulholland of the 116th Pennsylvania, would write later that while granting general absolution to soldiers who were about to go into battle was common in the Catholic countries of Europe, this was the first time it had ever occurred in the United States. Among the kneeling

IN 1891 PAUL WOOD PAINTED THIS SOMEWHAT ROMANTICIZED PAINTING ENTITLED, "ABSOLUTION UNDER FIRE."

FATHER WILLIAM CORBY, CSC, DID NOT WEAR A CASSOCK ON THE BATTLEFIELD BUT A BLACK CLERICAL SUIT.

AND THERE IS NO RECORD THAT TROOPS WERE BEING HIT BY ENEMY FIRE AS HE GRANTED THE IRISH BRIGADE GENERAL ABSOLUTION.

men, Mulholland recalled, "there was a profound silence . . . yet over to the left, out by the Peach Orchard and Little Round Top . . . the roar of battle rose and swelled and re-echoed through the woods."

Then the men rose from their knees and marched down the slope of Cemetery Ridge toward farmer John Rose's wheat field.

A BLIND ARMY

On June 22, 1863, Confederate troops marched into Pennsylvania, accomplishing at long last the invasion of the North that General Robert E. Lee had envisioned two years earlier. The 2nd Corps was under the command of General Richard Ewell of Virginia, a career army man who spent most of the 1850s serving in New Mexico where, in 1859, he was wounded during an engagement with Apaches led by the famous war chief Cochise.

Ewell was followed by General A.P. Hill of Virginia, who led his 3rd Corps into Pennsylvania on June 24, and then by General James Longstreet of Georgia and his 1st Corps, who arrived on June 25. Longstreet occupied the town of Chambersburg, Hill occupied the town of Cashtown, while Ewell's corps was encamped in open country between the towns of Carlisle and York. In all, Lee had brought 75,000 men into Pennsylvania.

The purpose of Lee's invasion was threefold: to resupply his army with the produce and livestock of the rich farms of southern Pennsylvania; to encourage the anti-war Democrats in Congress who were pressuring the Lincoln administration to sign a treaty with the Confederacy; and to score a victory on Northern soil so stunning that Britain or France or both would enter the war on the side of the South. But before he could engage the enemy, he must know where they were. Major General Jeb Stuart and his cavalry were the eyes of the Confederate army, but in those final days of June 1863, a series of rash decisions on Stuart's part left Lee and his Army of Northern Virginia blind.

Rather than locating the Army of the Potomac and immediately sending back a report to Lee, Stuart decided to make a full reconnaissance mission by riding completely around the Yankees. Along the way, he captured 140 wagons crammed full of supplies, along with their teams of horses and mules. The wagons slowed Stuart's progress, and the movement of the Union troops cut off his way back to Lee, and so the intelligence Lee needed was delayed.

But the Yankees were also suffering from a disadvantage. In late June, President Lincoln accepted the resignation of General Joseph Hooker and on June 28, appointed General George Gordon Meade commander of the Army of the Potomac.

Meade was a Pennsylvanian; now that a Rebel army had invaded his home state, Lincoln said he expected that Meade, like a feisty rooster, would "fight well on his own dung heap." Many of the Yankee troops did not share the president's opinion of Meade. He had no charisma and no gift for winning the affection of the ordinary soldiers, one of whom characterized the forty-seven-year-old Meade as "a damned old goggle-eyed snapping turtle."

Whatever Meade may have lacked in personality, he compensated for in drive: As 75,000 Rebels marched into Pennsylvania, the Army of the Potomac was encamped in Maryland, around the towns of Middletown and Frederick. On June 30, two days after his appointment, Meade gave the Army of the Potomac its marching orders. And so the Union army came up from the south while the Confederate army moved toward them from the north, until the two armies met at Gettysburg.

THE BURDEN OF THE DRAFT

More than 83,000 Union troops marched into Pennsylvania, but the Irish Brigade had fallen from its original strength of about 2,500 men to 530. The editors of the *Irish American* newspaper complained, "To keep them where they are now, in their reduced condition, is not merely a cruelty—it is a crime."

Repeatedly, General Thomas Meagher had written to Secretary of War Edwin Stanton requesting permission to recruit fresh volunteers to rebuild the Brigade, but Stanton's reply was stony silence. Meagher had a tendency to go over Stanton's head, writing directly to President Lincoln, who generally approved of Meagher's ideas. He would do so again even after he resigned his commission: In June 1863, Meagher wrote to Lincoln offering to raise 3,000 Irish volunteers. On June 16, Lincoln wrote back, "Shall be very glad for you to raise 3,000 Irish troops." As a man who understood the chain of command, Meagher should have known better, but it was part of his impulsive nature to run roughshod over the niceties. Edwin Stanton's response was to act as if the Irish general did not exist.

After resigning his commission in May 1863, Meagher returned home to New York, where Irish and non-Irish alike declared their support. On June 16, 1863, prominent New Yorkers, led by the mayor, George Opdyke, held a banquet in Meagher's honor at the Astor House, the most luxurious hotel in the city. Opdyke read a resolution, passed by the New York Common Council, honoring Meagher's military service. Then Alderman Terence Farley presented Meagher with the Kearny Cross, a new decoration for gallantry, named after General Philip Kearny, who had been killed in 1862 at the Battle of Chantilly in Virginia.

When it was Meagher's turn at the podium, he renewed his pledge of support for the war. "Let the army . . . beat back the enemy," he said, "crush the insurrection, restore the Constitution and reinstate the Union!"

Such sentiments did not go over well with many Irish immigrants across the North. They admired Meagher, and they resented the shabby way he and the Irish Brigade had been treated by the War Department, but they were tired of the war. The casualty rates were appalling.

The Emancipation Proclamation fulfilled the worst fears of the Irish: that soon they would be competing for jobs with four million newly liberated slaves. And the Conscription Act Lincoln signed in March 1863 especially antagonized the Irish: The provisions of the act permitted men of means to hire a substitute or to buy their way out of the draft completely for a one-time payment of $300. That meant the middle class and the wealthy would stay safe at home while poor working men must risk their lives on the battlefield. And because most Irish immigrants in the North were poor working men, they suspected—rightly—that the burden of the draft would fall on them.

THE BATTLE BEGINS

The Battle of Gettysburg began early in the morning of July 1, on Edward McPherson's farm, about 1 mile (1.6 km) west of the town of Gettysburg. About 2,900 Union cavalry under Brigadier General John Buford had taken up position on a ridge that overlooked McPherson's fields and the Chambersburg Pike. Buford had been born in Kentucky. His father owned slaves and had opposed Abraham Lincoln in the election of 1860. Buford's wife was a Southerner—when the war came, her family sided with the Confederacy. So did some of Buford's relatives—one of his cousins, Abraham Buford, was a brigadier general in the Confederate army. When the governor of Kentucky invited Buford to fight for the South, a friend asked Buford how he had replied. "I sent him word I was a Captain in the United States Army," Buford said, "and I intended to remain one!"

General Lee was still north of the town of Gettysburg drawing his three corps together; still uncertain of the number and location of the Union army, Lee did not want to risk battle until he had consolidated his 75,000. But on the morning of July 1, General A.P. Hill, curious to know where the Yankees were, sent two divisions—more than 14,000—into the Gettysburg countryside. This reconnaissance in force was led by Major General Henry Heth of Virginia. Heth was especially close to General Lee, who called him "Harry" (typically Lee addressed his generals by their rank and surname). At Gettysburg, Heth served with a member of his family—his cousin, George Pickett, who would lead the disastrous Pickett's Charge on July 3.

IN 1863, COLONEL PATRICK KELLY REPLACED GENERAL THOMAS FRANCIS MEAGHER AS COMMANDER OF THE IRISH BRIGADE. UNLIKE THE BOISTEROUS MEAGHER, KELLY WAS RESERVED. "WELL DONE, MEN," WAS CONSIDERED HIGH PRAISE FROM THE COLONEL.

COLONEL ST. CLAIR MULHOLLAND COMMANDED THE 116TH PENNSYLVANIA. HE WAS WOUNDED FOUR TIMES DURING THE WAR—

AT FREDERICKSBURG, THE WILDERNESS, PO RIVER, AND TOTOPOTOMOY CREEK. HE SURVIVED THE WAR TO RETURN HOME

TO PHILADELPHIA WHERE HE SERVED AT SEVERAL GOVERNMENT POSTS, WROTE SEVERAL BOOKS, AND BECAME REVERED

AS A GENEROUS CONTRIBUTOR TO CATHOLIC CHARITIES.

Heth had no idea how many men were with Buford, and Heth's ignorance worked to Buford's advantage. With his 2,900 dismounted cavalrymen firing breech-loading carbines (which were faster and easier to load than the Confederates' muskets), and a single battery of artillery, Buford managed to keep Heth's 14,000 men at bay for three hours, long enough for Union forces to seize the high ground above the town of Gettysburg on Cemetery Hill, at the northern edge of Cemetery Ridge, less than 3 miles (4.8 km) away.

Gettysburg in 1863 was a small town of about 2,400 inhabitants, many of them living in handsome red brick homes. It was named for Samuel Gettys, who had settled on the site of the town in 1761, building a tavern there that served travelers passing to and from Harrisburg (37 miles [59.2 km] away) and Baltimore (55 miles [88 km] away). Although surrounded by farm country, Gettysburg by 1860 was a thriving manufacturing center, dominated by tanneries and shoe factories. The Lutheran Seminary and Pennsylvania College (later Gettysburg College) brought a lively intellectual and cultural life to the town. And a railroad station linked Gettysburg to Washington, Philadelphia, and Baltimore.

On the afternoon of July 1, 1863, the town of Gettysburg became a battleground. Near the Diamond, the square that was the commercial heart of Gettysburg, two Confederate brigades met four Union regiments. The Rebels charged and the Yankees fled. The Rebels pursued them, taking more then 300 prisoners. Then the Confederates turned their attention to the town. Fifteen-year-old Tillie Pierce lived with her family in a large red brick house on Baltimore Street, one of the main thoroughfares. Peeping through the shutters she saw a mass of Rebels coming. "Clad almost in rags, covered with dust, riding wildly, pell-mell down the hill toward our home! Shouting, yelling most unearthly, cursing, brandishing their revolvers, and firing right and left. . . . And then the searching and ransacking began in earnest. They wanted horses, clothing, anything and almost everything they could conveniently carry away. Nor were they particular about asking. Whatever suited them they took."

As the Confederates occupied the town, some townsfolk hid Union stragglers in their cellars and attics. Although parts of Gettysburg were raked by musket fire and exploding artillery shells, Gettysburg suffered only one civilian casualty, twenty-year-old Mary Virginia Wade. Known to her family and friends as Jennie, she was baking bread in the kitchen of her sister's house on Baltimore Street when a musket ball pierced the door and struck her in the back, killing her instantly.

THE WHEAT FIELD

The Irish Brigade, with the rest of the 2nd Corps, marched to Gettysburg by way of the Maryland towns of Frederick Junction, Uniontown, and Taneytown. It arrived in Gettysburg at about ten at night on July 1 and camped in the fields that belonged to farmer Jacob Hummelbaugh, about 3 miles (4.8 km) from the town.

Since General Meagher's resignation in May, the Irish Brigade had been under the command of Colonel Patrick Kelly, a native of County Galway in the west of Ireland who had emigrated to America in 1850 and settled in New York City. Captain William L.D. O'Grady of the 88th New York described Kelly as a man with "the physique of a Hercules, broad and deep-chested. He was handsome, with a noble forehead, brilliant black eyes, fine nose, the blackest hair and beard and a dark complexion—which is not uncommon among the people of Galway and Limerick, who, in old days, were socially and politically in close alliance with Spain."

The Irish got about six hours of sleep, then they were roused at 4:30 in the morning on July 2 and marched along the Taneytown Road to Cemetery Ridge, near the fieldstone farmhouse of George Weikert. The Confederates were only 1,500 yards (1365 m) away, concealed by a patch of woods. The Rebels took a few potshots at the Yankees, and the Yankees returned fire, but that morning there was no fighting on this part of the battlefield. The Irish and their comrades in the 2nd Corps sprawled out on the grass to play cards or nap until they received orders. At about noon, Confederate skirmishers stepped out of the cover of the trees and opened fire on the Union troops. It was at this moment that Father Corby gave general absolution to the Irish Brigade.

The Irish were standing in readiness when General Daniel Sickles led his 3rd Corps a half mile (0.8 km) away from the Union line. Several officers of the Irish Brigade, including Colonel Kelly and Major Mulholland, observed Sickles's inexplicable behavior. The 3rd Corps' line stretched from the Devil's Den to the Peach Orchard, then to the Emmitsburg Road. Sickles had led his men into a position where his left and right flanks were fully exposed to the Confederates, and so was the left flank of the 2nd Corps. General Hancock, who stood nearby, remarked to his astonished officers, "Wait a moment, you will soon see them tumbling back."

Suddenly, Confederate General Longstreet attacked Sickles's men. The line was too thin, and under the furious Rebel assault it began to break up. Sickles had gotten himself into a desperate situation, but General Meade could not permit the destruction of the 3rd Corps in order to teach a foolish general a lesson. He sent orders to Hancock to send in a division to rescue the 3rd Corps. As the division moved out, the Irish were in the center. They entered John Rose's wheat field, where the grain stood chest high. To their left, Union and Confederate artillery pounded each other. In the woods to their right, they could hear volley after volley of deadly musket fire. But so far, they were unseen by the Confederates.

Ahead of the Irish were two regiments of South Carolinians on a knoll of boulders known as Stony Hill. When the Irish came into view, the South Carolinians fired down on them, but their aim was terrible—most of the musket balls passed harmlessly over the heads of the Irish Brigade. The Irish paused long enough to return fire, then charged across the 200 yards (182 m) of wheat field and up the hill. At the summit, they found dozens of Confederate corpses, the casualties of the first volley of what would become known as the Battle of the Wheatfield. Major Mulholland would recall, "Behind one large rock five men lay dead in a heap. They had evidently fallen at the first volley and all at the same time. One of them in his dying agony had torn his blouse and shirt open, exposing his breast and showing a great hole from which his heart's blood was flowing."

As the Irish advanced, the South Carolinians gave up more and more ground. The Rebels got off a good volley into the Brigade's ranks, but still the Irish came on. In some places, the Irish were firing on the Confederates at point-blank range— using his pistol, Sergeant Jefferson Carl shot and killed a South Carolinian only 6 feet (1.8 m) away.

With his men losing ground, Brigadier General Joseph B. Kershaw galloped to the rear for reinforcements from the Georgia brigade. It appeared that the Georgians would not arrive in time: The Irish pressed their advantage until the South Carolinians fell back to a stone wall near the Rose family's farmhouse. But then the Georgians appeared, smashing almost simultaneously into the Union's right and left flanks.

The Yankees, including the Irish, drew back into the wheat field. Now the Confederates lined up on either side of the field and poured deadly fire into the Union ranks, which abandoned any semblance of orderly retreat and ran through this gauntlet of musket fire. The Georgians were so eager to make each shot count that they moved in closer, narrowing the Yankees' escape route, but also endangering their own men. Ultimately, the Georgians stopped firing because they were hitting fellow Georgians.

Among the reinforcements sent to the wheat field were men from Cemetery Ridge. When they advanced, they left a gap in the Union line. An Alabama brigade spotted the opening and charged; General Hancock saw the gap, too, and sent to plug it with the only troops he had at the time, the 262 men of the 1st Minnesota.

The Alabamians had 1,600 men, yet the Minnesotans put up such a ferocious fight that the men of Alabama retreated. The skirmish lasted only five minutes, but cost the 1st Minnesota 215 men, killed or wounded.

The Battle of the Wheatfield lasted a three lethal hours. When it was over, the Confederates had lost more than 2,500 men, the Union more than 3,600, among them almost 200 members of the Irish Brigade.

COLONEL CHAMBERLAIN'S SURPRISE

The Confederates had driven the Union troops off Stony Hill and back through the wheat field. Elsewhere on the field, the two armies were scrambling for possession of Big and Little Round Top. These two rocky hills marked the end of the Union left flank. Colonel William C. Oates of Alabama believed if he could haul artillery to the summit of Big Round Top, he could clear the Union army off Cemetery Ridge and give Robert E. Lee a major victory. At twenty-eight, Oates was a handsome man who before the war had a promising law practice in Abbeville, Alabama. But his future had not always been so bright: His parents were dirt-poor farmers; as a teenager, he had a propensity to get into bloody brawls. For a time he was a vagabond, wandering aimlessly in Texas, until one of his brothers tracked him down, talked some sense into him, and brought him home.

But Oates wasn't the only man with an eye for high ground. General Meade sent two army engineers, General Gouverneur K. Warren, a former mathematics instructor at West Point, and Lieutenant Washington Roebling, who before the war had worked for his father, building suspension bridges. In 1865, Roebling would marry Warren's sister, Emily. Later, Roebling would design and begin construction of the Brooklyn Bridge; when caisson disease (now called decompression sickness) incapacitated him, Emily would see the grand project through to completion. From Little Round Top, Warren and Roebling recognized at once the danger to the Union line. Worse, they spotted Confederate troops heading into the ravine between the two Round Tops. Warren called for four regiments to hold Little Round Top.

As the Union regiments took up position on the rocky hill, the very last position, the end of the Union line, was assigned to the 20th Maine under the command of Colonel Joshua Lawrence Chamberlain, a professor of rhetoric from Bowdoin College. He was serving with his two younger brothers, Thomas and John. As they rode to Little Round Top, an artillery shell screamed past them. "Boys,"

TIMOTHY O'SULLIVAN, A 23-YEAR-OLD NEW YORK–BORN IRISH AMERICAN, WAS EMPLOYED BY MATHEW BRADY AS A BATTLEFIELD PHOTOGRAPHER. ON THE SECOND DAY OF THE BATTLE OF GETTYSBURG, HE TOOK THIS PHOTO OF SOME UNION CASUALTIES AT THE WHEATFIELD, WHERE THE IRISH BRIGADE LOST APPROXIMATELY 200 MEN.

Chamberlain said, "another such shot might make it hard for mother. Tom, go to the rear of the regiment and see that it is well closed up. John, pass up ahead and look out a place for our wounded."

Chamberlain's 350 men took cover behind rocks and trees. They had been in place scarcely ten minutes before General Oates's 15th Alabama charged up the slope. The Confederates were driven back, then came again, and again, each time more determined. Fighting was often hand-to-hand. "At times," Chamberlain wrote later, "I saw around me more of the enemy than of my own men." A musket ball struck the scabbard of Chamberlain's sword, knocking him to the ground, bending the sword and sheath, but doing no more harm to him than leaving a nasty bruise.

The men of Maine began to run out of ammunition. They scavenged among the pockets of the wounded and the dead, but even this gave the 20th Maine only a few more rounds, and the Alabamians were showing no signs of tiring. Then Chamberlain had an inspiration—a rarely used tactic for a charge. He had about 220 men fit to fight; he divided them into two groups—one would hold the line while the others he set at a right angle to it. At his command, the men at the right angle would pivot like a gate, striking the Alabamians on their flank and sweeping them down the hill. With his men in place, Chamberlain shouted, "Bayonets!" When bayonets were fixed to every musket and as the Alabamians came up the slope again, Chamberlain led the charge.

The unexpected assault on their flank confounded the Rebels. "Ranks were broken," Chamberlain recalled, "some retired before us somewhat hastily; some threw their muskets to the ground—even loaded—sunk on their knees, threw up their hands and called out, 'We surrender. Don't kill us!'"

Colonel Joshua Chamberlain and the 20th Maine had saved the Union line, but elsewhere on the battlefield the Yankees were taking a terrible beating. General Sickles was paying a high price for his ill-considered advance away from the main Union line. In farmer Joseph Sherfy's peach orchard, Sickles and his men came under artillery fire from two directions. Commanding one of the batteries was General E. Porter Alexander, whose guns had done so much damage to the retreating Federals at Chancellorsville. "An artillerist's heaven," he would write later, "is to follow the routed enemy after a tough resistance, and to throw shells and canister into his disorganized and fleeing masses. . . . There is no excitement on earth like it."

One of those shells struck General Sickles's right leg, nearly tearing it off completely. As he was carried to a field hospital, his men observed Sickles calmly smoking a cigar. Minutes later, army surgeons amputated the general's leg.

THE BARRAGE

The third day of battle began at 1:10 in the afternoon when the Confederates opened fire on the center of the Union line with 163 cannons. The roar of the guns was deafening, so thunderous, says historian Edwin Bearss, that they could be heard in Pittsburgh about 180 miles (288 km) away. The men of the Irish Brigade, like every other Yankee soldier on Cemetery Ridge, fell flat on the ground. But the Confederate artillerymen miscalculated the elevation and almost all of the shells and canisters flew over the Union lines into the woods about 100 yards (91 m) to the rear.

The Union's 118 guns did not reply until 1:30—General Henry Hunt, commander of the artillery and the finest artillery tactician in the United States—insisted that his gunnery crews calculate the elevation of their guns accurately and take careful aim before firing. Hunt believed that rapid firing produced sloppy, ineffective results; furthermore, it was a waste of expensive ammunition. There is a story that he once reprimanded an overeager gunner, saying, "Young man, are you aware that every round you fire costs $2.67?"

The Irish were assigned to support the artillery batteries positioned near the copse of trees on Cemetery Ridge. Between the pounding barrage of the Confederates and the deliberate return fire of General Hunt, in a matter of minutes, the open field between the two armies was so thick with smoke that Rebels and Yankees lost sight of each other. After two hours the guns fell silent, and as the dense clouds of smoke lifted, the Irish could see across the field, about 1 mile (1.6 km) away, approximately 13,000 men marching toward Cemetery Ridge.

General Lee had expected that his artillery would clear the Union guns from Cemetery Ridge, making it more vulnerable to an assault. He had instructed Colonel E. Porter Alexander that as the infantry began their assault on the ridge, he should wheel up his guns and when within 300 yards (273 m) of the Yankees, open fire. Lee believed the massed infantry attack combined with cannons firing at almost point-blank range would send Meade's army scurrying from the field. But Lee's plan had not gone as expected. Unknown to him or Colonel Alexander, the Confederate guns had overshot their targets. Furthermore, Alexander's guns were plagued by defective fuses and shells and canisters that either failed to explode or exploded prematurely, before they reached the Union lines. Such problems were endemic to the Confederate artillery, probably the result of faulty production at the South's artillery factories. There had been cases when Confederate shells, fired over the heads of advancing infantry, exploded prematurely, killing and wounding

Rebels rather than Yankees. Colonel Alexander stated candidly, "I have known of [the infantry] threatening to fire back at our guns if we opened [fire] over their heads."

"GENERAL LEE HAS ORDERED AND EXPECTS IT"

The most famous incident of July 3, 1863, Pickett's Charge, is something of a misnomer. For most of their advance on Cemetery Ridge, the 13,000 Rebels moved at a steady march; they did not charge until they were a couple hundred yards from the Yankees' position. And George Pickett was not the sole commander of the assault: He was joined by Brigadier Generals James Kemper, Richard Garnett, and Lewis Armistead, each of whom led his own brigade.

George Pickett of Virginia, known for his flowing, almost shoulder-length hair and lively manner, had graduated from West Point with George McClellan and Thomas "Stonewall" Jackson. In a class of fifty-nine cadets, Pickett had finished dead last. He owed his appointment to a friend of his father, an Illinois congressman named John Todd Stuart—a cousin of Mary Todd Lincoln and the law partner of Abraham Lincoln.

James Kemper's grandfather had been a member of George Washington's staff during the American Revolution. But James Kemper was a lawyer, not a soldier. He had volunteered for the Virginia militia in the 1850s, and as a member of the Virginia House of Delegates, he had been a strong advocate for building up the state's military, but Kemper had never seen a battle until he enlisted in the Confederate army.

Richard Garnett was a graduate of West Point and had been a renowned Indian fighter before the Civil War, but he arrived at Gettysburg under a cloud. In April 1862, Stonewall Jackson had ordered Garnett's arrest for "neglect of duty"—specifically for ordering his men to retreat during the Battle of Kernstown in Virginia. Garnett had hoped his reputation would be cleared at a court martial where

ROBERT KNOX SNEDEN'S MAP OF GETTYSBURG ON THE THIRD DAY OF BATTLE INDICATES THE LOCATION OF THE MILITARY UNITS BEFORE THE CULMINATING EVENT OF THE BATTLE— PICKETT'S CHARGE. ALSO SHOWN ON THE MAP IS THE WHEATFIELD, WHERE ON JULY 2 THE IRISH BRIGADE LOST NEARLY 200 MEN.
VIRGINIA HISTORICAL SOCIETY

he could explain that he had ordered the retreat because his men were almost completely surrounded and dangerously low on ammunition. But the trial was suspended when Lee began his campaign in northern Virginia.

Lewis Armistead's life was full of tragedy. He had married twice, and both his wives were dead. He had had three children, two of whom had died. And he had lost his family home and virtually all of his possessions in a disastrous fire. At Gettysburg, Armistead faced a potentially new tragedy—he would be fighting against one of his closest friends, Union General Winfield Scott Hancock.

When the guns had fallen silent, Pickett asked his commander, General Longstreet, "General, shall I advance?" Longstreet, who believed this assault over a mile (1.6 km) of open ground was folly, could not bring himself to answer. He bowed his head, which Pickett took as a "yes." As Pickett rode back to his men, concealed by Spangler's Woods below the Lutheran Seminary, Longstreet said to Colonel Alexander, "I don't want to make this attack. I believe it will fail. I do not see how it can succeed. I would not make it now, but that General Lee has ordered and expects it."

It was three in the afternoon. At Pennsylvania College, Professor Michael Jacobs recorded the temperature as 87°F (30.6°C). Pickett, on horseback before his division, cried, "Up, men, and to your posts! Don't forget today that you are from Old Virginia!" The men whooped and gave the rebel yell. Then General Garnett rode out to lead them across the field. Officers were ordered to go on foot, but Garnett's horse had kicked him, badly injuring his leg; he could not walk, but he would not stay behind. Although his fellow officers urged him not to ride, arguing that he would be a perfect target for Yankee sharpshooters, Garnett was resolute.

General Armistead drew his sword and called to his brigade, "Men, remember what you are fighting for. Your homes, your firesides, and your sweethearts! Follow me!" As the division stepped out from the shade and cover of the trees, General Kemper was also on horseback, perhaps in imitation of General Garnett's courage.

The ground they had to cover was farmers' fields. About halfway across the valley, there was a post-and-rail fence obstructing them. When they reached the Emmitsburg Road, they would be within range of the Yankees' muskets and cannons. And the Yankees were hunkered down on the ridge behind a stone wall— not as tall or as strong as the wall at Marye's Heights, but enough to give them cover. Lieutenant John Dooley of the 1st Virginia would recall how he felt as he began marching toward the Union center: "I tell you the enthusiasm of ardent breasts in many cases *ain't there*, and instead of burning to avenge the insults to our country, families and altars and firesides, the thought is most frequently, '*Oh*, if I could just come out of this charge safely how thankful *would I be!*'"

Historian Stephen Sears believes the first shots to strike the Confederates were artillery from opposite ends of the Union line, Little Round Top, and Cemetery Hill. Lieutenant Benjamin Rittenhouse, in command of the battery on Little Round Top, used percussion shells, which exploded on contact and could do frightful damage to a mass of men such as Pickett's division. There were thirty-nine guns on Cemetery Hill; their first volley smashed into a brigade of Virginians on Pickett's far left flank. On the hill that day was General Carl Schurz, an immigrant from Germany who had campaigned aggressively for Lincoln among German-Americans. Through his field glasses, Schurz saw "the gaps torn in their ranks, and the ground dotted with dark spots—their dead and wounded. . . . But the brave Rebels promptly filled the gaps from behind or by closing up on their colors, and unshaken and unhesitatingly they continued their onward march."

The fence bisecting the field brought the Rebels to a halt as they tried to dismantle it or climb over it. Now they were within range of the Yankee muskets, only 200 yards (182 m) away. General Alexander Hays, a Pennsylvanian who counted General Ulysses S. Grant as one of his closest friends, had packed his section of the stone wall with two brigades of troops. As the first wave of Rebels charged the wall, Hays's men released a deadly fire that killed or wounded dozens. Down by the Emmitsburg Road some Confederates had taken cover in a gully; they fired on Hays's men—crowded tightly, the Yankees were an easy target, and now they began to fall too: General Hays had two horses shot from under him, and of the twenty men on his staff, fourteen were killed or wounded. Nonetheless, the fire from the stone wall was too ferocious; no Confederate soldier got closer than 15 or 20 yards (13.7 or 18.2 m). The first charge failed.

"WE MUST GIVE THEM THE COLD STEEL!"

Kemper, Garnett, and Armistead's brigades were advancing on the Federal position near the copse of trees. There had been no fence on this part of the field to obstruct them, and the Union troops were not massed along the wall. As the Confederates prepared to charge, General John Gibbon rode calmly along the Union line. Gibbon had been born in Philadelphia but was raised in North Carolina. When the war came, three of his brothers enlisted in the Confederate army, but he had remained loyal to the Union. "Do not hurry, men, and fire too fast," he said, "let them come up close before you fire, and then aim low and steadily." As the brigades under

Kemper, Garnett, and Armistead charged, they were mown down by heavy cannon and musket fire. In a letter home, Edward Walker of Minnesota wrote, "It was Fredericksburg reversed—the first line went down in no time and others broke."

But Pickett's division rallied and, with what General Gibbon described as "a kind of savage roar," made their final charge on the stone wall, led by General Armistead. He had stuck his hat on the tip of his sword, and waving it over his head he shouted, "Come forward, Virginians! Come on, boys! We must give them the cold steel! Who will follow me?"

Incredibly, Armistead and 100 men breached the wall, and as they did, the men of the 71st Pennsylvania who had been stationed there fled. Some of Armistead's men seized a Yankee cannon and swiveled it around, but they found no ammunition so they could not fire on the retreating Pennsylvanians. But the 69th Pennsylvania, almost all of them Irish immigrants, would not give ground. The fighting was hand-to-hand. Then the 72nd Pennsylvania rushed into the fight. Suddenly, General Armistead was hit by three musket balls; clinging to a cannon, he slowly sank to the ground. Meanwhile, the Yankees drove Armistead's men back, step by step, over the stone wall.

From Cemetery Hill, General Schurz witnessed the retreat of Pickett's division. "First, little driblets," he wrote, "then larger numbers, and finally huge swarms of men in utter disorder hurrying back the way they had come."

Of the approximately 13,000 Confederates who had made Pickett's Charge, more than 1,100 were killed, more than 4,500 were wounded, and about 800 were taken prisoner. General Garnett was killed; General Kemper was wounded, but recovered; General Armistead's wounds were mortal, and he died two days later. Armistead's old friend, General Winfield Scott Hancock, had also been wounded, but he would recover.

AFTER THE BATTLE

At Gettysburg the Irish Brigade, already down to 530 men, lost about 200. Their casualties were a microcosm of the three days of battle, during which the Union lost about 21,000 and the Confederates lost between 23,000 and 28,000. Overnight, the 2,400 inhabitants of Gettysburg were overwhelmed by the task of burying the thousands of dead, nursing and feeding the thousands of wounded, and finding ways to dispose of more than 5,000 dead horses and mules.

Every church, every school, every house was used as a hospital. Sarah Keefauver Weikert, twenty-one years old, lived with her husband John and their daughter, Jennie, two years old, in a farmhouse at the bottom of Little Round Top.

They escaped to the home of friends. When the family returned after the battle, they found their house had been taken over as a hospital. "I looked into the front door, and there were so many dead men lying on the floor that it would have been impossible to have walked through the hall without stepping on the bodies."

After the Confederates retreated from the battered town on July 4, Gettysburg was flooded with visitors—families and friends of the dead and wounded who had come to recover bodies or tend loved ones. They slept on the floors of homes, in barns, and sometimes on the broad steps of public buildings. The Broadhead family nursed three wounded soldiers in their home, and provided shelter to twenty visiting strangers. Worse were the scavengers who wandered over the battlefield, rifling through the pockets of the dead for valuables or souvenirs. And always there was the stench of unburied men and undisposed-of horses and mules.

In the business of the days after the battle, it is not likely that the people of Gettysburg realized that something momentous had occurred in their town and the surrounding countryside: The course of the war was now virtually certain. Lee's invasion of the North had been turned back. The Confederacy's hopes for a major victory that would win them European alliances were crushed. And the Army of Northern Virginia had lost more than 23,000 men whom it could not replace.

On November 19, 1863, Abraham Lincoln would stand amid the fresh graves on Cemetery Hill to dedicate a new national military cemetery. In a speech only 272 words long, the president declared that the goal of the war was to defend "the proposition that all men are created equal," that from the tragedy of civil war the United States would experience "a new birth of freedom." How different from what General Meagher called for in his oration in New York in June 1863, to "crush the insurrection, restore the Constitution and reinstate the Union!" That, of course, had been the North's argument for going to war, but now President Lincoln had shifted the purpose of the war from preserving the Union to freeing the slaves. After the Battle of Gettysburg, the war was no longer a legal question—did the Southern states have the right to secede; now the war had a moral dimension—the abolition of slavery in America.

THE WALL OF FIRE:

The Irish Brigade at the Battle of the Wilderness

In 1864, the Irish Brigade faced extinction. After its casualties at Gettysburg, the Brigade had shrunk to about 330 men, and in 1864, their three-year enlistment would expire and they would be free to return home. To encourage veterans to reenlist, local, state, and federal governments offered bounties between $700 and $1,000—a fortune at a time when most laborers were happy to be paid a dollar a day.

To the relief of the officers of the Irish Brigade, almost all of the men of the 69th, 63rd, and 88th New York and the 28th Massachusetts reenlisted. (The men of 116th Pennsylvania had not been organized until 1862, so their enlistment would not run out until 1865.) To celebrate, the officers of the Irish Brigade threw a banquet for their enlisted men at Irving Hall, a popular venue in New York City for balls and concerts. The featured speaker of the evening was General Thomas Meagher, who assured the assembled crowd, "History has no power to bestow upon me any higher distinction than that I have been the general in command of the Irish Brigade."

But the Brigade was still short on men. To fill its ranks, recruiters turned to newly arrived Irish immigrants. Grinding poverty, a shortage of jobs, and the traumatic memories of the Famine drove thousands of Irish men and women to America. For these Irishmen, the enlistment bounties were almost irresistible, and the opportunity to serve in Irish regiments made the recruits feel at ease. One such recruit was Thomas McManus, who wrote to his family in Ireland, "The bounty [of $700] was very tempting and I enlisted the first day I came here." By St. Patrick's Day 1864, the Irish Brigade numbered about 2,000 men—down from the approximately 2,500 who had set out for Virginia in 1861, but certainly a tremendous improvement over the 330 men who had survived the Battle of Gettysburg.

Brigadier General Michael Corcoran (he had been promoted after the Battle of Gettysburg), the man who had been a lightning rod for new Irish recruits from the first days of the war in 1861, was not present at this latest recruitment. On December 22, 1863, while riding to his camp outside Fairfax, Virginia, Corcoran's horse slipped and fell, crushing him. He lingered for about twenty-four hours, dying the evening of December 23. Michael Corcoran was thirty-six years old.

His death came as a terrible shock to the Irish Brigade, whose men had loved and revered Corcoran since 1860 when he refused to march the 69th Regiment in a parade honoring the Prince of Wales. Captain David Conyngham, who knew Corcoran, wrote that his death "was a loss to America, for his name and reputation were talismanic to collect his [Irish] countrymen to his standard. He was a loss to Ireland, for the dearest wish of his heart was to live to strike for her independence; and from his experience as a soldier, his wisdom as a general, and his prudence and foresight as a man, who knows what he would have accomplished had he lived?"

Corcoran's body was sent home to New York City, where it lay in state for two days in City Hall. On the morning of December 27, a solemn military procession, which included the mayor of New York and the Common Council, escorted Corcoran's coffin to St. Patrick's Cathedral on Mulberry Street. Throngs of mourners had filled the church to capacity, and the overflow stood in the churchyard among the white marble headstones. Sixteen pallbearers, among them General Thomas Meagher, followed the hearse.

THE DECLINE AND FALL OF GENERAL MEAGHER

Within weeks of resigning his commission as commander of the Irish Brigade, Meagher had second thoughts. On July 13, 1863, he wrote to his old nemesis, Secretary of War Edwin Stanton: "I have now to request permission to withdraw my letter of resignation, and beg to renew the offer of my services to the government which accompanied the letter." True to form when it came to correspondence from Meagher, Stanton did not reply. The U.S. Army kept Meagher in limbo between the military and civilian worlds for almost a full year. In spring 1864, he was called to Washington and asked to return to duty. He was not given his old command of the Irish Brigade; he was not given any assignment at all, aside from orders to rendezvous with the Irish at City Point, Virginia.

Meagher arrived on August 12, 1864, promptly got drunk, and stayed drunk until August 18, when the commander of the City Point post, Colonel Theodore B. Gates, sent Meagher a note informing him that the U.S. Army would no longer provide him with quarters. Humiliated and hung over, Meagher rode out of camp, but he stayed in the neighborhood.

September 4, 1864, marked the third anniversary of the formation of the Irish Brigade, and Meagher assigned himself the task of organizing a formal celebration. He had some of the men erect a rustic chapel and altar in the woods, where Father William Corby said Mass. Meagher had invited General Winfield Scott Hancock and his generals to the festivities and after Mass the secular portion of the anniversary celebration began, with Meagher as master of ceremonies. There was a dinner with music, followed by speeches by several of the generals, and a grand oration by Meagher. He praised the men of the Irish Brigade, who had never disgraced themselves in battle, never lost their regimental colors to the enemy, and had always proven themselves to be valiant sons of Ireland and true, patriotic Americans. Then he wrapped up his remarks by calling for three cheers for the guest of honor, General Winfield Scott Hancock.

The anniversary celebration had its desired effect—it brought Meagher to the attention of the top army brass. On September 11, General Ulysses S. Grant, the new commander of the Union army, issued an order that Meagher should be assigned to Nashville. It was a mixed blessing: Meagher's resignation was rescinded and he was back in active service, but he was not attached to the Irish Brigade. Worse, he would serve under General William Tecumseh Sherman. The two men had never gotten along, especially after Meagher described Sherman as an "envenomed martinet," and the insult got back to Sherman.

Sherman assigned Meagher to the Provisional Brigades, composed of soldiers who were not entirely fit for combat—men recuperating from wounds or illness, replacement troops who had not completed their training. While Sherman swept through Georgia, Meagher's Provisional Division, as it was called, did guard duty along the railroad between Chattanooga and Knoxville, Tennessee. Then Sherman, who had spent a very pleasant Christmas in the newly captured city of Savannah, ordered Meagher to bring his division by steamboat and railroad to New Bern, North Carolina. It was a long, circuitous route via Pittsburgh and Annapolis, and Meagher, as well as some of his officers and men, relieved the tedium by drinking heavily. To make matters worse, Meagher did not arrange transport so that his entire command would travel together. At one point, 2,000 of his men were missing (they were in Nashville, waiting for a transport train) and Meagher could not explain to his superior officers where they were. This dereliction of duty compounded by Meagher's habitual drunkenness taxed the patience of the Union army's commanders. On February 24, 1865, with the approval Secretary of War Stanton, General Ulysses S. Grant ordered that Meagher should be relieved from duty and sent back to New York. The military career of the founder of the Irish Brigade was over.

LINCOLN FINDS A COMMANDER

After three frustrating years of war, Abraham Lincoln believed that he had at last found the right man to command the Union armies: forty-two-year-old Ulysses S. Grant. Grant had been born in Ohio where his parents owned a farm, but it was his father's leather tanning business that brought the Grants financial security. Grant received an appointment to West Point, where horsemanship and mathematics were his best subjects—he graduated in the middle of his class. In 1848, after fighting in the Mexican War, Grant married Julia Dent—it was a love match that endured for the rest of their lives. In 1852, the army sent Grant to a post in California. Without Julia and their two young sons, Grant became depressed and sought comfort in the bottle. In 1854, his superior officers pressured him to resign. He returned home and tried his hand at a variety of jobs—from farming to real estate management—but failed at them all. When the Civil War began in 1861, Grant was working as a clerk in his family's leather shop. It has been said that the only thing Grant was good at was war. In 1861, he brought the Union its first important victories at Fort Donelson and Fort Henry in Tennessee. In 1862, he won the Battle of Shiloh. In 1863, he captured Vicksburg, thereby depriving the Confederacy access to the Mississippi River, and then he won the Battle of Chattanooga.

On March 8, 1864, Grant arrived at a reception at the White House, where he and Lincoln met for the first time. Noah Brooks, a journalist from Sacramento who had become a close friend of the president, described the general's appearance that evening. Grant was "rather slightly built," with "stooping shoulders, mild blue eyes and light brown hair and whiskers, with a foxy tinge to his moustache. He has a frank, manly bearing, wears an ordinary-looking military suit, and doesn't put on any airs whatever." From the buzz of excitement that suddenly erupted among his guests, Lincoln guessed that Grant had arrived, and hurried over to greet him.

After being introduced to Mrs. Lincoln, the general found himself mobbed by the other guests, all of whom wanted to meet him and shake his hand. Because Grant stood only five feet, eight inches (1.7 m) tall, most the people at the reception could not see him. So everyone could get a good look, he was compelled to climb up on a sofa, which he did, blushing all the while. Four days later, Lincoln formally appointed Grant General in Chief of All United States Armies.

Grant's plan was to strike the Confederacy's two great armies—General Lee's Army of Northern Virginia and General Johnston's Army of Tennessee—virtually simultaneously. Grant would assume personal command of the Union armies in the east while General William Tecumseh Sherman would command the Union armies in the west. Grant stated that his goal was to give the Confederacy no other option than surrender by using "the greatest number of troops practicable against the armed force of the enemy [and] to hammer continuously against the armed force of the enemy and his resources, until by mere attrition, if in no other way, there should be nothing left to him."

In every major battle of the Civil War, the Union troops had outnumbered the Confederates. Grant's plan was not to simply outnumber the Rebels, but to overwhelm them. Furloughs were cancelled, and thousands of officers and men were ordered to report to their regiments. State and territorial governors were obliged to send their militias. By the end of April, the Army of the Potomac had swollen to more than 100,000 men, ready to march with Grant on his Overland Campaign to find and crush Robert E. Lee.

But Lee had a plan of his own. Whenever possible he would not meet Grant on open ground, but would take up his position in some well-defended place, forcing Grant to attack him. In November 1864 there would be a presidential election, and Lee hoped that Union casualties would be so staggering that the people of the North would turn against Lincoln and elect a candidate who would make peace with the South and recognize the independence of the Confederacy.

Lee's Army of Northern Virginia had spent the winter of 1863–64 fortifying the region south of the Rapidan River, a kind of Maginot Line to defend Richmond, the Confederate capital, about 60 miles (96 km) away. To reach Richmond, Grant had to break through this line.

The logistics of moving an army of more than 100,000 men, plus 4,300 supply wagons and 850 ambulances, was daunting, but the job was assigned to the right man. Major General Andrew Humphreys was a sullen, short-tempered, foul-mouthed Pennsylvania topographer who did not care much for people but did enjoy solving problems such as getting a massive army from point A to point B as swiftly and with as little trouble as possible.

Humphreys's solution was to divide the army into two wings, one crossing the Rapidan at Germanna Ford and the other at Ely's Ford. The two forces would move through the Wilderness, then reunite on the Orange Turnpike. From there, instead of attacking Lee's fortifications head-on, the army would swing around to the west, coming up on Lee's left flank, which would force the Confederates to leave the safety of their breastworks and fight on open ground, where Grant's superior numbers would crush Lee's 60,000 men.

IRISH BRIGADE GENERAL THOMAS SMYTH WAS MORTALLY WOUNDED OUTSIDE FARMVILLE, VIRGINIA. HE DIED ON

APRIL 9, 1865, THE DAY LEE SURRENDERED TO GRANT. SMYTH, A NATIVE OF COUNTY CORK, IRELAND,

WAS THE LAST GENERAL TO DIE DURING THE CIVIL WAR.

Lee had known for weeks that Grant was planning to move south—Lee's scouts delivered regular reports on the arrival of fresh Union troops and supplies at the Federals' camp on the north bank of the Rapidan River. On May 2, 1864, Lee rode to the summit of Clark's Mountain, which offered a commanding view of the countryside—including the Union camp. Seeing the Yankees bustling about, the general predicted that they were preparing to cross the Rapidan. Back at his headquarters Lee telegraphed a warning to President Jefferson Davis: "Look to see [the Federals] operating against Richmond, and make . . . preparations accordingly."

On the night of May 3, Lee was awakened by a courier from Clark's Mountain: The Yankees were on the march, but it was too dark to see where they were headed. After sunrise it became clear—the Union army was heading for Germanna Ford and Ely's Ford. Lee ordered General Richard Ewell to the Orange Turnpike, General A.P. Hill to Orange Court House, and General Richard Anderson to the Rapidan River to prevent the Yankees from pivoting and attacking the Confederates from the rear.

"BUSHWHACKING ON A GRAND SCALE"

In February 1864, command of the revitalized Irish Brigade was given to thirty-one-year-old Colonel Thomas A. Smyth. A native of Balleyhooley in County Cork, Smyth had emigrated to Philadelphia in 1854, then settled in Wilmington, Delaware, where he worked as a wood carver and carriage maker. Smyth commanded the 1st Delaware Infantry, which had fought with the Irish Brigade at the Sunken Road at Antietam, charged Marye's Heights at Fredericksburg, and withstood Pickett's Charge at Gettysburg. As an Irishman and a veteran commander, Smyth was the natural choice to lead the Irish Brigade, especially after the death of General Michael Corcoran, who had been killed in a riding accident in December 1863.

On May 3, the Irish Brigade left their camp at Stevensburg, Virginia. The next morning, at Ely's Ford, the Irish crossed the Rapidan River, wading through hip-deep water. Late that afternoon they camped beside the scorched ruins of the Chancellor House, the site of the Battle of Chancellorsville, and the place where the men of the Irish Brigade had rescued the artillery abandoned by the 5th Maine Battery. In the fields and woods around the burned house lay the bones of men no one had taken the trouble to bury, as well as battered equipment, tattered caps and knapsacks, and rusted weapons—the debris of the battle.

Camped on the same ground with the Irish was the 11th New York Light Artillery. A raw recruit, seventeen-year-old Private Frank Wilkerson, wrote of that night, "The dead were all around us. Their eyeless skulls seemed to stare steadily at us. . . . An infantry soldier who had, unobserved by us, been prying into the shallow grave he sat on with his bayonet, suddenly rolled a skull on the ground before us, and said in a deep, low voice: 'That is what you are all coming to, and some of you will start toward it tomorrow.'"

On the morning of May 4, the Irish took the Catharpin Road to the Brock Road, which led them into the Wilderness, a dense, almost impenetrable tangle of forest and brush and bogs covering more than 70 square miles (181 square km) of Spotsylvania County. To accommodate artillery and supply wagons, sappers cleared 20-foot-wide (6 m) roads through the forest and threw bridges over streams such as Wilderness Run. Intelligence reports had informed the Union commanders that Lee was in the Wilderness, too, but as the Yankees marched through they were not sure of the Rebels' actual location. General Winfield Scott Hancock, commander of the 2nd Corps, and General Gouverneur K. Warren, commander of the 5th Corps, ordered their men to march slowly and in tight formation and be ready for an attack that might come at any moment.

When Yankee scouts reached the Orange Turnpike, one of the few major roads through the Wilderness, they paused to take a look around, but the surrounding countryside was silent and empty. Then one of the scouts noticed a small cloud of dust to the southwest, in the neighborhood of the hamlet of Verdiersville. The scouts waited and watched until they could see Confederate infantry marching in the direction of Robertson's Tavern, a landmark on the Orange Turnpike. The Rebels were not staying behind their breastworks as Grant had expected; instead, they were on the offensive. Union skirmishers, moving ahead of the army, walked out of the forest and into Saunders Field, a cornfield bisected by the turnpike. The skirmishers got close to the Rebels—so close that one of them, eighteen-year-old Charles Wilson of Massachusetts, was shot and killed by a Rebel marksman, making Wilson the first casualty of the Battle of the Wilderness.

The Rebels on the Orange Turnpike numbered about 17,000 men and were under the command of General Richard Ewell. South and running parallel to the turnpike was the Orange Plank Road, where General A.P. Hill was leading approximately 22,000 men. Ewell's men stopped short of Saunders Field and began to dig trenches and throw up a rough fortification of fallen trees. General Warren sent in 5,000 Union troops led by General Charles Griffin to attack Ewell. In the 1850s, Griffin had fought the Navajo in the New Mexico Territory. His fellow officers found him short-tempered and irascible, yet Griffin had proven leadership skills, which had contributed to the Union victories at Gaines' Mill and Malvern Hill during the Seven Days Campaign in 1862.

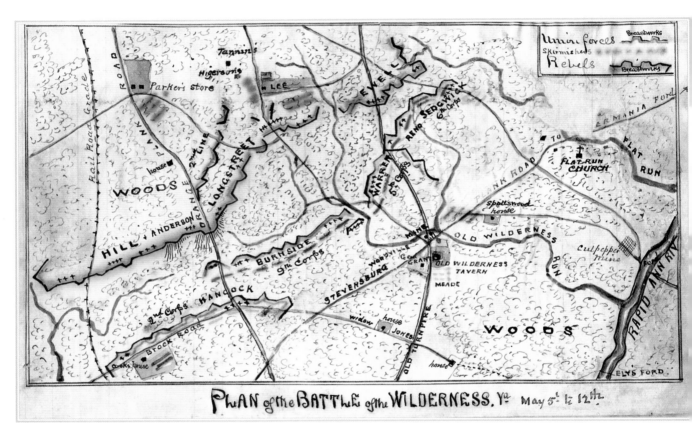

PLAN of the BATTLE of the WILDERNESS, Va. May 5t 1 12th

ROBERT KNOX SNEDEN'S MAP DEPICTS THE LOCATION AND MOVEMENTS OF THE UNION AND CONFEDERATE ARMIES AT THE BATTLE OF THE

WILDERNESS, MAY 5 TO 6, 1864, AS WELL AS AT THE BATTLE OF SPOTSYLVANIA COURT HOUSE, MAY 8 TO 12, 1864. THE IRISH BRIGADE WAS

WITH THE 2ND CORPS, COMMANDED BY GENERAL WINFIELD SCOTT HANCOCK.

Griffin sent in his 5,000 in a frontal attack on the Confederates. As they moved through the cornfield, the Yankees found that it was not all smooth ground—there was a swale, a deep depression similar to a ravine, cutting through the field. To reach Ewell's men in the woods, they had to scurry up the steep slope of the western side of the swale. As they reached the crest, the Confederates 20 yards (18 m) away opened fire. Worse, the Confederates had flanked the attacking Yankees. With Rebel musket fire tearing through their ranks from two directions, Griffin's men panicked and fled back down into the swale and toward their lines. The Union lost more than 500 men in Saunders Field, and hundreds more were wounded.

About 4 miles (6.4 km) from Saunders Field, at the intersection of the Orange Plank Road and Brock Road, the Union division under Brigadier General George Getty was caught in withering musket and artillery fire from Confederates concealed in the forest. Hundreds of Union men fell in a matter of minutes—a sight so sickening that one of the Confederates who participated in the slaughter characterized it as "bushwhacking on a grand scale."

General Winfield Scott Hancock brought up his corps and Brigadier General John Gibbons led his division into the fight, where both were mauled by the Confederate guns. Sparks from thousands of muskets and dozens of artillery set the dry undergrowth of the Wilderness ablaze, so now both Confederates and Union men were staggering about, choking on clouds of smoke, trying to escape the flames. All around them they heard the screams of the crippled and the badly wounded who could not get away from the fire. And when the blaze swept over a dead or dying man and ignited the cartridges in his pouch, dozens of musket balls flew in every direction, wounding and killing more men.

During the fight in Saunders Field, the Irish had been among the brigades held in reserve on or near Brock Road. At about five in the afternoon Colonel Smyth received orders to take the Irish Brigade into the fight. Three hundred yards (270 m) into the woods, they encountered a brigade of North Carolinians. Skirmishers from the 28th Massachusetts fell back to join the main body of the Irish Brigade and the 1st Brigade, a collection of men from Pennsylvania, New York, and Michigan. The two brigades advanced, striking the North Carolinians on both flanks until the Rebels fled into the woods. The Yankees followed, and met another line of Confederates. Neither side would give ground. "The fighting," a Union soldier recalled, "became simply terrific. The musketry was continuous and deadly along the whole line." One of the Irish, Sergeant John Cassidy of the 116th Pennsylvania, was shot in the chest, the musket ball drilling through his lungs. The fighting was too hot for anyone to help him get to a field hospital, so as Cassidy shambled away he complained loudly about being left to fend for himself. One of his friends replied, "Why Cassidy, there's a man with all of his head blown off, and he's not making half as much fuss as you are!"

Then two Union regiments, the 66th New York and the 20th Indiana, surprised the North Carolinians, hitting them on their left flank. The Rebel line broke, and one Confederate, Berry Benson, recorded that the Orange Plank Road was "jammed with a disorderly, flying mass of Confederates." Later General Winfield Scott Hancock would praise the Irish Brigade's conduct on the first day of the Battle of the Wilderness, saying, "[The men of the Irish Brigade] were heavily engaged and although four-fifths of its members were recruits it behaved with great steadiness and gallantry."

The fight continued until dark, when the two Union brigades were called back to Brock Road.

"I AM HAPPY!"

In the early morning of May 5, Union forces followed General James Wadsworth in a frontal assault on Lee's center. Wadsworth was a wealthy New Yorker—in fact, one of the wealthiest men in the state. He owned so many estates and farms that managing them was his full-time occupation. In 1861, he enlisted in the New York state militia and received a commission as major general. Wadsworth had no military training, but he learned quickly—in 1862, he was appointed commander of the 1st Division, 1st Corps. His insistence that his men must have good food and tents for shelter won him the affection of the troops, but they also respected him—here was a wealthy gentleman who had left the comforts of his estate to fight for the Union, and he insisted upon doing so without pay. And there was one other thing that distinguished James Wadsworth—at fifty-six, he was the oldest commander of a division in the Army of the Potomac.

Under the ferocity of Wadsworth's attack, Lee's center broke. Nearly 700 Texans rushed forward to fill the gap as their commander, General John Gregg, shouted, "The eyes of General Lee are upon you!" And Lee was there, so close that as the Texans raced past he stood up in his stirrups, waved his hat over his head, and cried, "Texans always move them!" Then Lee spurred his horse, Traveler, and rode beside the advancing Texans. To see Lee literally at their side filled the Texans with reckless courage. They plugged the gap in the Confederate center and held it until reinforcements from General Longstreet's corps came up to support them.

THIS HAND-COLORED LITHOGRAPH OF THE BATTLE OF THE WILDERNESS, PUBLISHED BY THE RENOWNED FIRM OF CURRIER & IVES,
DISPLAYS SOME PARTISAN ZEAL IN ITS REFERENCES TO THE "GREAT HERO, LIEUT. GENL. U.S. GRANT" AND "THE REBEL HORDES."
WHEN HE HEARD OF THE UNION CASUALTIES OF 17,000 FOLLOWING THE BATTLE, GRANT SHOWED NO EMOTION,
BUT RETIRED TO HIS TENT WHERE HE WEPT FOR THE LOSSES.

Gen U S Grant at Wilderness Va May 7th 1864.

EDWIN FORBES SKETCHED GENERAL
ULYSSES S. GRANT GREETED BY
CHEERING UNION TROOPS AT THE
BATTLE OF THE WILDERNESS, THE
FIRST OFFENSIVE OF HIS OVERLAND
CAMPAIGN TO CRUSH THE ARMY OF
NORTHERN VIRGINIA. THE BATTLE
WAS THE FIRST DEMONSTRATION OF
GRANT'S STRATEGY FOR WINNING
THE WAR: THROW AS MANY TROOPS
AS POSSIBLE INTO BATTLE, IN
THE KNOWLEDGE THAT TENS OF
THOUSANDS OF FRESH RECRUITS
WERE AVAILABLE IN THE NORTH,
WHILE EVERY CONFEDERATE LOST
WAS IRREPLACEABLE.

The fighting was desperate, so much so that the Rebels feared for the safety of their commander. "Lee, to the rear!" they chanted. "Lee, to the rear!" Finally, a sergeant sprinted toward the general, grabbed the reins of his horse, and led him off the battlefield.

The Confederate center held, but of the almost 700 Texans who had come to its rescue, only 223 survived.

When Longstreet arrived at six that morning, he did not simply hold the line; he counterattacked. For two hours, Yankees and Rebels fought each other in the tangle of the Wilderness and in the fields of Widow Catherine Tapp's farm. Longstreet's men did not drive the Union men back, but they did halt the drive to shatter the Confederate's center. Lee was so pleased with Longstreet's success that morning that he deferred all further orders to him. Couriers who galloped up to Lee with requests for reinforcements or questions about the placement of a particular brigade were told, "Well, let's see General Longstreet about it."

Between eight and ten that morning, the fighting shifted from the Tapp Farm to the Orange Plank Road, about half a mile (0.8 km) away. Longstreet's chief engineer rode up with surprising news—he had discovered an unfinished railway link that was not marked on the map. The engineer assured the general that the roadbed offered a clear passage through the Wilderness directly to Hancock's left flank. Longstreet decided to exploit it. He assembled four brigades and sent them racing down the line. Concealed by the forest, the Confederates took the Union troops entirely by surprise. Lieutenant Colonel Charles Weygant called on the men of the 124th New York to stand and fight. "I might as well have tried to stop the flight of a cannon ball," he wrote later, "by interposing the lid of a cracker box." There were so many Rebels, and they came on so swiftly that the Yankees, fearing they would be taken prisoner, turned tail and ran. "The terrible tempest of disaster swept down on the Union lines," Weygant recorded, "beating back brigade after brigade, and tearing to pieces regiment after regiment, until upwards of twenty thousand veterans were fleeing, every man for himself, through the disorganizing and already blood-stained woods, toward the Union rear." Years later, recalling that day, Hancock would tell Longstreet, "You rolled me up like a wet blanket."

The stunning success of the attack on Hancock's men delighted General Micah Jenkins. Beaming with joy, he told Longstreet, "I am happy! I felt despair for the cause for some months, but am relieved, and feel assured that we will put the enemy back across the Rapidan before night."

General Longstreet and his party were riding along a path back to headquarters when someone concealed in the woods opened fire: Men of the 12th Virginia had mistaken Longstreet's entourage for Yankee cavalry. Officers shouted, "Friends! These are friends!" Another volley came crashing out of the woods, and suddenly General Longstreet slumped over his horse's neck. The general had been struck in the throat, the musket ball exiting behind his right shoulder. His staff lifted him down and leaned him against a tree while a British observer galloped off to find a surgeon.

Longstreet's staff and his men, as well as General Lee, feared they were about to witness a repeat of the Stonewall Jackson tragedy—the loss of a great and beloved commander. The wound was not fatal, Longstreet would recover, but with Longstreet out of the fight, the Confederates lost their momentum. The four brigades that had rolled up Hancock's line were themselves scattered—in their pursuit of the Yankees they had broken into small groups to take prisoners. There could be no follow-up attack until those four brigades were reassembled in battle formation, but the rumors that Longstreet was dying took the heart out of his officers, who should have rallied Longstreet's men.

THE BURNING BREASTWORKS

Longstreet passed his command to Major General Charles Field. A member of Kentucky's plantation aristocracy, Field had taught cavalry tactics at West Point, but in 1861, he resigned from the academy to serve in the Army of Northern Virginia. It took Field most of the afternoon to collect enough men for an assault on the Union breastworks at Brock Road—the Irish Brigade had spent the previous night hauling logs and piling them up chest high.

Field gathered his men in the forest, where they were invisible to the Yankees. About 4:15 in the afternoon, the Union troops heard the high-pitched rebel yell, then saw thousands of Rebels explode out of the woods. Musket and cannon fire from the Union breastworks crashed into the charging Confederates, but instead of falling back they dropped to their knees, or fell on their bellies, and returned fire. The standoff between Rebels and Yankees lasted only half an hour, and then sparks from the muskets and cannons fell on the dry brush along the Orange Plank Road. Little tongues of flame shot up along the road, then a strong breeze blew across the field and the fire sprang to life. Pushed forward by the wind, the wall of flames and thick clouds of smoke roared toward the Union line. The breastworks caught fire, but by then most of the Union men had retreated, driven back by the heat and smoke.

The Irish Brigade was among the troops who stayed at their post. Corporal Samuel Clear of the 116th Pennsylvania recalled, "The Irishmen stood their ground, firing blind volley after volley through the blazing barrier."

Elsewhere, the Rebels breached the burning breastworks. Leaping through the flames, their faces blackened with soot, they resembled devils, and the Yankees ran faster. It appeared that Hancock's men would be routed for the second time in the same day, but then the Union artillery opened fire, halting the Confederate's advance. Meanwhile, Union reinforcements—three regiments and a brigade—came running along Orange Plank Road. Many of the fleeing Yankees rallied and counterattacked. Charles Weygant recorded that the Union men charged, "with clubbed muskets, swords, and bayonets, right at the now totally demoralized Confederates, who broke for the rear, and fled in the widest disorder . . . down through the woods again."

After the battle at the breastworks, the fighting petered out. General Grant would not order any more attacks. "I do not hope to gain any decided advantage from the fighting in this forest," he told Horace Porter, one of his aides. "I did expect excellent results from Hancock's movement early this morning, when he started the enemy on the run; but it was impossible for him to see his own troops, or the true position of the enemy, and the success gained could not be followed through in such country."

By sundown on May 6, the second day of the Battle of the Wilderness, the Confederates had virtually destroyed Grant's right flank and taken two Union generals prisoner. Union casualties for May 5 and 6 totaled 17,000 men, about 500 of them members of the Irish Brigade. As he received these reports, Grant appeared to be unmoved—it was against his nature to display his emotions before others. Newspaperman Charles Dana of the *New York Tribune* had noticed this personality trait of Grant. "He keeps his own counsel," Dana wrote, "padlocks his mouth, while his countenance in battle or repose . . . indicates nothing—that is, gives no expression of his feelings and no evidence of his intentions." But alone in his tent, Grant wept like a child.

As for Lee, he had lost approximately 13,000 men.

For three years, whenever the Army of the Potomac had lost a battle, it retreated to northern Virginia or to Maryland. On the morning of May 7, Grant led his men south, deeper into Virginia. Grant sent Lincoln a telegram: "Whatever happens, we will not retreat."

Grant led his army in a sweeping movement to the southeast, forcing Lee to come out and intercept him or risk being flanked. For the next year, the two commanders would jockey for advantage—Grant trying everything he could imagine to draw Lee into a fight, Lee taking every opportunity to hunker down in some fortified place that Grant had to attack and capture before he could advance again.

Some historians characterize the Battle of the Wilderness as a draw, others as a Confederate victory. It was the first demonstration of Grant's new strategy for winning the war: Throw as many troops as possible into battle, certain in the knowledge that there were tens of thousands of fresh men who could be recruited in the North, while every man Lee lost was irreplaceable. Time and mathematics were on Grant's side.

10

"HOLD ON WITH A BULLDOG GRIP":
The Irish Brigade at the Siege of the Petersburg

All morning on June 16, 1864, Union troops watched as Confederate reinforcements manned the parapets and trenches of the defenses of Petersburg, Virginia. At six in the evening, the order came to attack. The Irish Brigade, fighting with the 2nd Corps, jogged over open ground, past the Hare family's clapboard house, east of the city's fortifications. It came under terrible fire from artillery and muskets, yet when it was only 100 yards (91 m) from the breastworks, the Irish doubled their pace. With bayonets fixed they stormed up the Rebels' defenses; within minutes the fighting was hand-to-hand. The Confederates defending this portion of the fortifications retreated, and the 2nd Corps found themselves in possession of three redans (V-shaped parapets that projected from the breastworks), along with cannons and prisoners.

The Irish lost about 100 men in the attack, including their commander: Colonel Patrick Kelly, forty-two years old, was shot through the head. A reporter for the *Irish American* newspaper in New York, who was at the scene, described the reactions of Kelly's men. "Strong old veteran soldiers wept like children," the reporter wrote, "and wrung their hands in frenzy." Captain David Conyngham, who served under Kelly, eulogized him as "Gentle, brave, and unassuming, no truer man nor braver officer fell during the war."

Kelly's body was taken back to New York City, where he was buried beside his wife, Elizabeth, in First Calvary Cemetery in Queens. Over the decades, the Kellys' headstone—if they ever had one—disappeared. In 1998 the Galway Association of New York and the Irish Brigade Association erected a new monument at the gravesite.

A LOST OPPORTUNITY
With a population of more than 14,000, Petersburg was the third largest city in Virginia. But it was Petersburg's industries rather than its population that made it

essential to the war. Petersburg was vital to Richmond and to the Confederacy at large. Its iron foundries made weapons, particularly cannons. The smelting works made lead musket balls, and the mills produced gunpowder. Its textile factories turned out bolts of cotton cloth for uniforms. All of these goods were shipped throughout the South via the five railway lines and three major roads that ran in and out of the city.

General George McClellan's 1862 Peninsula Campaign demonstrated how vulnerable Petersburg was to attack, and so the city's Common Council voted to build defensive works around the city. Captain Charles H. Dimmock, an engineer in the Confederate army, directed the project. Dimmock was a native of Massachusetts, sixty-two years old, who, after a busy career building roads, railways, and canals from Delaware to Arkansas, settled in Richmond, where he joined the state militia and served three terms on the city council. When the Civil War began, Dimmock fought in defense of his adopted state.

Initially, about 200 slaves and free black men were put to work digging trenches, raising earthworks, and constructing emplacements for artillery. But a work crew of 200 was insufficient for such an ambitious project, so slaves were rounded up from neighboring farms and plantations, and 4,000 Confederate troops were also assigned to the project.

The Dimmock Line, as the fortification was called, was completed in 1863. The Line stood 2 miles (3.2 km) outside the city limits and stretched for 10 miles (16 km) in a semicircle around Petersburg. Mounted in the zigzag of trenches and other defense works were 55 batteries of artillery. Unfortunately, General Pierre G.T. Beauregard had only about 3,200 troops to defend the Dimmock Line, and many of them were "second class militia," young boys and old men who were not fit for regular duty in the Confederate army. General Grant characterized the South's second class militia policy as "robbing the cradle and the grave."

In June 1864, Grant marched on Petersburg with an army of approximately 112,000 men. His goal was to cut off the railroads that carried weapons, ammunition, and other supplies from the factories of Petersburg to Richmond, as well as precious European goods such as medicine that Confederate blockade runners unloaded at the port of Wilmington, North Carolina. Grant was confident that once he had taken Petersburg, Richmond would fall and the war would be over.

Using pontoon bridges and ferryboats, Grant's army crossed the James River, approaching Petersburg from the northeast. In the vanguard of the army was General William Smith of Vermont with a force of 16,000 men. Smith was an army

THE YANKEES LAID RAILROAD
TRACK SO THEY COULD BRING IN
"THE DICTATOR," SHOWN HERE,
AN 8.5-TON CANNON KNOWN
AS A TRENCH MORTAR OR
RAILROAD MORTAR, BECAUSE
A TRAIN WAS THE ONLY WAY
IT COULD BE TRANSPORTED.

engineer who before the war had built lighthouses along the Florida coast. While in Florida he contracted malaria, and he suffered from the aftereffects of the illness, including fever and exhaustion, for the rest of his life.

At seven in the evening on June 15, Smith attacked the Dimmock Line, and within two hours captured a 2-mile (3.2 km) stretch of Petersburg's defenses, including four cannons and hundreds of prisoners. As Beauregard's men fell back, another 16,000 Union men arrived on the scene. Inexplicably, Smith did not capitalize on this opportunity: Rather than attack the Confederates and perhaps capture the entire Dimmock Line in one night, Smith stayed where he was. That night Beauregard received about 7,000 reinforcements from Cold Harbor, Virginia, 26 miles (41.6 km) away.

THE LONGEST SIEGE

From early May until mid-June 1864, Grant and Lee had fought ten tough battles in Virginia, from the Wilderness to Spotsylvania Court House to Yellow Tavern to Cold Harbor. In six weeks, Grant lost approximately 55,000 men; Lee, about 32,000. Both generals followed the strategies they had adopted since spring: Grant tried to maneuver Lee's army onto an open battlefield, while Lee tried to remain within well-fortified positions, the better to defend Richmond. Even when Grant marched on Petersburg, Lee remained near Richmond, just in case Grant's move was a feint, tempting Lee to pursue him so he could swing around and capture the Confederate capital.

Between June 15 and 18, the Union army tried to repeat the success it had enjoyed its first night outside Petersburg: It made attempt after attempt to capture the Dimmock Line, but each time the Confederates drove the Yankees back. The fighting on June 18 was especially deadly. The 1st Maine Heavy Artillery went into battle with 900 men and lost 632. Among the wounded was Joshua Chamberlain, the hero of Little Round Top—he was shot twice through the bladder, but he would recover. After the loss of 10,000 men, Grant called a halt. "I will make no more assaults . . . but will give the men a rest, and then look to extensions toward our left, with a view to destroying Lee's communications on the south and confining him to a close siege." That same day, Lee arrived in Petersburg with approximately 60,000 men.

As Alan Axelrod, historian of the Battle of Petersburg, puts it, "Within Grant's innocuous sounding phrase, 'then look to extensions toward our left', was a whole world of hard labor." After a few days' rest, Grant put his army to work digging a system of trenches that ran parallel to Lee's. The Union's 26 miles (41.6 km) of trenches were 6 to 8 feet (1.8 to 2.4 m) deep and about 10 feet (3 m) across, according to Axelrod, with the earth piled in mounds and reinforced with logs. Each trench had a firing step where a trooper stood to take aim at the enemy. Once he'd fired, he stepped down to reload—off the firing step, he was completely out of sight of the enemy.

The Yankees also laid railroad track so they could bring in "the Dictator," an 8.5-ton cannon known as a trench mortar or a railroad mortar (because a train was the only way to transport such a massive gun). It had a short, thick barrel that fired 200-pound (90.7 kg) shells a distance of 2 miles (3.2 km)—far enough to strike at least the outskirts of Petersburg. As the Union army dug the track, Grant received a message from President Lincoln. "Hold on with a bulldog grip," he said, "and chew and choke as much as possible."

With the trenches dug and the artillery in place, the siege of Petersburg was begun—it would drag on for 292 days, the longest siege in American history.

THE TUNNEL

Like his father, Lieutenant Colonel Henry Pleasants was an engineer. He had been born in Buenos Aires, Argentina, where his father had found work, but the family soon moved back to Pennsylvania, their home state. As a young man, Pleasants became interested in coal mining and developed a new technique he called "deep-shaft mining," which gave miners access to thicker seams of coal far below the surface. As mining companies adopted his technique, Pleasants began to prosper. He married, but soon after the wedding Pleasants's wife died unexpectedly of some undiagnosed illness that the doctor described simply as "a fever." In July 1861, with nothing to hold him at home, thirty-one-year-old Pleasants joined the 48th Pennsylvania Infantry. By 1864, he had risen to the rank of lieutenant colonel and was given command of the 48th.

At Petersburg, Pleasants had about 100 miners with him. Shortly after the Union's failed June 18 attack on the Dimmock Line, Pleasants was standing opposite a portion of the Confederate defenses, an artillery battery known as Elliott's Salient, about 400 feet (121 m) away, when he overheard a soldier say, "We could blow that damned fort out of existence if we could run a mine shaft under it." That offhand observation gave Pleasants an idea.

He approached Generals Grant and Burnside with a plan to dig a tunnel beneath Elliott's Salient. He would pack kegs of gunpowder at the end of the tunnel, directly beneath the artillery. When the gunpowder exploded, it would destroy the artillery and blow a gap in the Confederate defenses through which Union troops would charge, capturing the Dimmock Line and the city of Petersburg. Grant and Burnside approved the plan, and Pleasants's men started digging on June 25.

A major concern was the presence in the tunnels of "mephitic vapors," as Burnside called them. "Mephitic vapors" was the nineteenth-century term for noxious gases such as methane and carbon dioxide, which Pleasants knew tunneling released from the soil. To solve the problem he installed two wooden pipes in the tunnel, one like a chimney with a fire burning beneath it. The chimney drew the poison gases out and through the other pipe drew fresh air in.

Pleasants had begun his tunnel more than 100 feet (30 m) from where he had first studied Elliott's Salient, at a place where the Confederates could not see his miners at work. Nonetheless, the Rebels could hear the sound of excavation beneath their feet. They began digging several countermines to find and destroy the Yankee tunnel, but their miners missed it. As the work progressed, Pleasants modified his plan to include two lateral tunnels that would run about 20 feet (6 m) in either direction under the Salient. On July 27, the digging was finished and the miners carried 320 kegs of gunpowder—about 4 tons (4,000 kg) of explosives—into the lateral tunnels. Then they laid down a 98-foot (29.7 m) fuse.

At 3:15 on the morning of July 30, Pleasants lit the fuse. It should have set off the explosion in fifteen minutes, yet an hour passed and nothing happened. Two men of the 48th Pennsylvania volunteered to enter the tunnel to pinpoint the problem. They found that the fuse had burned out where it split off into the two lateral galleries. They lit the two fuses, then raced for the surface.

At 4:45, a tremendous roar split the night as earth, cannons, and men were hurled into the air. A soldier from Michigan who witnessed the blast wrote of "a heaving and lifting of the fort and the hill on which it stood; then a monstrous tongue of flame shot fully two hundred feet [61 m] in the air, followed by a vast column of white smoke . . . then a great spout or fountain of red earth rose to a great height, mingled with men and guns, timbers and planks, and every other kind of debris, all ascending, spreading, whirling, scattering." At least 278 Confederates were killed or wounded in the blast, and before the void that had been Elliott's Salient was a crater about 170 feet (51.6 m) long, 70 feet (21.2 m) wide, and 30 feet (9 m) deep.

THE CRATER

General Burnside had planned that two brigades of United States Colored Troops under the command of Brigadier General Edward Ferrero would lead the attack.

THE CONFEDERATE WORKS AT ELLIOTT'S SALIENT, SEEN HERE IN AN INTERIOR SHOT, WERE THE TARGET OF
LIEUTENANT COLONEL HENRY PLEASANTS' 500-FOOT-LONG MINE. PORTIONS OF THE CRATER CREATED BY
THE EXPLOSION CAN STILL BE SEEN AT THE PETERSBURG NATIONAL BATTLEFIELD.

Richmond Va.
Church Hill Edinburgh.

11 May 1870

My dear Willie

After a long interval I resume the Chicauny letters. We have been great rain all night, and it still continues so that we cannot go out

Yesterday we were in Petersburgh — a small town that sustained a memorable siege in the Civil War. On elevated but nearly level ground near the town the earthen forts remain with little change. There is one place, where a huge crater — like a saucer in shape — is hollowed out in the middle of an earth fort of the defence. It is where the federals sprung a mine.

From the side of a natural ravine, between their lines, the federals drove a mine — through the soft clay — and piled an immense quantity of gunpowder under the centre of the confederate fort. They sprung it — the fort

he saw another soldiers cemetery on the opposite side of the town, which contains twenty thousand graves. But it was not so impressive to the sense, because it has not the wooden pillars for grave stones. Each grave has a low post, with a gine number — precisely like plants in a nursery.

A few miles farther out there are cemeteries ... belonging to the federals.

These silent ranks told more powerfully the warning against war than I have ever heard it before.

We are invited out to a gentleman's county seat to day — 5 miles distant — and we start at night by train, hoping to arrive in Washington to-morrow morning

The writing is not very careful: I am doing a good deal yet to day, and one is apt to weary

Let brotherly love continue.

Before the war, Ferrero had been a choreographer in New York's theaters and had written a book titled *The Art of Dance*. Like dance steps, Burnside had spelled out exactly what he wanted, and had spent two weeks training the black troops to split at the edge of the crater and race around its edge, one on the left, the other on the right, then straight into the gap opened by the explosion. General Meade objected to Burnside's decision to use black soldiers. If they suffered heavy casualties, black leaders and abolitionists in the North would say the army had used the black troops as cannon fodder. Burnside, unwilling to let two weeks of training go to waste, appealed to Grant, but Grant agreed with Meade. Instead, the first assault would be led by Brigadier General James H. Ledlie's 1st Division, composed overwhelmingly of Massachusetts men, plus two New York regiments, two Pennsylvania regiments, and one Maryland regiment.

What happened next is difficult to ascertain. Some historians believe that Ledlie's men had not been instructed to advance along the edge of the crater, and that Ledlie, who may have received these instructions, was at the rear, drunk. Other historians suggest that the shock of the explosion temporarily addled the Union men—they lost all common sense and developed a kind of mob mentality. The mob explanation may be correct, because as the first Yankees advanced they charged down into the crater rather than around it. Tragically, all the other Yankees followed them. When they tried to climb out at the opposite end, they found the slope too steep, and the soil—mostly clay and sand—too loose to provide a foothold or handhold.

By now a South Carolina regiment and a North Carolina regiment had moved forward to plug the gap made by the explosion. Union troops that managed, somehow, to scramble out of the crater were met by withering musket and canister fire from Confederate artillery. To escape, many Yankees leapt back into the pit, and now the Rebels lowered the barrels of their cannons and fired mortars into the blue-coated mass at the bottom of the crater. Confederate Brigadier General William Mahone, who was commanding Southern troops at the gap, likened shooting Yankees at the bottom of the pit to "a turkey shoot."

Burnside sent in the two black brigades, who forgot their training and also ran down into the crater. They became a particular target for the Confederates: One of Mahone's officers cried to his men, "Boys, you have hot work ahead; they are Negroes—show no quarter!" To escape the carnage, Yankees, white and black, surrendered, and there were ugly incidents of Confederates killing in cold blood black troops who had laid down their arms.

The Battle of the Crater raged for eight hours and cost General Grant 3,800 men, the highest proportion being among the black troops, which lost more than 1,300 men. General Lee, on the other hand, suffered 1,500 casualties.

Grant and Meade blamed Ledlie and Burnside for the debacle. Both were put on permanent leave, the equivalent of being dismissed from the service. In a telegram to Army Chief of Staff Henry W. Halleck about the Battle of the Crater Grant said, "It was the saddest affair I have witnessed in war. Such opportunity for carrying fortifications I have never seen and do not expect again to have."

THE DESERTERS

The Irish Brigade was spared the fiasco at the crater. On June 20, four days after its assault on the Dimmock Line, it was ordered southwest with the 2nd Corps to the Weldon Railroad, one of the lines Grant wanted to sever. The Brigade was deployed along the Jerusalem Plank Road, near the Johnson family's farm. Two days later, General Mahone unexpectedly attacked the 2nd Corps' left flank, where the Irish were positioned. The Rebels fought hard, and the Irish lost about 100 men in the surprise attack, but ultimately they drove them off.

To the chagrin of veterans of the Irish Brigade, it was revealed that ten of their new recruits who had recently deserted went over to the Rebels and divulged the details of the placement of Union pickets outside Fort Davis.

Once again the Irish Brigade was running low on men. Between the Battle of the Wilderness in early May and the just-completed skirmish on Johnson's farm, the Brigade had lost about 1,200 men. Of the Brigade's ten officers, six had been killed and the surviving four were seriously wounded. The 28th Massachusetts, which had eighty-seven men on the first day Grant's army entered the Wilderness, was down to eight. Headquarters decided to reorganize the Irish Brigade. The three original New York regiments—the 69th, 63rd, and 88th—would remain together as the Consolidated Brigade, while the 28th Massachusetts and the 116th Pennsylvania were reassigned to other brigades.

Colonel St. Clair Mulholland of the 116th wrote that his "regiment left the Irish Brigade with regret. They had participated in all the glories and triumphs of that famous brigade for two years, and although the One Hundred and Sixteenth was composed almost entirely of American-born citizens, the men had learned to love and esteem the men of the Emerald Isle." Command of the Consolidated Brigade was given to Major Richard Moroney, a native New Yorker and a veteran of the Mexican War. Moroney had been wounded in the Battle of the Wheatfield at Gettysburg; a year earlier his valor had been praised by General Thomas Meagher in his official report regarding the conduct of the Irish at Antietam.

To bring the Consolidated Brigade back to full strength (or at least close to it), Colonel Robert Nugent and Lieutenant Colonel James McGee traveled to New York to recruit more men. In September and October about 800 recruits—all of them volunteers, draftees, or substitutes hired to take the place of other men—arrived at Petersburg. They were raw, with little training, but their numbers brought the Brigade's numbers up to about 1,400. On November 1, 1864, General Nelson Miles dissolved the Consolidated Brigade, and the men of the 69th, 63rd, and 88th New York regiments became once again the Irish Brigade. Command passed to Colonel Nugent, who had served with the Irish from its formation in 1861. In an address to the reformed Irish Brigade Nugent said, "Never has a regimental color of [the Irish Brigade] graced the halls of its enemies. Let the spirit that animates the officers and men of the present be that which shall strive to emulate the deeds of the old brigade."

On the evening of October 30, men from the 69th were assigned to picket duty opposite Fort Davis, one of the fortifications that defended Petersburg. In the middle of the night, a Confederate raiding party took the Irish by surprise, capturing 168 men of the 69th and 246 men from a nearby regiment, the 111th New York. But before the Rebels could march their prisoners back to Confederate lines, Lieutenant Murtha Murphy sounded the alarm. The men of the 69th and 111th opened fire, but few of the prisoners escaped. In the skirmish, Murphy suffered a head wound.

Among the prisoners was Sergeant Thomas McGrath, a popular veteran who had served with the Irish since 1861. A man of great courage, he had been wounded at Malvern Hill, Fredericksburg, Gettysburg, and Spotsylvania. As a prisoner of the Confederates, McGrath would try to escape three times—unfortunately, none of the attempts were successful.

The surprise raid and the capture of so many men set off an investigation. To the chagrin of veterans of the Irish Brigade, it was revealed that ten of their new recruits who had recently deserted went over to the Rebels and divulged the details of the placement of Union pickets outside Fort Davis. One of the deserters was captured: Private John Nicholas was a Canadian whom an American draftee had paid to be his substitute. Nicholas was tried by a court martial and hanged.

Before Petersburg — at

ALFRED WAUD'S SKETCH SHOWS
THE PETERSBURG BATTLEFIELD
MOMENTS AFTER THE MINE UNDER
ELLIOTT'S SALIENT EXPLODED AND
UNION ARTILLERY OPENED UP ON
THE CONFEDERATE DEFENSES.

"DON'T LEAVE ME, FOR GOD'S SAKE!"

There was more to the siege of Petersburg than day after tedious day of sitting in muddy trenches. Lee had stretched his forces in a thin line, 25 miles (40 km) long, from Richmond south to Petersburg. Time and again Grant sent troops to hammer the Confederates, hoping to break through. He also sent General Philip Sheridan with two cavalry divisions to lay waste to the Shenandoah Valley, one of the most fertile, most productive farming regions in the South, and General Lee's most important source for fresh food. For this mission, Grant wanted a man who would be merciless, and Sheridan was a fine choice: A five-foot-five-inch (1.7 m) hothead, he had been suspended for a year from West Point for threatening to run through a fellow classmate with a bayonet.

Lee was not passive either. Grant had cut the Weldon Railroad line and Lee wanted it back. On August 25, Lee sent about 9,000 men under Generals A.P. Hill and Henry Heth against the 9,000 men under the command of General Winfield Scott Hancock at Ream's Station, right on the Weldon line. The Yankees had trenches and a three-sided earthworks, each side about 1,000 yards (910 m) long. But the eastern end of their defenses was open.

On August 25, the Irish Brigade was busily tearing up the Weldon line's tracks. Suddenly, at 5 p.m., Confederate artillery opened fire, pounding the Union position, terrorizing the raw recruits. Then six brigades—about 6,000 Confederates—attacked. General Miles's men behind the earthworks laid down a deadly fire that mowed through the charging Rebels. The Confederates hesitated and were on the verge of falling back when two Union regiments positioned in the center of the earthworks suddenly leapt up and ran: Almost all of them were novice soldiers who were too frightened to stand and fight. Miles ordered another brigade up to fill the gap, but these men, also new recruits, flopped facedown on the ground and refused to move.

Seeing more and more Yankees desert their posts, the Confederates divided their forces in two and slammed into the Union's right and left flanks. Hancock rode to every weak spot in his line—and there were plenty of them—trying to rally men, urging them to return fire. "We can beat them yet," he cried. Then, he shouted after his fleeing troops, "Don't leave me, for God's sake!"

As Confederates poured over the earthen wall on the left, General Miles ordered an artilleryman, Lieutenant George K. Dauchy, to aim his three guns at the advancing Rebels. Dauchy fired all three at once, slashing through the Confederates. Meanwhile, Miles had rallied the 61st New York, which attacked and drove the Rebels out from that portion of the earthworks.

ALFRED R. WAUD, A STAFF ARTIST FOR THE *NEW YORK ILLUSTRATED NEWS*, SKETCHED UNION TROOPS IN THEIR RIFLE PITS DURING THE

SIEGE OF PETERSBURG. LIKE THE IRISH BRIGADE, WAUD WAS PRESENT AT EVERY BATTLE FROM BULL RUN TO APPOMATTOX.

Creeping up on Hancock's men was Lieutenant General Wade Hampton. The son and grandson of veterans, one of the wealthiest men in the South, and the largest slave owner in South Carolina, Hampton led a dashing cavalry division. Now he ordered his men to dismount and attack the Yankees on foot. Once again, panic spread through the Yankee lines. At nightfall, after three hours of discouraging battle, Hancock ordered a retreat. He had lost about 2,400 men, more than 2,100 of whom were taken prisoner. Of those prisoners, 84 were from the Irish Brigade.

Ten days later, at the celebration marking the fourth anniversary of the formation of the Irish Brigade, General Miles told the assembly that although the Confederate attack took the Irish by surprise—like all the other Union troops at Ream's Station—they dug in and fought hard, repulsing the Rebels time and again. Miles said that Ream's Station could have been a Union victory, thanks to the Irish Brigade, had not Confederate reinforcements arrived to drive back the Union men.

THE FALL OF PETERSBURG

General Lee had hoped the Northern electorate would turn Lincoln out of the White House and bring in a man who would accept the Confederacy as a fait accompli and end the war. Lincoln himself feared that he would lose the election to his old nemesis, George B. McClellan, the Democrats' candidate. Yet Lincoln swept to victory, winning 212 electoral votes to McClellan's 21, and 2,218,338 popular votes to McClellan's 1,812,807. Among Union soldiers, 78 percent voted for Lincoln—a sharp slap in the face to their old commander, McClellan.

In October 1863, Lincoln had issued a proclamation establishing the last Thursday of November as a national day of thanksgiving. For Thanksgiving Day 1864, the army commissary sent flocks of fresh turkeys and chickens and mountains of fresh fruit to Grant's men outside Petersburg. Out of respect for the Yankee holiday, Confederate guns were silent throughout the day. While Grant's army feasted, Lee's dispirited troops were short on food and warm clothing—as usual—but they were also low on morale. They were not beating the Yankees. The Northern Democrats' peace platform in the late election had been soundly defeated. And from home came distressing letters that told of poverty and hunger. At Petersburg, Lee's men began to desert. The rate of several dozen slipping away after dark escalated so that by April 1865, Lee was losing several hundred men every night. Believing the war was lost, Lee's veterans abandoned the Confederate cause to return to their primary loyalty—their families.

On March 29, Grant began his final assault on Petersburg. For five days, Yankees and Rebels fought along the tracks of the Southside Railroad, in the neighborhood of an intersection known as Five Forks. On April 2, 1865, Grant's army broke through the Confederate lines 6 miles (9.6 km) southwest of Petersburg; the Rebels could not turn them back. Before he hurried his men out of the city, Lee sent a message to Jefferson Davis informing him he was evacuating Petersburg and recommending that the president evacuate Richmond.

At 4:30 in the morning on April 3, the first Union troops, a regiment from Michigan, marched into Petersburg with two American flags—one they raised over the courthouse, the second over the post office. Later that morning, Lincoln arrived in Petersburg. For ninety minutes, he and Grant sat on the porch of the Wallace family's house discussing the general's next move and the president's policy once the Confederacy surrendered. It was a brief conference for such weighty issues, but Grant could not linger. Lee would try to head south to join up with General Joseph E. Johnston's army in North Carolina; to end the war, Grant had to block Lee's path and keep him isolated. The two men shook hands. Then the president went back to Washington and the general went in pursuit of Robert E. Lee.

"HERE IS WHAT IS LEFT OF US":
The Irish Brigade at Appomattox

On Sunday morning, April 2, 1865, a messenger walked up the main aisle of St. Paul's Episcopal Church in Richmond, stopped at the Davis family's pew, and handed an envelope to Jefferson Davis. The Confederate president drew out a telegram from General Robert E. Lee informing him that General Ulysses Grant had broken Lee's line and Lee had abandoned Petersburg. "I advise that all preparation be made for leaving Richmond tonight," Lee concluded. The enemy was only 25 miles (40 km) away from the Confederate capital. A member of the congregation, Sallie Putnam, observed that as Davis stepped out of his pew, he "was noticed to walk rather unsteadily out of the church."

As Davis prepared the Confederate government to leave the capital, word spread from house to house that Richmond was to be evacuated. Soon the streets out of town were thronged with vehicles of every sort, crowded with passengers and piled high with household goods. Mingled among the wagons and buggies were swarms of pedestrians, burdened down with bundles, valises, and small children.

The treasury dumped the worthless Confederate currency in a pile outside the old capitol building and burned it. City officials called for the destruction of all beer, wine, and liquor, which flowed down the gutters in an alcoholic stream. The guards at the state penitentiary deserted their posts, and soon the convicts had broken out of their cells and were rampaging through the business district, looting shops and saloons. They discarded their prison uniforms and stole clothing out of shops, or right off clotheslines, so they could blend in with the mass of people leaving Richmond.

Someone gave the order to set fire to the tobacco warehouses. Mayor Joseph Mayo, anxious that the fire would spread to the rest of the city, countermanded the order, but the soldiers charged with burning the tobacco would not listen. Running with torches from warehouse to warehouse, they set off a conflagration that swept across Richmond. Sallie Putnam, who had begun her day serenely in church, spent

Sunday night watching "the devouring flames . . . [leap] from building to building, as if possessed of demonic instinct and intent upon wholesale destruction."

All through the night the fire raged, and the next morning it reached the arsenal. With a tremendous roar, the artillery shells exploded, the force of them leveling the arsenal, blowing out windows, and adding a fresh terror to those citizens of Richmond who had resolved to remain in their homes.

Captain George A. Bruce of the 13th New Hampshire Infantry remembered that morning very differently. As he approached Richmond from Petersburg, Bruce recalled, "It was a refreshing march in the pleasant hours of a delightful morning." Along the road, he met Confederate deserters who offered to sell to the Yankees their arms and equipment. One of the deserters said, "I guess the Confederacy is about played out at last."

"HAS THE ARMY DISSOLVED?"

Lee, hoping to rendezvous with the army of General Joseph E. Johnston in North Carolina, was marching southwest with what remained of the Army of Northern Virginia, 30,000 men. The Union's 2nd Corps, with the Irish Brigade at the head of the column, went in pursuit. At the village of Jetersville, Virginia, the Irish Brigade met General Philip Sheridan, the Irish-American cavalry officer whose scorched-earth policy in the Shenandoah Valley had done so much damage to the Confederacy's economy. Colonel Robert Nugent, the Brigade's commander, learned from Sheridan that the Rebels were about 10 miles (16 km) to the northeast, at Amelia Court House, a hamlet on one of the railway lines out of Richmond. Here Lee had ordered a halt in the hope that, before evacuating Richmond, the Confederate war department would have sent him a trainload of supplies. When the Irish learned they would attack the Rebels with Sheridan, they cheered.

The morning of April 5, the 2nd Corps and Sheridan's cavalry followed country roads to Amelia Court House. They were at a neighboring village, Amelia Springs, when they saw Lee's baggage train ahead of them. General Nelson Miles, who was in command of the 1st Division 2nd Corps, called for a battery of artillery to be rolled up to the head of the column, and gave the order to shell the Confederate baggage train. It was the beginning of a running battle that drove the Confederates westward.

On April 6, at Little Sailor's Creek, the Confederates' heavy baggage wagons became mired in the deep mud. Lee and General James Longstreet, who were at the head of the column, did not realize that their supply train had fallen behind, that their army was split in two. As Sheridan's cavalry attacked, General Richard S. Ewell ordered the wagons onto the dry Jamestown Road, and then once downstream, found

THE SON OF IRISH IMMIGRANTS, A GRADUATE OF WEST POINT, AND THE COMMANDER WHO RAVAGED THE SHENANDOAH VALLEY—
ONE OF THE MOST PRODUCTIVE FARM REGIONS IN VIRGINIA—GENERAL PHILIP SHERIDAN WAS A HERO TO THE IRISH BRIGADE.

a fording place, and hurried the wagons across. As the last wagons rolled onto the opposite shore, Ewell turned around and saw about 15,000 Union infantry and cavalry, with artillery, in battle formation near a farmhouse owned by the Hillsman family.

The Irish, who had been at the forefront of the running skirmish all day, were among the Union infantry that charged into Sailor's (or Sayler's) Creek, but wading through the waist-deep water slowed their advance. On the opposite side of the stream, clerks and wagon drivers grabbed muskets and joined Ewell's rear guard to fight off the Yankees. Union artillery opened fire, and canister raked through the Rebels' ranks. Confederate battalion commander Major Robert Stiles ordered his men to lie flat on the ground until the artillery was silent. One of the last shells struck a Confederate at the waist, nearly cutting him in two. The impact hurled "him bodily over my head," Stiles recalled, "his arms hanging down and his hands almost slapping me in the face as they passed."

A few moments later the shelling ceased and the Union men, in close formation, moved slowly toward the Confederates. As they drew near Stiles called out, "Ready!" and his men all rose up on one knee. He cried, "Aim!" and each man brought his musket to his shoulder. Then he shouted, "Fire!" The first rank of advancing Union troops crumpled to the ground. As the Confederates leapt to their feet and charged, the survivors turned and ran.

"Quicker than I can tell it," Stiles wrote, "the battle degenerated into a butchery, and a confused melee of brutal personal conflicts. I saw numbers of men kill each other with bayonets and the butts of muskets, and even bite each other's throats and ears and noses, rolling on the ground like wild beasts."

A corporal, a member of the Irish Brigade, whose brother had been killed days earlier at Petersburg, took cover in a thicket and shot and killed nine Rebels.

The Yankee infantry charged again, surged up the far bank of Sailor's Creek, and completely surrounded Ewell's men. Sheridan and Miles captured virtually all of Lee's supplies and 7,700 men, including General Ewell, General Custis Lee (Robert E. Lee's son), and seven other Confederate generals. Lee and Longstreet did not learn of the disaster until survivors who escaped the Yankees came racing up the road to rejoin the remnant of the Army of Northern Virginia. "My God!" Lee exclaimed, "has the army dissolved?"

Overall, the Irish Brigade's casualties at Sailor's Creek were insignificant—about a dozen men slightly wounded. But the Irish did suffer one major loss: Thirty-two-year-old Colonel Thomas Smyth, who had been commander of the Irish Brigade at the Wilderness, was shot through the face, the musket ball embedding itself in his neck. He died three days later. "It would be impossible to picture the grief this

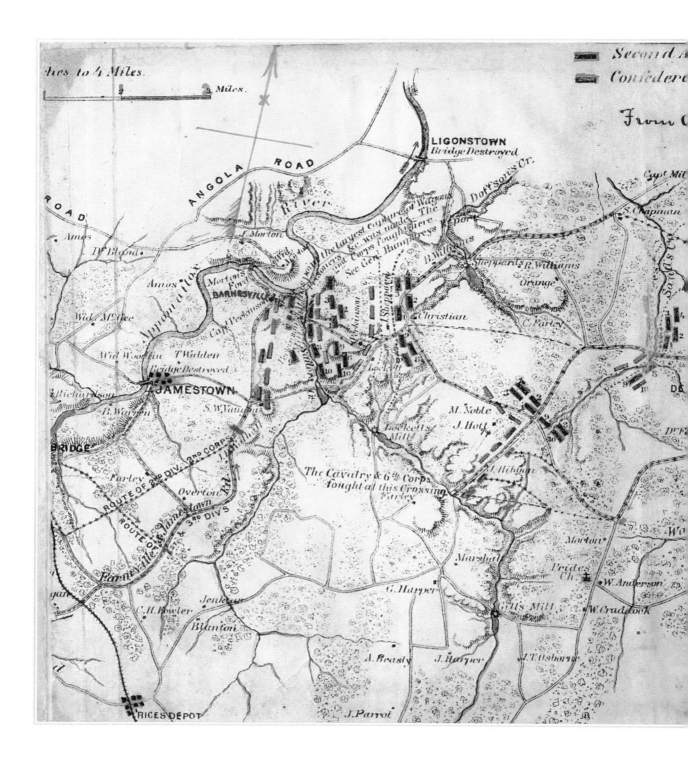

Corps   ————— *Line of the Enemy's Retreat.*

rces   ‡‡‡‡‡‡‡ *Line of Pursuit.*   ▣ *Forts*

Skirmish Line ••••••••••••••

al Plans of U.S. Topog Engineer Department

THIS MAP TRACES GRANT'S PURSUIT
OF LEE'S EVER-DWINDLING ARMY
FROM APRIL 6 TO 8, AND THE BATTLE
OF SAILOR'S CREEK, WHERE THE
FEDERALS CAPTURED ONE FOURTH OF
LEE'S ARMY. HISTORIANS CONSIDER
SAILOR'S CREEK THE DEATH KNELL OF
THE CONFEDERACY.
VIRGINIA HISTORICAL SOCIETY

unexpected calamity caused to his immediate command and to the Brigade, by whom he was almost idolized," wrote Captain David Conyngham, who had served under Smyth. "Everything else was forgotten, and even victory itself could not repay the survivors for the loss of such a gallant commander."

THE GENERAL'S HEADACHE

The next day, both General Miles and General Lee decided to divide their forces. The 1st Division, which included the Irish Brigade, and the 3rd Division would continue to pursue and harass Lee. The 2nd Division would march west on the village of Farmville, where supplies had arrived by train from Lynchburg.

Lee sent about 9,000 men with Longstreet to Farmville with orders to collect the supplies, cross the Appomattox River, and then burn the bridges. Lee, with the remaining 13,000 men, would cross at High Bridge, where there was a railroad bridge spanning a ravine 6 miles (9.6 km) east of Farmville and an adjacent bridge for wagons, horses, and pedestrians. He hoped that by destroying the two bridges, he would stop or at least slow the Union advance.

But shortly after Longstreet and his men arrived in Farmville, and just as rations were being distributed to Rebels at the head of the column, the Yankees attacked their rear. Longstreet ordered his men out of Farmville and to make for the river. It was pandemonium at the railroad bridge, part of which was already burning. As men and horses jostled each other to get across the wagon bridge, Union artillery opened fire. Major Edward M. Boykin recalled that shells that missed the retreating troops were still dangerous: "They [ricocheted] high up the hillsides . . . bursting and hurling fragments in every direction."

Meanwhile, Miles's 1st and 3rd Divisions had followed the Danville Road to High Bridge. Lee's entire force had already crossed over safely; the railroad bridge had been partially destroyed and Confederate engineers were setting fire to the wagon bridge when the Yankees arrived. General Miles's men opened fire, and the Rebels scattered.

The Union troops occupied Farmville, and late in the day, General Grant arrived. Perhaps sensing the war was almost over, that victory was at hand, the Union troops staged a jubilant torchlight procession through Farmville after dark. From the front porch of the Prince Edward Hotel, Grant watched the procession.

Earlier that day, Grant had sent a courier under a white flag of truce to General Lee's headquarters at Cumberland Church, only 3 miles (4.8 km) away. The courier bore a letter from Grant inviting Lee to surrender. Lee read the note silently to himself first, then aloud to his staff. Longstreet insisted that it was too early to consider surrender, and Lee agreed, but in his reply to Grant, Lee asked what terms of surrender the Union commander proposed.

The next morning, Lee led his army toward Appomattox Station, where he learned that another supply train from Lynchburg was waiting for him. That day Yankee troops did not attack Lee's rear; he had no word that the Yankees had gotten ahead of him to obstruct his march westward. In a confident mood, Lee wrote another note to Grant. "To be frank," Lee wrote, "I do not think the emergency has arisen to call for the surrender of this army." Upon reading Lee's note, Grant developed a migraine.

That evening, as Grant took to his bed with a mustard plaster on the back of his neck to relieve his aching head, General George Armstrong Custer led his cavalrymen into Appomattox Station. They attacked the handful of Rebel troops guarding the supply train, and once the supplies were captured, they attacked and captured a small Confederate camp on the edge of town. Custer's cavalry was now in control of the Lynchburg Road. In a matter of minutes, Lee lost his supplies and his escape route west.

"THE ARMY OF NORTHERN VIRGINIA PASSED OUT OF EXISTENCE"

Word of the loss of the supplies and that General Custer's cavalry was in possession of the Lynchburg Road came to General Lee late that night. Generals Longstreet, William N. Pendleton, Gordon, and Fitzhugh Lee (Robert E. Lee's nephew) gathered around their commander for what General Gordon called "the last sad Confederate council of war." Beside a campfire the generals sprawled on blankets on the grass or sat on their saddles as Lee summarized their situation. The generals discussed surrender—"the long-dreaded inevitable"—as Gordon put it, but none of them could bring themselves to admit that surrender was their only option. There was desperate talk of going into hiding in the mountains of Virginia and Tennessee, of becoming a guerilla army that would wear down the Yankees until they recognized Southern independence. But to reach the mountains, they had to first get away from Grant's army. And so General Lee resolved to make one more attempt to break free.

On the morning of April 9, Palm Sunday, a force of 8,000 men composed of Fitzhugh Lee's cavalry, Gordon's infantry, and a battery of artillery prepared to drive through Grant's line and make straight for the Tennessee border, 200 miles (320 km) away.

General Grant was up before sunrise that morning, pacing in the yard of the Prince Edward Hotel, still in excruciating pain from his migraine. An hour or so later, only a few miles away, Lee's army made its last reckless assault on the Yankees. Cavalry led by Fitzhugh Lee dashed around the Union's left flank, while Gordon's

TWENTIETH-CENTURY AMERICAN
ARTIST TOM LOVELL PAINTED LEE'S
SURRENDER IN THE PARLOR OF
THE MCLEAN FAMILY'S HOUSE AT
APPOMATTOX. THE SECOND FIGURE ON
THE RIGHT IS COLONEL ELY S. PARKER,
A SENECA INDIAN. WHEN HE HAD
FIRST VOLUNTEERED TO FIGHT FOR
THE UNION, HE WAS REBUFFED BY THE
GOVERNOR OF NEW YORK AND THE
SECRETARY OF WAR. HE APPEALED
TO ULYSSES S. GRANT, SEATED, WHO
SECURED PARKER A COMMISSION.

infantry and artillery struck the enemy head-on. They smashed through the Union line, and captured two cannons. The Confederate advance halted momentarily as the Rebels cheered and waved their regimental colors. Then General Gordon saw more Union troops coming up on his right and rear. The artillery kept the Yankees at bay, but more Yankees were coming. Then Colonel Charles S. Venable of General Lee's staff rode up asking for a progress report. "Tell General Lee," Gordon replied, "that my command has been fought to a frazzle." Between the retreat from Petersburg and the last effort to get through the Union lines, Lee had lost about 1,200 dead and 6,000 wounded (Grant had lost more than 1,300 dead and 7,700 wounded).

When Venable carried the message to Lee, he said, "Then there is nothing left for me to do but go and see General Grant, and I would rather die a thousand deaths." Nonetheless, he sent a note to Grant, requesting a parlay to "ascertain definitely what terms were embraced in your proposal of yesterday with reference to the surrender of this army." The moment Grant read the note, his migraine vanished.

Grant replied, "Your note of this date is but this moment (11:50 a.m.) received, in consequence of my having passed from the Richmond and Lynchburg road to the Farmville and Lynchburg road. I am at this writing about four miles [6.4 km] west of Walker's Church, and will push forward to the front for the purpose of meeting you. Notice sent to me on this road where you wish the interview to take place will meet me."

The two generals met in the parlor of the McLean family's red brick farmhouse in Appomattox Court House. The McLeans were new to the neighborhood: Their original farm had stood at Bull Run, the site of the first battle of the Civil War. After the second battle of Bull Run, Wilmer McLean decided to move his family to a quiet corner of western Virginia. He would say later, "The war began in my front yard and ended in my front parlor."

Lee arrived first. He had taken the time to change into a fresh uniform. From his belt hung a long sword, its hilt studded with jewels, and at the heels of his polished boots were gold spurs. Grant arrived minutes later, fresh from the field, in a mud-spattered uniform, no sword, no spurs. They had met once before, in the 1840s, during the war with Mexico. Lee had made an impression on Grant. "I have always remembered your appearance," he said, "and I think I should have recognized you anywhere." Grant had made less of an impression on Lee. "I have often thought of [our meeting]," Lee said, "and tried to recollect how you looked, but I have never been able to recall a single feature."

Then the two generals got down to business. Grant wrote the terms of surrender, which permitted officers to keep their swords and sidearms, and all Confederates to keep their personal baggage as well as any horses or mules they owned. Lee wrote a

IRISH INHABITANTS OF NEW YORK CITY CONTRIBUTED THE FUNDS FOR THE MEMORIAL TO THE 63RD, 69TH, AND 88TH
NEW YORK REGIMENTS AT GETTYSBURG. THE MONUMENT, DEPICTING AN IRISH WOLFHOUND AND CROSS,
WAS CARVED BY WILLIAM RUDOLF O'DONOVAN, A SELF-TAUGHT SCULPTOR WHO HAD BEEN BORN IN VIRGINIA
AND FOUGHT FOR THE CONFEDERACY DURING THE WAR.

formal letter accepting Grant's terms, then asked for rations for his men and fodder for their animals. Grant turned over to Lee the trains full of supplies that General Custer had captured the night before. During the drafting of the terms of surrender, the atmosphere in the McLeans' parlor was subdued. As Lee rose to leave, Grant and several of his officers followed the general outside. As Lee mounted his horse and prepared to ride back to his camp, Grant and his officers removed their hats—a final gesture of respect and courtesy for Robert E. Lee.

As Lee drew near his headquarters, Confederate infantrymen ran down the road to meet him. Reining in his horse, he stopped to speak to the men. "I have done the best I could for you," he said. "My heart is too full to say more."

Three days later Lee's men marched to Appomattox Court House for the formal surrender. William Swinton, a correspondent for the *New York Times*, witnessed the ceremony. "The troops stacked their arms and deposited their accoutrements," he wrote. "Paroles were then distributed to the men, and the Army of Northern Virginia passed out of existence."

"WHERE ARE THE OTHERS?"

On the evening of April 14, 1865, as President Abraham Lincoln and his wife, Mary, prepared to attend a performance of a comedy, *Our American Cousin*, at Ford's Theater, the Irish Brigade was encamped near the village of Burkeville, Virginia, in Nottoway County. The next morning, as the troops assembled for dress parade, the adjutant of each regiment read aloud the dispatch that had just arrived—President Lincoln was dead, killed by the assassin John Wilkes Booth only five days after Lee's surrender. It is strange that no document survives that describes the reaction of the Irish to the assassination. Captain David Conyngham devoted only a single sentence to it: "At Burkesville [*sic*] the army was stunned and horrified at the news of the atrocious murder of President Lincoln." Note that he said "the army," indicating that the assassination was a collective tragedy the entire army and the entire nation experienced together. Nonetheless, it would be interesting to learn how the Irish Brigade mourned the assassination of its commander in chief.

On May 2, 1865, the Irish Brigade, along with the rest of the 2nd Corps, began to march to Alexandria, Virginia, where it went into camp. There the men washed their uniforms and polished their muskets and the brass buttons on their jackets for the North's formal victory celebration—the Grand Review.

May 22 was a warm, sunny spring day, and it seemed that the entire population of Washington had turned out to line Pennsylvania Avenue. Beginning on Capitol

Hill, the Army of the Potomac marched up the boulevard, past a throng of spectators that waved hats and flags and handkerchiefs, sang patriotic songs, and cheered themselves hoarse. At two in the afternoon, Colonel Robert Nugent, riding a black horse, led the Irish Brigade past the reviewing stand erected in front of the White House: There President Andrew Johnson, General Grant, and General Meade stood among a small crowd of congressmen and foreign ambassadors. As they had on the day they charged Marye's Heights at Fredericksburg, each Irishman wore a sprig of green boxwood in his cap.

On July 2, the Irish disembarked in New York Harbor. Two days later, a division of the New York State National Guard led the 700 veterans through the streets of Manhattan, where thousands of Irish and non-Irish crowded the sidewalks. A reporter for the *Irish American* newspaper wrote that the men of the Irish Brigade appeared "strong and hearty; their faces, bronzed by the exposures of the field, were, along the march, wreathed in smiles, as cheer after cheer rent the air, welcoming them back to citizenship and their former homes."

General Thomas Meagher was not prominent at the march—the disgrace of his dismissal from the army was too new. Instead, he waited for the Irish Brigade at Irving Hall, where he made a brief speech in which he called upon the archdiocese of New York to erect in the Brigade's honor a cathedral and a tall round tower, such as those Irish monks built in the early Middle Ages.

The Irish Brigade never got a cathedral or a round tower, but on July 2, 1888, the first monument to the Irish was dedicated at Gettysburg, exactly twenty-five years after the Battle of the Wheatfield. Set at the edge of the wheat field, the monument is a Celtic cross, carved from green granite, with an Irish wolfhound lying at the foot of the cross. That day the Brigade's two chaplains, Father Corby and Father Ouellet, said Mass for the few dozen veterans of the Irish Brigade who had come to Gettysburg for the dedication. Looking over the small congregation of elderly and middle-aged men, Father Corby said, "Here is what is left of us. Where are the others?"

EPILOGUE

THE LEGACY OF THE IRISH BRIGADE

The courage and sacrifice of the Irish Brigade during the Civil War helped diminish prevalent anti-Irish prejudice in America. The Irish assimilated into American society through respectable occupations such as law enforcement, the construction trades, teaching, operating saloons and restaurants, and especially through Democratic political machines. Among these Irish American Democratic "pols" was Patrick J. "PJ" Kennedy (1858–1920), a successful Boston saloonkeeper who served as a Democratic Party ward boss in East Boston and in 1892 was elected to the Massachusetts Senate. Kennedy's colleague in Democratic politics, John Francis "Honey Fitz" Fitzgerald (1863–1950), was twice elected mayor of Boston. In 1960, the grandson of PJ and Honey Fitz, John Fitzgerald Kennedy, would be elected president of the United States, succeeding where another Irish Catholic Democrat had failed—Al Smith, in the 1928 presidential election.

The Irish also did well in the entertainment business. The great American playwright Eugene O'Neill was the son of James O'Neill, a nineteenth-century matinee idol who played the title role in *The Count of Monte Cristo* more than 6,000 times. In the early decades of the twentieth century, it was said that George M. Cohan, born of Irish Catholic parents, was "the man who owned Broadway": He was a singer, dancer, songwriter, playwright, and producer whose musical comedies dominated New York's theater district. His songs "You're a Grand Old Flag," "Over There," and "Give My Regards to Broadway" have become American classics. And when the movies came along, many of Hollywood's brightest stars were Irish: Bing Crosby, Spencer Tracy, James Cagney, Errol Flynn, Tyrone Power, Helen Hayes, Maureen O'Hara, and Grace Kelly.

In the first half of the twentieth century, some of the best-respected, most popular writers in America were of Irish descent, including F. Scott Fitzgerald, Flannery O'Connor, and James T. Farrell.

In sports, John L. Sullivan, Gene Tunney, and Jack Dempsey dominated boxing, and in professional baseball there was "Wild Bill" Donovan, "Dirty Jack" Doyle, and "Kid" Gleason.

A NATIVE OF KILLENAULE IN COUNTY TIPPERARY, DAVID POWER CONYNGHAM EMIGRATED TO NEW YORK, WHERE
HE JOINED THE IRISH BRIGADE IN 1861. HE ROSE TO THE RANK OF CAPTAIN. IN 1866 CONYNGHAM PUBLISHED *THE IRISH BRIGADE
AND ITS CAMPAIGNS*, THE FIRST HISTORY OF THE FAMOUS BRIGADE.

LIBRARY OF CONGRESS

All of these successes in all of these fields—and others as well—eventually eliminated the concept that the Irish were unwanted outsiders. In the twentieth century, anti-Irish prejudice had virtually disappeared, but there was still a persistent streak of anti-Catholic prejudice in America that John Kennedy had to confront when he ran for president in 1960.

THE FIGHTING 69TH

After the triumphal parade through Manhattan on July 4, 1865, the Irish Brigade was dissolved. But its legacy was carried on by the 69th New York Infantry. In 1917, as the United States prepared to enter World War I, the 69th called for volunteers: According to the regiment's Catholic chaplain, Father Francis Duffy, of the 2,002 men who enlisted in the 69th, 95 percent were Irish Catholics. Among the new recruits was the poet Joyce Kilmer. In 1941, when the 69th prepared to enter World War II, Irish Catholics still comprised 70 percent of the regiment—and among them was Christopher Kilmer, the poet's son.

In 1940, Hollywood released a movie about the regiment's exploits during World War I. *The Fighting 69th* starred Pat O'Brien as Father Duffy and James Cagney as a smart-mouthed, cowardly private who in the end proves himself to be as courageous as any of "the Fighting Irish."

On September 11, 2001, half of the men of the 69th, now part of the New York Army National Guard, were assigned to the recovery and rescue operation at Ground Zero, while the other half secured New York's bridges and tunnels. Initially, the 69th's armory was thrown open to families and friends seeking information about loved ones who had been in the World Trade Center, but the throng of anxious people overwhelmed the armory's facilities, and the information center was moved to the piers along the Hudson River. In 2004, some members of the 69th were sent to Iraq as part of Operation Iraqi Freedom; most of them were back home in 2006.

Today, the 69th is not as Irish a regiment as it once was, yet it still has the honor of leading New York's St. Patrick's Day Parade.

General Thomas Francis Meagher

On August 2, 1865, President Andrew Johnson offered Meagher the governorship of the Montana Territory (which later entered the Union as the state of Montana). Meagher accepted immediately, hoping the post would restore his battered reputation. Instead, he found fresh troubles in Montana. The administration of the territory was in the hands of Republicans (Meagher, unlike most Irish immigrants, was a Republican), but most of the citizens were Democrats, and many were originally from the South. Under pressure from the voters, Meagher called for an election. The result: the Democrats won a sweeping victory that gave them an overwhelming majority in the territorial legislature. The Republicans were so angry that Meagher began to receive death threats.

On July 1, 1867, Meagher arrived at Fort Benton, Montana, to pick up a shipment of weapons. He spent the afternoon and evening aboard a steamboat with an old friend. After dark, Meagher seemed to become increasingly agitated. He excused himself, and a few moments later his friend heard a splash, followed by a cry for help. Meagher was never seen again, his body was never recovered, and it has never been established whether his death was an accident or suicide. At the time of his death, Meagher was forty-four years old.

Colonel Robert Nugent

Colonel Nugent remained in the army, seeing action in the 1870s during the Great Plains War against the Sioux. In 1879, he retired and settled in Brooklyn. He was active in veterans' associations, especially the Grand Army of the Republic. In his final years, his health was poor, a result of the wounds he had suffered at Fredericksburg. He died at age seventy-six at his home in 1901.

Captain David P. Conyngham

After the war, Conyngham wrote *The Irish Brigade and Its Campaigns*, the definitive account of the Brigade in its day, and still essential reading for any student of the Irish Brigade. Conyngham served as a correspondent for several New York newspapers and wrote historical novels, as well as a history of Ireland's saints and martyrs. On April 1, 1883, he died unexpectedly of pneumonia; Conyngham was forty-three.

St. Clair Mulholland

The Story of the 116th Regiment of Pennsylvania Volunteers in the War of the Rebellion is only one of several works of military history Mulholland wrote after the war. He was active in both Civil War veterans' organizations and Irish American historical societies. In 1894, President Grover Cleveland appointed Mulholland pension agent in Philadelphia, responsible for the payment of disability and death benefits to veterans and their families. He died of heart disease at age seventy-one in 1910.

Father William Corby, CSC

The men of the Irish Brigade presented Father Corby with a chalice as a memento of his service as their chaplain. In 1866, Father Corby, thirty-three years old, was appointed president of Notre Dame College. In 1872, he was transferred to Sacred Heart College in Watertown, Wisconsin, to help the school become financially stable. In 1877, he was back at Notre Dame serving as president once again. After the disastrous fire of 1879, Father Corby worked tirelessly to rebuild the school: He is revered as Notre Dame's "second founder." At his death at age sixty-four in 1897, veterans of the Irish Brigade served as his pallbearers, and over his coffin was draped the Brigade's flag.

Appendix

THE IRISH BRIGADE'S MEDAL OF HONOR RECIPIENTS

The Medal of Honor was born during the U.S. Civil War. On December 9, 1861, Senator James W. Grimes of Iowa introduced a bill calling for the creation of a "medal of honor . . . which shall be bestowed upon such petty officers, seamen, landsmen and marines as shall distinguish themselves by their gallantry in action and other seamanlike qualities during the present war." The limitation to the Navy was amended on February 17, 1862, when Senator Henry Wilson of Massachusetts proposed a bill calling for awarding a medal of honor to members of "the Army of the United States who shall distinguish themselves in battle." President Abraham Lincoln signed both bills into law.

The original Army Medal of Honor consisted of a red, white, and blue ribbon from which was suspended an eagle clutching a cannon and a sword in its talons, and beneath the eagle a large, five-pointed star. On the back of the star were the words, "The Congress To" followed by an empty space where the recipient's name could be engraved.

This was not the first time Congress had authorized an award to recognize distinguished service in the military. On March 3, 1847, Congress passed a bill calling for the creation of a Certificate of Merit, which would be presented by the President of the United States to a "soldier [who] distinguishes himself in the service." The soldier would also receive a pay raise of $2 per month.

The first man to be awarded the Medal of Honor was Private Francis E. Brownell of the 11th New York Infantry. On May 24, 1861, 24-year-old Colonel Elmer Ellsworth of the 11th New York removed a large Confederate flag that was flying from the top of the Marshall House hotel in Alexandria, Virginia. As Ellsworth descended the stairs with the Rebel flag in his hands, James W. Jackson, the owner of the Marshall House, killed Elllsworth with a blast from his shotgun. Brownell immediately raised his musket and shot and killed Jackson.

Of the 1,522 veterans of the Civil War who were awarded the Medal of Honor, seven were members of the Irish Brigade.

Major James Quinlan

James Quinlan was born in Clonmel, County Tipperary, Ireland, in 1833. He was living in New York City in April 1861 when President Abraham Lincoln called for 75,000 volunteers to defend the Union against the Confederates. Quinlan enlisted with the Engineer Company of the 69th New York State Militia and fought at the first battle of Bull Run. After the formation of the Irish Brigade in September 1861, Quinlan transferred to the 88th New York Infantry, where he achieved the rank of major.

In June 1862, the Army of the Potomac was retreating eastward across Virginia to Harrison Landing and the safety of the Union gunboats on the James River. The retreat, or as the Union commander, George B. McClellan called it, "change of base," took seven days, and each day Yankees and Rebels clashed—hence the name Battle of the Seven Days.

At Savage's Station, in order to move more quickly, Union troops burned their supplies in huge bonfires. At the same time, to inflict damage on the Confederates, they blew up the railroad bridge two miles (3.2 km) outside the town.

By four in the afternoon of Sunday, June 29, 1862, most of the Army of the Potomac had passed through Savage's Station. General Edwin Vose Sumner and his 2nd Corps were still in the town: There was a Union hospital in Savage's Station with 2,500 men too severely wounded to be moved. Sumner was reluctant to leave the wounded to be taken prisoner by the Confederates, but he did not know how he could transport them to safety either. He was still debating the question with himself when Rebel artillery, mounted atop a nearby hill, opened fire on Sumner's men. More Confederate troops arrived by way of the Williamsburg road and attacked the 2nd Corps at five in the afternoon.

The Rebel attack was met by two regiments of the Irish Brigade, the 69th New York and the 88th New York—Major Quinlan was in command of the 88th. Under the cover of Union artillery, which lobbed shells into the Confederate lines, the Irish surged forward against the enemy. The fighting was hand-to-hand and raged for two hours before at last the Rebels broke and ran. Quinlan led his men in another charge up the hill where some of the Confederate artillery was positioned. The Irish overwhelmed the gun crews and captured two cannons, which they spiked, then hacked to pieces.

In spite of the successes of the Irish in the Battle of Savage's Station, Sumner could not remain there—he was now essentially the rear guard of the Army of the Potomac and could not hold back the entire Army of Northern Virginia. At midnight he ordered a retreat, leaving behind the wounded in the hospital. As the 2nd Corps moved out, Major Quinlan and the 88th New York covered their retreat.

The official statement that led to Major Quinlan receiving the Medal of Honor reads, "The conduct of Major Quinlan on that occasion was that of a self-sacrificing soldier. He dashed into the very face of death, so far as he could know, thereby relieving the troops massed in a cul de sac from the battery's devastating fire, and probably discouraging the enemy for the day, for the fighting was not renewed after the silencing of their guns until past nightfall. Major Quinlan deserves the badge of gallantry to be awarded to the most brave and intrepid on the field."

James Quinlan died in New York City in 1906.

Private Peter F. Rafferty

Peter Rafferty was born in Ireland in 1845. He was seventeen, living in New York City, when he enlisted in the 69th New York. On July 1, 1862, the 69th and the 88th New York were at Malvern Hill, Virginia, outside Richmond, when they were ordered to turn back an advancing column of Confederates. The 69th was deployed first; when it exhausted its ammunition it fell back, and the 88th stepped forward.

The 69th was ready to return to the fight when its commander, Colonel Robert Nugent, spotted a Confederate detachment advancing on the 69th and the 88th's flank—it was from the 9th Louisiana Infantry, the famous Louisiana Tigers. Nugent ordered both regiments to charge, and they drove the Tigers from the field. In the fight, Rafferty was wounded in the right thigh. Captain Thomas Leddy ordered Rafferty to the rear, but he did not want to go: There were no surgeons there to treat his wound, no ambulances to take him to a field hospital. Furthermore, Rafferty was afraid that if the Irish Brigade were ordered into battle elsewhere he would be isolated from them, and in the worse case scenario, might even be taken prisoner by the enemy. "I'm all right," he told the captain. "I'll stay and fight it out with the boys."

The Tigers regrouped and 1,000 of them attacked 1,000 men of the Irish Brigade. Once again the Irish drove them off. In this second fight Rafferty was shot through the foot, and two musket balls struck him in the face, shattering his jaw bone and severing part of his tongue. He was left for dead on the field, then was captured by the Confederates and kept in Libby Prison in Richmond, Virginia. In prison, Rafferty was left with no medical treatment for five days, until a group of Sisters of Charity came to Libby to tend the wounded Yankees. He was released several months later in a prisoner exchange and was discharged from the army in March 1863 as an invalid.

Peter Rafferty's Medal of Honor citation reads, "Having been wounded and directed to the rear, declined to go, but continued in action, receiving several additional wounds, which resulted in his capture by the enemy and his total disability for military service."

Lieutenant Louis J. Sacriste

Louis J. Sacriste was born in Delaware in 1843. He enlisted in the 116th Pennsylvania Volunteers, which became part of the Irish Brigade (although most of the men in the 116th were not Irish).

At Chancellorsville on May 3, 1863, the Irish Brigade was placed in battle formation near the Chancellor family's home. As the 116th formed up, the Fifth Maine Battery rolled up its artillery on the Pennsylvanians' left and opened fire on the Confederates. The Confederates, under General J.E.B. Stuart, had thirty pieces of artillery, which they trained on the Irish Brigade. "The man on my right was literally cut in two by a shell," Sacriste recalled later, "the man on my left had both legs cut off; the man in my front had a piece of his skull carried away, and the ground was covered with the dead and wounded."

The Confederates aimed for the Maine Battery, and in less than an hour killed or wounded all the gunners, except Corporal Charles Lebrooke and Private John F. Chase, who remained at their posts, reloading and firing as fast as they could. One Confederate shell struck an ammunition chest, and the explosion set fire to the Chancellor house. Under such deadly fire the Union lines broke and men sprinted away from the battlefield.

Seeing the Yankees in retreat, the Confederates advanced. Sacriste called to the men of the 116th to save the Maine guns. They ran to the battery and rolled one cannon to safety. The rest of the Irish Brigade joined them, and saved every cannon and caisson from falling into enemy hands.

The Medal of Honor citation also mentions a second act of valor performed by Lt. Sacriste. Early in the morning of October 14, 1863, Sacriste and twenty-five picked men of the 116th were at the picket line, guarding the First Division, which was crossing Cedar Creek with its baggage train. Confederates attacked the pickets, and by eleven in the morning had them cut off from the rest of the division and nearly surrounded. Colonel James A. Beaver, who was in command of the picket line, sent Sacriste with a message to all the officers, informing them of the retreat route and directing them to fall back slowly. As Sacriste set out, he overheard a man say, "That's the last you will see of Sacriste."

The fighting was hot all along the line, but Sacriste delivered his message to each officer. When everyone had pulled back, Sacriste saw a detail of the 140th Pennsylvania Volunteers that he had missed. He went back in, delivered the retreat message to the lieutenant in command, and all the men of the 140th escaped unharmed.

Louis J. Sacriste's citation reads: "Saved from capture a gun of the 5th Maine Battery. Voluntarily carried orders which resulted in saving from destruction or capture the picket line of the 1st Division, 2d Army Corps."

James M. Seitzinger

James M. Seitzinger was born in Gordon, Pennsylvania, in 1846. His grandfather had served in the War of 1812, and his great-grandfather had fought for American independence during the Revolutionary War.

In 1864, 17-year-old James enlisted in the 116th Pennsylvania Volunteers, along with his father, Israel Seitzinger. Father and son would fight together at the battles of the Wilderness, Cold Harbor, Spotsylvania, and Petersburg.

At Cold Harbor, on the morning of June 3, 1864, the Irish Brigade, along with the other men of the 2nd Corps, suffered tremendous casualties: In less than half an hour the 2nd Corps lost 3,000 men, killed or wounded. To escape the deadly Confederate fire, the survivors lay flat on the ground—and the Rebels kept them pinned down there; any man who stood or even tried to crawl to safety was shot by Rebel sharpshooters.

The officers of the 2nd Corps called for a counterattack, and as the men rose to attack the Confederate positions, the 116th's colorbearer, Sergeant T.A. Sloan, rushed forward and was instantly shot dead. James Seitzinger lifted the regimental flag from the ground and waving it over his head, shouted to his father, "Go in, Pop! I'm coming!"

James Seitzinger could not hold the flag long—he was small and slightly built, and the flag was too heavy for him. Sergeant Peter Kelly took the flag from him and charged with the rest of the Irish Brigade.

After the battle, Seitzinger's commanding officer, Captain Frank R. Leib, recommended him for a Medal of Honor: "In the charge on Cold Harbor on the morning of June 3, 1864, our color sergeant was shot down and through the midst of the shot and shell, James M. Seitzinger, then a private, grabbed the colors and waving it called to the regiment to follow. If in your judgment you deem him worthy of a Medal of Honor, it would be well bestowed on a gallant soldier."

Two months after the Battle of Cold Harbor, James Seitzinger was wounded twice at the siege of Petersburg, Virginia, but he and his father Israel both survived the war. Israel Seitzinger died in 1894, and James Seitzinger in 1924.

The citation for James Seizinger's Medal of Honor reads: "When the color bearer was shot down, this soldier seized the colors and bore them gallantly in a charge against the enemy."

Colonel St. Clair Mulholland

St. Clair Mulholland was born in Lisburn, County Antrim, Ireland, in 1839. He was a boy when he came to America with his parents; they settled in Philadelphia. In his late teens he joined the Pennsylvania militia, and when the Civil War began, Mulholland joined the 116th Pennsylvania Volunteers, which became part of the Irish Brigade. In 1862 he received a commission as lieutenant colonel.

On May 4, 1863, at the Battle of Chancellorsville, men of the Irish Brigade saved several Union cannon from being captured by the Confederates. That night, as the Union army withdrew from the field, General Winfield Scott Hancock chose Mulholland to cover the retreat. Both officers expected that Mulholland and his men would be taken prisoner by the Rebels, and if that proved to be the case, Hancock promised to do all in power to arrange for Mulholland's release through a prisoner exchange.

With 400 men of the 116th Pennsylvania, Mulholland kept the Confederates at bay. When the Army of the Potomac was safely on the opposite bank of the

Rappahannock River, Mulholland led his men across, too. He returned to the main body of the Union army with almost all of his men—only a handful had been captured by the Rebels.

For his rear-guard action against the Confederates at Chancellorsville, Mulholland was awarded the Medal of Honor. His citation reads: "In command of the picket line held the enemy in check all night to cover the retreat of the Army."

After the war Mulholland returned to Philadelphia, where he was appointed chief of police. He held several federal government posts as well, he wrote histories of the 116th Pennsylvania and of Medal of Honor recipients, and he was active in Catholic charities. St. Clair Mulholland died in 1910.

Timothy Donoghoe (also spelled Donoghue and Donahue)

Very little information survives regarding Medal of Honor recipient Private Timothy Donoghue. He was born in Ireland in 1828 (some sources say 1825). In the 1850s he served with the British military in India, where he and his wife Angelina had a son, Patrick. After Angelina's death in 1859, Donoghoe was mustered out; he and his son settled in Liverpool, England, where Donoghoe became a police officer. In 1862 he married Esther Bason, and several months later the family emigrated to New York City. Soon after their arrival Donoghoe enlisted in the 69th New York Infantry.

On December 13, 1862, at the Battle of Fredericksburg, Donoghoe saved the life of a wounded officer. His citation reads: "Voluntarily carried a wounded officer off the field from between the lines; while doing this he was himself wounded."

The wound in his thigh left Donoghoe disabled, and he was assigned to the Veterans Reserve Corps. After the war Donoghoe returned home to New York City; he and Esther had six children together. Timothy Donoghoe died in New York in 1908.

George W. Ford

Even less information is available about First Lieutenant George W. Ford. He was born in Ireland in 1840, emigrated to New York, and in 1861 enlisted in the 88th New York Infantry. On April 6, 1865, at the Battle of Sailor's Creek in Virginia, Lieutenant Ford captured a Confederate flag.

BIBLIOGRAPHY

Abels, Robert. *Early American Firearms*. New York: The World Publishing Company, 1950.

Alexander, Edward Porter. *Military Memoirs of a Confederate*. New York: Charles Scribner's Sons, 1907.

Axelrod, Alan. *The Horrid Pit: The Battle of the Crater, the Civil War's Cruelest Mission*. New York: Carroll and Graf, 2007.

Baumgartner, Frederic J. *From Spear to Flintlock: A History of War in Europe and the Middle East to the French Revolution*. New York: Praeger, 1991.

Bayor, Ronald H., and Timothy J. Meagher, editors. *The New York Irish*. Baltimore: The Johns Hopkins University Press, 1996.

Bearss, Edwin C. *Fields of Honor: Pivotal Battles of the Civil War*. Washington, D.C.: National Geographic, 2006.

Beyer, Walter F., and Oscar F. Keydel, compilers. *Deeds of Valor: How America's Heroes Won the Medal of Honor*, Volume I. Detroit: The Perrien-Keydel Company, 1901.

Bilby, Joseph. *Remember Fontenoy! The 69th New York and the Irish Brigade in the Civil War*. Hightstown, NJ: Longstreet House, 1997.

Bilby, Joseph G., and Stephan D. O'Neill. *My Sons Were Faithful and They Fought: The Irish Brigade at Antietam—An Anthology*. Hightstown, NJ: Longstreet House, 1997.

Boritt, Gabor. *The Gettysburg Gospel: The Lincoln Speech That Nobody Knows*. New York: Simon & Schuster, 2006.

Boyle, William J. *The Story of St. Michael's*. 1934.

Brooks, Victor. *Marye's Heights, Fredericksburg*. Conshohocken, PA: Combined Publishing, 2001.

Bruce, Susannah Ural. *The Harp and the Eagle: Irish-American Volunteers and the Union Army, 1861–1865*. New York: New York University Press, 2006.

Burlingame, Michael. *Abraham Lincoln: A Life*. Baltimore: The Johns Hopkins University Press, 2008.

Burton, William L. *Melting Pot Soldiers: The Union's Ethnic Regiments*. Bronx, NY: Fordham University Press, 1998.

Concannon, John J. "Colorful and Gallant: General Michael Corcoran." The Wild Geese Today—Erin's Far-Flung Exiles. www.thewildgeese.com/pages/corcpt2.html.

Conyngham, David Power. *The Irish Brigade and Its Campaigns*. Bronx, NY: Fordham University Press, 1994.

Davis, William C. *The Battlefields of the Civil War*. Baltimore: Salamander Books, 1999.

Davis, William C., and the Editors of Time-Life Books. *Death in the Trenches: Grant at Petersburg*. New York: Time-Life Books, 1986.

Demeter, Richard. *The Fighting 69th: A History*. Pasadena, CA: Cranford Press, 2002.

Donald, David Herbert. *Lincoln*. New York: Simon & Schuster, 1995.

Encyclopedia Virginia. www.encyclopediavirginia.org.

Gannon, Joseph E. "The Deadliest Day: The Irish Brigade at Bloody Lane, September 17, 1862." The Wild Geese Today. www.thewildgeese.com/pages/antietam.html.

Gavin, Lieutenant General James M. "Great Advances That Changed War." *Life* (February 17, 1961).

Harman, Troy D. *Lee's Real Plan at Gettysburg*. Mechanicsburg, PA: Stackpole Books, 2003.

Hughes, Major-General B.P. *Firepower: Weapons Effectiveness on the Battlefield, 1630–1850*. Conshohocken, PA: Sarpedon, 1997.

Mathless, Paul, editor. *Voices of the Civil War: First Manassas*. New York: Time-Life Books, 1997.

Mathless, Paul, editor. *Voices of the Civil War: Fredericksburg*. New York: Time-Life Books, 1997.

McCarter, William. *My Life in the Irish Brigade*. North Augusta, SC: Savas Publishing Company, 1996.

McGreevey, John T. *Catholicism and American Freedom: A History*. New York: W.W. Norton, 2003.

"Michael Corcoran." Irish Identity. www.irishidentity.com/geese/stories/corcoran.htm.

"Military Re-enacting: Part II—Uniforms and Equipment, Company A, 69th NYSV (1861–1863)." The 69th NYSV Historical Association. www.69thnysv.org.

Morris, Roy Jr. "Battle of the Wilderness." *Military History* (April, 1997).

Mulholland, St. Clair Augustine. *The Story of the 116th Regiment of Pennsylvania Volunteers in the War of the Rebellion*. Philadelphia: F. McManus Jr., & Co., 1903.

National Park Service. www.nps.gov.

"The Obsequies Of Gen. Michael Corcoran." *New York Times*, December 28, 1863.

O'Donnell, Edward T. *1001 Things Everyone Should Know about Irish-American History*. New York: Broadway Books, 2002.

O'Neill, Stephan D. "Antietam." The Sixty-ninth. www.sixtyninth.net/index.html.

O'Reilly, Francis Augustine. *The Fredericksburg Campaign*. Baton Rouge: Louisiana State University Press, 2006.

Quinn, Peter. "The Tragedy of Bridget Such-A-One." *American Heritage* (December 1997).

Rable, George C. *Fredericksburg! Fredericksburg!* Chapel Hill: University of North Carolina Press, 2002.

Rhea, Gordon C. *The Battle of the Wilderness, May 5–6, 1864.* Baton Rouge: Louisiana State University Press, 1994.

Sears, Stephen W. *Gettysburg*. Boston: Houghton Mifflin, 2004.

Sears, Stephen W. *Landscape Turned Red: The Battle of Antietam*. Boston: Houghton Mifflin, 1983.

Shaw, Richard. *Dagger John: The Unquiet Life and Times of Archbishop John Hughes of New York*. Mahwah, NJ: Paulist Press, 1977.

Smith, Robin. *American Civil War Zouaves*. Oxford, UK: Osprey Publishing, 1996.

Sommers, Richard J. *Richmond Redeemed: The Siege at Petersburg*. New York: Doubleday, 1981.

Stevens, George Thomas. *Three Years in the Sixth Corps*. Albany: S.R. Gray Publisher, 1866.

Stiles, Robert. *Four Years under Marse Robert*. New York: Neale Publishing Company, 1903.

Thomason, John W. *Jeb Stuart*. Lincoln: University of Nebraska Press, 1994.

Wallace, Lee A. Jr., and Martin R. Conway. *A History of Petersburg National Battlefield*. Washington, DC: National Park Service, 1983.

Ward, Geoffrey C., with Ric Burns and Ken Burns. *The Civil War: An Illustrated History*. New York: Borzoi Books, 1990.

Warren, Craig A. "'Oh, God, What a Pity!': The Irish Brigade at Fredericksburg and the Creation of Myth." *Civil War History* 47, No. 3 (2001).

Wheeler, Richard. *A Rising Thunder: From Lincoln's Election to the Battle of Bull Run: An Eyewitness History*. New York: HarperCollins, 1994.

Wheeler, Richard. *Witness to Appomattox*. New York: Harper & Row, 1989.

Woodhead, Henry, editor. *Voices of the Civil War: Chancellorsville*. New York: Time-Life Books, 1996.

Wylie, Paul R. *The Irish General: Thomas Francis Meagher*. Norman: University of Oklahoma Press, 2007.

ABOUT THE AUTHOR

Thomas J. Craughwell is the author of more than twenty books on history, religion, and popular culture, including *The Buck Stops Here* (Fair Winds Press, 2009), *Stealing Lincoln's Body* (Harvard University Press, 2007), and *Saints Behaving Badly* (Doubleday, 2006). He has written articles for the *Wall Street Journal*, the *New York Times, American Spectator, U.S. News & World Report, Emmy* magazine, and *Inside the Vatican*. He has appeared on CNN, BBC, FOX, EWTN, and the Discovery Channel. In 2009, the History Channel produced a documentary based on *Stealing Lincoln's Body*. In 2010, he was elected to the Board of Advisors of the Lincoln Forum. He writes from his home in Bethel, Connecticut.

ACKNOWLEDGMENTS

My sincere thanks to the generous, helpful, and patient staff of Fair Winds Press, particularly my editor, Cara Connors, and my very skillful copy editor, Karen Levy. And finally, my thanks to Will Kiester—a great friend and an inspired publisher.

INDEX

Fontenoy, Battle of, 59

Forbes, Edwin, *126–127*, *135*, *176–177*

Ford, George W., 225

Ford's Theater, 212

Fort Benton, Montana, 217

Fort Corcoran, Virginia, 44

Fort Davis, Texas, 192, 193

Fort Donelson, Tennessee, 167

Fort Henry, Tennessee, 167

Fort Lafayette, New York, 23

Fort Macon, Battle of, 108

Fort Macon, Virginia, 108

Fort Sumter, South Carolina, 8, 26, 27, 38, 41, 44, 47, 50

Fox, William F., 8

Frank Leslie's Illustrated Newspaper, *55–56*, *126–127*

Franklin, William, 111, 116

Frederick, Pennsylvania, 147

Frederick Junction, Maryland, 152

Fredericksburg, Battle of, 11, *74*, *78–79*, 106–123, *110*, *112–113*, *115*, *118–119*, 124, 139, 141, 143, 162, 170, 193, 213, 225

Fredericksburg, Virginia, 11, *74*, *78–79*, 106–123, *110*, *112–113*, *115*, *118–119*, 124, 138, 139, 141, 143, 162, 170, 193, 213, 225

freedmen, 183

Freeman's Journal, 23

French, William H., 92, 95, 114, 116

Frontier Guards, 51

G

Gaines' Mill, Battle of, 80

Gaines' Mill, Virginia, 80

Galway Association of New York, 182

Gardner, Alexander, *88*, *94*

Garnett, Richard, 159, 160, 161, 162

"Garryowen," *84–85*, 114

Gates, Theodore B., 165

Georgetown College, 44

Georgia, 46, 95, 101, 103, 114, 116–117, 120, 153, 166

German-Americans, 161

Germanna Ford, 168, 170

Getty, George, 173

Gettys, Samuel, 151

Gettysburg, Battle of, 144–163, *155*, *158–159*, 164, 193

Gettysburg, Pennsylvania, 8, 144–163, *155*, *158–159*, 164, 170, 193

    monument in, *211*, 213

Gibbon, John, 114, 161

    The Artillerist's Manual, 111

Gibbons, John, 173

Gleason, "Kid," 214

Glendale, Virginia, 81

Glover, Ann, 17

Goodwin, John, 17

Gordon, John B., 95, 99, 100, 207, 210

Gossen, John, 44

the Grand Review, 212–213

Grant, Julia, 167

Grant, Ulysses S., 161, 166–168, *176–177*, 180–181, 183, 186–187, 191–192, 198–200, 206–210, *208–209*, 212–213

Gregg, John, 174

Gregg, Maxcy, 114

Griffin, Charles, 171, 173

Ground Zero, 216

Guiney Station, Virginia, 129, 141

gunpowder, 183, 187–188

H

Hagerstown Turnpike, 91

Haggerty, James, 47

Hall, Irving, 164

Halleck, Henry W., 192

Hampton, Wade, 198

Hancock, Winfield Scott, 73, 116, 144, 152–153, 160, 162, 166, 171, 173–174, 178, 180, 196, 198, 224

Harpers Ferry, Virginia, 89, 103

Harrisburg, Pennsylvania, 87, 151

Harrison, William Henry, 81

Harrison's Landing, Virginia, 81, *88*, 220

Hawkins, Rush, 120

Hay, John, 51

Hayes, Helen, 214

Hays, Alexander, 161

Hazel Grove, Virginia, 133

Heaney, Elizabeth, 40

Heaney, John, 40

Henry, Anson, 143

Henry, Judith Carter, 46

Henry family, 46

Henry House Hill, 46, 47, 53, 58, 59, 62

Henry II, 30

Henry VIII, 30–31

the *Herald*, 16

Heth, Henry, 133, 148, 151, 196

Hibernia Hose Company, 14, 16

Hibernian Hall, 40, 41

High Bridge, Virginia, 206

Hill, A.P., 77, 80, 81, 103, 146, 148, 170, 171, 196

Hill, Daniel Harvey, 70, 86, 92, 100

Hillsman family, 203

Holmes, Oliver Wendell Jr., 92

Holmes, William, 103

Homer, Winslow, *42–43*

Hood, John Bell, 80, 91

Hooker, Joseph, 76, 81, 91, 109, 116, 120–121, 124–125, 128–130, *131*, 138–139, 146

Howard, Oliver O., 116

Howe, Julia Ward, "The Battle Hymn of the Republic," 108

Huger, Benjamin, 75

Hughes, John, 16–17, 20, 23, 26, 37, 41, 44–45

Hummelbaugh, Jacob, 152

Humphreys, Andrew A., 120, 168

Hunt, Henry, 157

I

Indiana, 174

Ireland, 8–9, *10*, 11, 28, *33*, 35, 38, 67, 84, 98

    politics in, 30–34

    Potato Famine in, 18, 20

    remembering, 13–27